NEWS *of* G

T*h*

CHURCH TIMES
Christmas Collection

JAMES ALISON • JOHN BARTON

RICHARD COLES • STEPHEN COTTRELL

CATHERINE FOX • PAULA GOODER

MALCOLM GUITE • MARK OAKLEY

PÁDRAIG Ó TUAMA

BARBARA BROWN TAYLOR

JANE WILLIAMS • LUCY WINKETT

TOM WRIGHT and others

edited by
HUGH HILLYARD-PARKER

CANTERBURY
PRESS
Norwich

First published in 2021 by the Canterbury Press Norwich
Editorial office
3rd Floor, Invicta House,
108–114 Golden Lane, London EC1Y 0TG, UK

www.canterburypress.co.uk

Canterbury Press is an imprint of Hymns Ancient & Modern Ltd
(a registered charity)

Hymns Ancient & Modern® is a registered trademark of
Hymns Ancient & Modern Ltd
13A Hellesdon Park Road, Norwich, Norfolk NR6 5DR, UK

British Library Cataloguing in Publication data
A catalogue record for this book is available from the British Library

ISBN 978 1 78622 406 4

Designed and typeset by Hugh Hillyard-Parker
Copyedited by Rosamund Connelly
Printed and bound in Great Britain by CPI Group (UK) Ltd

ACKNOWLEDGEMENTS

The images on pages 4, 7, 10, 11, 51, 81, 95, 99, 113, 125, 139, 149, 154, 169, 183, 185 (left), 187, 188, 195, 213, 219, 221, 225, 233, 242, 249, 261, 265 (left & centre) are public domain artwork downloaded from Wikimedia Commons under its generic Creative Commons licence.

The images on the following pages are licensed under the Creative Commons Attribution licences indicated: CC 1.0 Universal Public Domain Dedication: p.255 donated to Wikimedia Commons as part of a project by the Metropolitan Museum of Art; p.265 (right) Chester Dale Collection, National Gallery of Art, Washington; CC Attribution 2.5 Generic licence: p.242; CC Attribution-Share Alike 4.0 International licence: p.69 Yelkrokoyade; p.76 Didier Descouens; p.107 European Southern Observatory/Y. Beletsky; p.185 (right) Carole Raddato, Frankfurt, Germany; p.244 Livioandronico2013; p.245 José Luiz Bernardes Ribeiro; CC Attribution only licence CC BY 4.0: p.236 made available by Wellcome Images (images@wellcome.ac.uk, http://wellcomeimages.org)

Other images: pp.41, 198 Alamy; p.151 © Hugh Hillyard-Parker

Text permissions:
We are grateful to the following for permission to reproduce copyright material:
p.3, R. S. Thomas, "Kneeling" from *The Collected Later Poems: 1988–2000*. Copyright © 2004 by R. S. Thomas. Reprinted by permission of Bloodaxe Books Ltd; p.12, David Higham Associates, for the verse from Eleanor Farjeon's carol "People, look east" (permssion sought); pp.39, 88, Malcolm Guite, *The Singing Bowl* (Canterbury Press, 2013); p.105, Estate of W. H. Auden (permission sought); p.114, Malcolm Guite, *Waiting on the Word* (Canterbury Press, 2015); p.217, Malcolm Guite, *Sounding the Seasons* (Canterbury Press, 2012); p.180, Pádraig Ó Tuama, *Sorry for Your Troubles* (Canterbury Press, 2013); pp.20, 47, 259, Kenneth Steven, *Out of the Ordinary* (Canterbury Press, 2020).

Contents

WORSHIP AT CHRISTMAS

CHRISTMAS FEATURES

CHRISTMAS IN THE ARTS

THE TWELVE DAYS OF CHRISTMAS

EPIPHANY TO CANDLEMAS

Introduction

by **Paul Handley**

THE editing of a weekly newspaper allows no time to reflect on what has appeared. Every issue, however carefully commissioned, praised, grumbled about, subbed, argued over, subbed again, illustrated, laid out, and trimmed or stretched to fit, is instantly consigned to history when it goes to press on a Wednesday evening, added to the pile of 8000-plus issues produced since 1863 by my predecessors (and rather too many by me).

It is an unlooked-for pleasure, then, to be re-acquainted with articles that have appeared in the *Church Times* in the past twenty or so years, skilfully chosen by Hugh Hillyard-Parker. None was forgotten — though when we approached their authors for permission to use them in this collection, several struggled to remember their offspring — but when you are concerned about headlines and deadlines, you can sometimes fail to appreciate the sheer quality of the material with which you're working. Conversations really are along the lines of 'What's x's article about?' – 'It's about 150 lines too long.'

So much of what is included in the paper is designed for the swift communication of news and ideas: short sentences and paragraphs; front-loaded stories in case readers don't have time to get to the end; pictures for people with even less time. Our two exceptional issues each year, though, are at Christmas and Easter, when we reckon — I fear erroneously — that our readers have more time to absorb longer pieces, which take account of the uncertainties and ambiguities that make these two great festivals so rich and fascinating.

Both those issues have their practical challenges: the Christmas double issue — largely dictated by early Christmas-posting dates — is a case of fitting twice the usual amount of work into an ordinary working week. (Easter is a little better: not such a big issue, but we publish a day early in Holy Week — and then have to deal with two bank holidays while putting the next issue together.)

This, then, is the workaday world in which these pieces were generated, rather — though it's a presumptuous analogy — like the workaday world in which our Saviour was generated. The fact that they shine with insight, expertise, and wisdom is an indication of how blessed the *Church Times* has been over the years to have such excellent, thoughtful, patient (and generally prompt) contributors.

Now that these pieces are in book form, all that urgency can drop away, leaving reflections, stories, explorations, and revelations that can work at their own pace, in a way that their modest authors never dreamed would happen. Who would have guessed how enduring good news would be?

Paul Handley has been Editor of Church Times *since 1995.*

Editor's note: all the pieces in this book first appeared in the Church Times *at Christmas, between 2000 and 2020, the vast majority in the annual Christmas double issue. The year of first appearance is given at the end of each article.*

The God-bearer waits

Being favoured by God was as much to be feared as to be embraced, says **Paula Gooder**

THE last month of pregnancy is a time filled with a mass of emotions, both positive and negative. The waiting is nearly over. The longed-for event is about to arrive. All the hopes and dreams that have built up over nine months are about to be fulfilled; but this is accompanied by the knowledge that the only way to achieve these dreams is through the pain and suffering of labour.

The future is both known (a baby is about to be born) and unknown (what sex the baby will be and what she or he will be like). Excitement is tinged with fear, anxiety with hope. This mix of emotions can only be heightened in a culture where infant and maternal mortality rates are high. Mary, like many other mothers-to-be both then and now, must end her period of waiting facing her fear with courage and optimism.

It is appropriate, therefore, in Advent that we spend the last weeks watching and waiting with Mary, remembering not only the waiting that she did as she awaited Jesus's birth, but the waiting that she had to do for the whole of his life, and beyond. No parent-to-be can properly comprehend before birth the lifetime of joy, anxiety, delight, guilt, pleasure, and fear that awaits once the baby has been born. This is a maelstrom of emotion that grows stronger rather than weaker as the years go by. Mary's accepting "Let it be to me according to your word" (Luke 1.38) brought with it so much more than she could have ever expected; but it is this that shapes her waiting and our accompaniment of her in this last week of Advent.

"'GREETINGS, favoured one! The Lord is with you.' But she was much perplexed by his words and pondered what sort of greeting this might be … Then Mary said, 'Here am I, the servant of the Lord; let it be with me according to your word.'" (Luke 1.28-9 and 38)

What would you have said in response to Gabriel's message that you were about to bear a child? My response would have included a great deal more arguing than Mary's equivalent of "All right, then," and almost certainly more than a few rude words. Perhaps the account has been pared down, and between the "How can this be?" in verse 34 and the "Here am I" in verse 38 there was much shouting, crying, and outrage.

It is hard to comprehend the devastation of a message like this. If Mary was betrothed to Joseph, but still unmarried, she was probably in her early

1

teens. Pregnancy outside marriage was regarded with horror in first-century Jewish society; although it was unlikely that she would have been stoned, since stoning occurred only on the rarest of occasions, she would have become an outcast from society, and her reputation would have been in ruins.

So how could she say "Let it be with me according to your word"? How could she bring herself to accept the angel's message with such equanimity? If we read the story more carefully, though, it appears that she did struggle with Gabriel's announcement, but earlier in their conversation.

It is fascinating to notice that Mary appears much more perturbed when the angel first greets her than when she has learned the content of the message. After Gabriel's initial greeting, we are told in the NRSV that Mary was "perplexed" by the greeting, and "pondered" what sort of greeting this might be; or in the NIV that she was greatly "troubled" and "wondered", or again in the New Jerusalem Bible that she was "deeply disturbed" and "asked herself" what sort of greeting this might be.

The NRSV translation has clearly downplayed Mary's emotion at this point, but even the other translations do not quite communicate the potential anxiety behind the words. The Greek word "*dietarachthe*" means "deeply agitated", and "*dielogizeto*" can have the feeling of "argued" as well as "pondered" or "wondered". We need to add this to the fact that "*dielogizeto*" is in the imperfect tense, which implies ongoing action.

So Mary did not just say, "I wonder … never mind, it's OK —"; her state of wondering, pondering, and arguing went on for a while. Rather than a mild crinkle of the brow and a small question mark above her head, Mary seems to have been taken aback, disturbed, unnerved, anxious, troubled (and other such emotions) by the appearance of Gabriel.

THE Annunciation to Mary is not often understood as a calling so much as a declaration, but a closer examination of it reveals that this is exactly what it is. In the way that many judges and prophets were called in the Hebrew Scriptures of the Old Testament, so Mary is called here to a task of gargantuan proportions.

Mary may not, at this point, grasp the world-changing, life-changing significance of her calling, but then few of us do when we say that first tentative yes to God's summoning. She would, however, grasp the immediate significance of her own personal disgrace and exclusion from the community, and deserves our admiration for saying yes anyway. What seems important about Mary's calling is that she understands that being favoured by God is as much to be feared as embraced. It is truly wonderful to be beloved by God, but with this comes challenges beyond our imaginings. It seems to me that Mary has it the right way round: the message that God has chosen her is far more frightening than what he has chosen her for.

MARY is someone whose whole life was shaped by waiting. We find in her an example of someone who had no choice but to wait: from the moment of our first encounter with her, she was called into the way of waiting for Jesus's birth, for him during his life, and, most of all, for his death.

Much of Mary's waiting was neither for something good promised by God, nor for something long expected — as it has been for other characters, such as John the Baptist — but for something she dreaded most. This form of waiting brings a new depth to waiting so far explored.

Mary is a character about whom we know a great deal and very little, all at the same time. We know that events of enormous impact affected and shaped her life, but we do not know what she made of them. We know that for a large portion of her life she was forced to wait, but, again, we do not know how she coped with this. Was she someone who found depth and comprehension in her waiting, or irritation and frustration?

As so often with biblical characters, we are forced to accept how little we know or are going to know about them; so Mary is something of a mystery, and will remain so. She stands, an often silent figure in the Gospels, waiting for Jesus's birth and death, in great joy as well as in great suffering, and symbolises for us the agony as well as the glory of waiting.

MANY Advent wreaths have a fifth and final white candle, which is lit on Christmas Day and which symbolises Jesus Christ, the one for whom Abraham and Sarah, the prophets, John the Baptist, Mary, and indeed we, ourselves, have been waiting for so long.

It is in Jesus Christ that we discover a perfect fulfilment of everything for which we have waited — as well as for those things for which we have not waited. Jesus brings both completion and surprise in our waiting, and points us forward to a life-long waiting that can only find fulfilment in the end of all things. Perhaps most surprising of all, however, is the discovery that the one for whom we wait has been present all along; silently waiting with us in joy as well as in sorrow, in delight as well as in agony, drawing us further into the glorious paradox of God, who summons us to wait for that which has already happened and to remember that which is still to come.

It is this paradox that, as the completion of our waiting draws near, may cause us to pray, with R. S. Thomas:

Prompt me, God;
But not yet. When I speak,
Though it be you who speak
Through me, something is lost.
The meaning is in the waiting.

(2008)

O Sapientia: O Wisdom

Jane Williams reflects on the first antiphon from
'The Great Os' of Advent, the prophetic titles ascribed
by Isaiah to the coming King of Kings

IN the last few days before Christmas, the custom is to praise the child who is about to be born, highlighting aspects of his character as they have been known throughout the ages. The child of Bethlehem is not a new God, but the one, true God, our creator, who has been calling human beings from the moment we were made. What we see in Jesus is the fullness of the character of God.

This icon praises the wisdom of God, through which creation came into existence, and which

Holy Wisdom (icon, 1670s)

is found, personified, in Jesus. It is unusual to find a depiction of it, but the title is one that is often ascribed to Jesus. When the earliest Christians were searching back through Scripture for references to Jesus, the figure of Wisdom in Proverbs 8 and in the Wisdom of Solomon 7 resonated.

Proverbs 8 describes Wisdom's role with God in creation, and the joy that they share; Wisdom is God's "darling and delight", "playing over his whole world" (Proverbs 8.30-31, REB), and the Wisdom of Solomon says that Wisdom is "the flawless mirror of the active power of God, and the image of his goodness" (Wisdom 7.26, NEB). The similarity to the Christian understanding of the relationship between Father and Son made these obvious texts to go to.

IN the icon, the figure of Jesus stands just above Wisdom, claiming and affirming her as an insight into his own character. Mary and John the Baptist stand either side of Wisdom, and also attest to her as the likeness of Jesus, with all the authority of the mother and the forerunner. Wisdom sits on the seven pillars on which the universe is founded; she is dressed in vivid colours, making herself available to us, full of energy and passion. There is nothing insipid about Wisdom: she is forceful and attractive. The attention and praise that are given to her are channelled upwards to the figure of Christ, and from him still farther up to the Father's throne, where the angels echo earth's praise.

There is no embarrassment at all about the identification of the feminine Wisdom with Jesus — that seems to be a relatively modern preoccupation. Augustine talks easily about the "breasts of the Father" from which we are fed; Julian of Norwich describes Jesus as a mother pelican, tearing her own breast to feed her children; Jesus describes himself as a mother hen; Hosea pictures God as a mother helping her infant with its first toddling, unsteady steps. The images that best help us to catch glimpses of the character of God are used without gender distinction.

IN Advent, we are encouraged to meditate on the wisdom of God, recognising that it is both deeply engrained in the universe and yet also alien and elusive. It is God's wisdom that is coming to birth in a baby who has no power and no status, who will live a short, unsuccessful life and die a painful and shameful death.

This is the wisdom of God at work. We trace its contours in the life of Jesus: the little boy who understands the Scriptures better than the experts in the Temple; the young man who unerringly calls a motley crew of disciples to him, entrusting them with the good news for the world; the teacher who sees into the heart of the rich young ruler, of Zacchaeus, of the woman at the well; the fierce opponent, who challenges all those who try to keep God boxed in; the strategist, who avoids capture and death until the perfect moment.

This is wisdom embodied. It can be misunderstood, ignored, rejected, but it cannot be defeated, as the resurrection shows. It is the reality of the universe.

Learning to live in the wisdom of God is learning to attend to and trust what God has made. There is no conflict between "knowledge" and "wisdom": both are about what is true, and how to honour it and live in tune with it. The early Christians called Jesus both "wisdom" and "word", *Sophia* and *Logos*. The universe is rational; it is meant to be open to our exploration and delight, and we flourish when we live by its rhythms and needs.

The universe, like us, takes its character from the one through whom it came into existence. At its heart, there is delight, joy, generous communication. Now, in Advent, we respond with praise and find ourselves living in wisdom. God is coming to invite us to play in the presence of the Son, for the joy of all that is made.

(2018)

O Rex Gentium: O King of the Nations

Jane Williams reflects on the penultimate antiphon
from 'The Great Os' of Advent

BLAKE's depiction of the creation of Adam is by no means a celebration of life. Blake was deeply ambivalent about the theological narrative that seems to say that we are created good but constantly judged for being unable to live up to our origins. It is as though we are blamed for being what we are.

This painting is full of pain and bitter symbolism. The winged creator figure, whom Blake called Elohim, rather than God, has a look of fierce, abstracted effort on his face, as he wrenches Adam out of the ground. His left hand is clenching the earth, as though he is having to tear it away from Adam. Adam, too, looks full of terrible sorrow, his left hand desperately reaching back into the watery darkness beneath him, which represents the homely nothingness he longs for, and from which he is being forcibly removed.

Even as the earth begins to recede, the human form is already manacled to its deathly destiny. Already, the serpent is coiled around Adam's leg, which ends in a hoof. He is an unclean thing, bereft of choice, from the start. Adam longs to be uncreated, disembodied, returned to nothingness, rather than burdened with this earthly life in which no freedom from sin is possible.

BLAKE's tragic vision of human destiny rings true: from this terrible beginning flows a human race constantly forced, almost against its will, to wage war on each other and wreak havoc on the earth.

At Advent, we call out to Jesus as the King of the Nations, the one who can take the responsibility of this tragic history from our shoulders, and lift from us the weight of rule and governance that we are so incapable of exercising well. There is no sense that Blake intended this echo, yet the racked figure of Adam seems to prefigure that of Jesus, laid out on the cross, his arms outstretched, his hands waiting for the impact of the hammered nails.

Just as Blake's Adam is made unclean by his creation, as symbolised by his cloven hoof, so too was Jesus's punishment designed to declare him unclean — "anyone hung on a tree is under God's curse" (Deuteronomy 21.23). Paul picks up the reference in Galatians 3.13, with the extraordinary statement that Christ becomes "a curse for us".

THE bitter, enslaved humanity that Blake seems to show us is one that Jesus deliberately takes on himself. If this is indeed what it is to be human, then

*Elohim
creating
Adam,
William Blake
(1795)*

this is where Jesus will go. But Jesus comes to this state as "King of the Nations". Adam is not the fount of the human race, the matrix through which its meaning must be read — Jesus is. If we can imagine Blake's picture of creation being mapped on to one of the crucifixion where the human figure is now Jesus, then what we are seeing is what is described in Ephesians 2.15-22: Jesus is making a new humanity. The fragmented pieces of the old humanity are nailed to the cross and put to death, so that what is reborn is the new nation of which Jesus is king.

We are no longer "strangers and aliens", as Blake's Adam is to his hated existence; instead, we are "members of the household of God". Sad, egocentric, embittered, and self-obsessed as we are, we have tended to assume that Jesus became human like us, but now, illuminatingly, we discover that we are invited to become human like him. Jesus is the original, in whose likeness we are dreamed. As we wipe away the clinging soil, unwind the grave clothes, what we find is our humanity, rejoicing. Ours is not a fearful legacy, where we are called to be what we cannot be, and judged when we fail. Instead, we are invited home, where all our sins are forgiven, nailed to the tree.

THE Advent assertion that Jesus is King of the Nations is one that reclaims the creation vision of the oneness of the human family, all made from the same dust, all tracing our blood lines back to one progenitor, all given a joint share in the one world. In Jesus, all of this comes together.

Here, again, we find we are one human race, not fragmented by enmity; sharing one world, not fighting to break it into pieces; knowing one source, owing allegiance to one king.

So look again — Adam or Jesus? Life torn from the earth, or life offered to the earth? Desolation or restoration? Expulsion or homecoming?

(2018)

O Emmanuel: 'With us' always

Kenneth Stevenson considers the significance of the
seventh of the great 'O' antiphons

Emmanuel
O Emmanuel
O Emmanuel, our king and lawgiver,
the hope of all the nations and their Saviour:
Come and save us, O Lord our God.

THIS seventh and final antiphon in the series comes across as much a summary of the sequence as a composition in its own right. By its succinctness, it speaks of the Advent message of the Coming Lord. But it reads surprisingly differently from the others, since it is made up of seven titles in all: Emmanuel, king, lawgiver, hope, Saviour, Lord, and God. Such an assembly of titles is unique in the series.

"Emmanuel" echoes the main biblical source (Isaiah 7.14), being the Hebrew word for "God with us". "God with us" is the Advent message that transcends all others. In spite of the difficulties of life as we know it, the consequences of human sin and wilfulness, God is still prepared to take us seriously, and be "with us" — not estranged from us, not retaliating at us because we refuse to walk in his ways.

"Emmanuel" is, above all, the title that best expresses the message as Advent points us towards the three prongs of the future — daily discipleship, the annual commemoration of the nativity, and the ultimate coming of Christ at the end of time. Each one of those three dimensions to the life of faith circumscribes our daily living, so that each day does not exist in some kind of isolation, but is part of a coherent whole, for all that things often appear to be otherwise. Daily, yearly, eternally — these are the dimensions of the Advent message.

That is another part of Advent's riddle. I can just about cope with the daily Coming, and I have got used to the annual rhythms of the year, different as each one is when the days arrive. But the end of all time? Instead, I have had to consider my own death as a reality for the first time in the past two years, because of serious illness.

Yet even that is too individual, too specific, too unrelated to the other people towards whom I am beckoned by those seven Advent antiphons. In their studied and compressed eloquence, they stand as a sevenfold challenge to the culture in which we live, where — in the West — we have become so affluent, yet underneath lies a ferment of unanswered questions, unresolved fears, unnecessary unhappinesses, a condition described by Oliver James as "affluenza" (*Affluenza,* Vermillion, 2007).

As I watch and wait upon the Lord, I know in my heart of hearts that that ferment is not where I really belong, because I belong somewhere else. I may not be ready for it when I do die. But I believe that, whatever sense I can make of the Four Last Things, death, judgement, heaven, and hell, we are — somehow, by the grace of God — destined for another shore, and a greater light.

Michael Ramsey writes of these truths in his usual perceptive manner:

The hope of the beatific vision is crossed by the hope of the vindication of the divine design not only in us but in all things. And the hope of the resurrection of the body, when the body of our low estate is transformed into the body of Christ's glory, is the reminder of our kinship with the created world which the God of glory will redeem in a new world wherein the old is not lost but fulfilled. (*The Glory of God and the Transfiguration of Christ,* Longman, 1949)

(2007)

Word from Wormingford

We wait expectantly — but for whom?
asks **Ronald Blythe**

ADVENT. Season of name-giving — and such names! Who giveth these names? Heaven only knows. Poets, saints, youths, ancient folk. What shall we call him? Adonaï — a name for God? Dayspring bright? Desire of nations? Key which opens what cannot be closed? Emmanuel, of course.

In the congregation, a baby is long overdue, spinning out womb-days in order to have an Advent birth. What shall we call him or her? Something beautiful. No flowers in church, but all this name-calling. Outside, murk and final sunshine, slippery leaves, and noisy rooks. Inside, I say the sublime Advent collect, the one about putting away works of darkness and putting on the armour of light. Shall we sing Eleanor Farjeon's carol of the Advent?

> *Furrows, be glad. Though earth is bare,*
> *One more seed is planted there:*
> *Give up your strength the seed to nourish,*
> *That in course the flower may flourish.*
> *People, look east, and sing today:*
> *Love, the Rose, is on the way.*

Quite a lot of charlock is being grown, and brassy yellow alternates with rich browns in the landscape. Trees and hedges are semi-bare, but the air has a sultriness tinged with frost. Norfolk friends are held up by fogs. The white cat takes up winter quarters, this time on my garden-tools table in the boiler room, her tail wound around a hot pipe. She sleeps deeply 23 hours a day, and, apart from six square meals, will not come to until late March. Who would? I would, for one.

I would not mind missing Christmas, but to miss Advent! Ages ago, Advent was as strict a fast as Lent, the Second Coming in mind. Now, a confusion of natural and supernatural birth, plus this intense welcoming of the gloriously named Child, plus, it has to be said, an absence of judgemental terror and awe, makes the severity of a flowerless sanctuary a liturgical pointer to winter. Little more.

Richard Mabey arrives, and we talk shop. The years of our friendship are quite amazing. We go back a bit, as they say. We sit by the stove, and the ash logs spit at us. A chicken sizzles in the oven. He and Polly have brought champagne and apple tart. Thus we slummock in the old room as the light fails, careful not to bore one another with current toil, the flames illuminating our three faces.

Polly has returned from Zambia, and from an encouraging account of her son's refrigerator, its hairy contents, and its almost archaeological sell-by dates. Her son runs a wild-animal reserve, and an elephant can, literally, be in the room.

But pythons, tigers — what are these to her son's fearful groceries, mouldering away in the icy darkness? When they have gone, I find some pâté right at the back of my fridge; quite good, but dated 2009. Oh, the waste, the strength of character needed to cast it forth! The fridge stands in a brick-floored dairy, so cold in itself as to compete with this newfangled gadget for keeping food edible for ages. Though not for ever.

Apart from Adonaï-Dayspring-Desire of Nations, what else will Advent bring us? There will be Gaudete Sunday, when, as in mid-Lent, a rose-coloured vestment may be worn. For me, the pulsating season itself will always be enough.

(2011)

The unborn Jesus arrives incognito

George Pattison examines the details of *The Census at Bethlehem*, by Pieter Bruegel the Elder

The Census at Bethlehem *(1566) by Pieter Bruegel the Elder,*
Royal Museums of Fine Arts of Belgium

THE Census at Bethlehem, a painting in the Royal Museums of Fine Arts of Belgium, in Brussels, may well be the most "secular" of all Bruegel's religious paintings. In fact, it is hard to see anything obviously religious about it at all.

Although the title identifies it as a familiar moment in the Nativity story, we might be forgiven for thinking that it was merely a genre painting, illustrating winter life in a 16th-century Netherlandish town. And, at one level, this is what it is. Bruegel is doing what he does so well — bringing to life the sights, sounds, and even smells of his age: the slaughter of a pig outside the inn where the taxes are being collected; children skating and tobogganing on the ice; a group of soldiers huddled round a fire; workmen erecting a wood-framed shelter; pack-bearers struggling across a frozen river; and much, much more.

And, while any competent painter could use a covering of snow to suggest winter, Bruegel's bare trees, outlined against a stippled brown sky, his weary flocks of crows, and the dark red of the setting sun make us feel the cold seeping into our bones. This is indeed a bleak midwinter.

We could stop here, and it would be enough. Bruegel would have given us a picture we can pore over, relish, and return to again and again, always discovering new details to delight and fascinate. Note how the outer fortifications of the town are shown as broken and crumbling away, as if to suggest that — for all its perpetual motion — this is a world that is passing away, eking out its cold existence in the shadow of past glories. But there is more.

IF we look again, slightly to the right of centre, we notice the unassuming figure of a young woman seated on a donkey, apparently just arriving in town: Mary. And, once we see her, the balance of the whole picture changes. But what is it about her that holds our gaze and makes her the true focus of this busy scene, the still centre of this teeming world?

Perhaps it is just that — her stillness. This is a picture full of movement. Everyone is up and doing, or watching what others are doing — bustling, shoving, peering, staring; in short, a heaving mass of humanity.

But Mary is not involved in, or attentive to, any of this. Her head is slightly bowed, and her face — again uniquely — is turned towards us, the viewers. But she is not exactly looking at us, either. Rather, she seems absorbed in herself, pondering the words she treasures in her heart, and brooding on the mystery she carries in her womb: the Word becoming flesh.

Nor are any of the crowd giving her a second glance. She passes unnoticed through their midst. If only they knew that it was through her — this quiet, unassuming young woman — that a new and eternal light would shine into this bleak midwinter world, then, surely, they would look.

Karl Barth spoke of the "secularity of the Word", and Søren Kierkegaard of the divine "incognito" — and what picture could better reveal this, the true humility of the incarnation, arriving without a fanfare, unobserved, unrecognised, but full of grace for all the world.

(2012)

Brief encounter:
a true Advent story

by **Dennis Bailey**

"ONLY in Africa!" The speaker, a pilot, caught my eye and shook his head. At the head of the disorderly check-in queue at Kigali Alport was a pregnant nun. Large with life, she straightened her spine, adjusted her sun-bleached habit, and, ignoring the stares, she crossed the hall and climbed the staircase to passport control and the departure lounge.

Predictably, the airport computers were down, prolonging the formalities and making chaos of the seating arrangements aboard the weekend's only direct flight to Johannesburg. Normally this would have provoked me to fury, but, having upgraded to business class in an attempt to use my frequent-flyer miles before they expired, I kept my nose buried in J. M. Coetzee's *Disgrace*.

An hour later, lubricating my throat with the last of the drinks that came with the upgrade, I ignored the call to board and distanced myself from the usual fracas at the boarding gate. I couldn't help but smile at the sight of the nun being escorted unhurriedly, ahead of everyone else — though I doubted she'd booked in business class.

But as luck would have it — or higher forces would design — by the time I had sauntered across the blistering tarmac and climbed the stairs into the aeroplane, all but one of the seats in business class had been taken. And it was the one next to the pregnant nun, whose company everyone else had avoided.

I stowed my laptop and slumped into the seat beside her. She smiled and greeted me in Kinyaiwanda. I had learned enough of the local lingo to reply, then I settled back to my novel.

"Going home for Christmas?"

I nodded, and felt constrained by convention to enquire: "You?"

She shook her head. "Rwanda's my home."

I guessed she was no older than 30, though she had the complexion of an infant. And her physique was quite clearly more congruent with her condition than her vocation. From her intense study of the emergency information card and her attention to the flight attendants' instructions on take-off, it was obvious that she was a novice passenger. Prudently, I located the discreet paper bag.

But, despite the roller-coaster climb through the central African cumulus, the nun remained a glowing picture of health and contentment. A cloud of condensation grew on the window beneath her nose.

Eventually she turned from the window and glanced at me.

"My first flight."

Like most of those who travel for a living, I hate flying. Not that being airborne is any scarier than driving in Africa. It's all the stuff that goes with flying I find so disagreeable — like being sociable when you'd rather slip into alcohol-induced sleep. As Rwanda doesn't feature on the average tourist's itinerary, it was inevitable that my neighbour would ask the purpose of my visit to Kigali.

"We're in the same business, sort of," I said.

"We are?" Her voice had a playful lilt. "And what sort of business might that be?"

"I'm a priest," I began, but, on observing her widening eyes, qualified it. "Sort of."

"And what sort of priest might you be, Father?"

The sort that's intrigued to be sitting beside a knocked-up nun, I thought, but manfully resisted.

"I'm not paid by a church, but I am ordained."

"I didn't ask who paid you." Then she smiled. "I meant, of which Church are you a priest."

The implied rebuke seemed an affront. What kind of nun was she, after all?

"I was ordained in the Anglican Church, though I'm more comfortable in the company of sinners than saints these days," said I, turning on the defensive tone to which my wife regularly objected. "I'm a writer. I call myself a media and development consultant." Sounded grand, but it was really a euphemism for unemployed. To deflect her pursuit of the truth, I asked "You?".

She almost smiled. "Isn't that obvious?" And she savoured my embarrassment. I had assumed she was a member of a lay order that didn't insist on the vows that normally went with the garb.

"Nuns are women too, Father," she said.

"Hardly usual, though?"

"Not usual," she conceded in a whisper.

Thus she began her story, told quite matter-of-factly over the next few hours, with the agony camouflaged and sparing me the gore. Though rape is endemic in Africa, it is the last thing one expects a nun to undergo. But, caught up in the backlash of Rwanda's epic genocide, even the religious become victims of hatred and revenge.

"So you're going on your way to have the child in South Africa?"

"My child."

I nodded, to acknowledge the correction.

"Yes, discreetly, in a private clinic in Johannesburg," she continued, happily leaving the past for the excitement of the unknown ahead. "I'll be there until Easter. Then I will return to Rwanda, and care for my baby for as long as the Lord allows."

I took this to mean for as long as her Order could cope. "And then?"

"The child will be cared for."

I had little doubt that Mother Church would do her duty by such a special child. However, I couldn't help wondering how her community would cope with an infant that refused to conform to the rhythm of the religious life.

"You seem to have come to terms with it all very well."

"I'm not sure being raped is something anyone comes to terms with, Father," she said putting me in my place. "Though I'm grateful to God for the unexpected privilege of motherhood."

Before my natural cynicism cast a shadow over such poise, I made a further mistake: "You believe there's something quite special about this child don't you, Sister?"

"Doesn't every mother?"

They do, but I hadn't expected to be reminded of it by a nun. I marvelled at the miracle of birth and rebirth taking place in the seat beside me. Having worked amid the torment of Rwanda's genocide for a year, I was inspired by her resilience and resolute spirit. I tried to imagine what the fruit of her womb could become to a community torn apart by hatred and violence. Should God become one of us, the transport awaited in seat number 1A.

HAVING cleared immigration at Johannesburg airport, we strolled through Nothing-To-Declare, relishing the covert stares of the customs officials whose embarrassment seemed greater than their curiosity.

"You haven't told me your name, Sister," I said, handing her a card with my details on it.

"You haven't asked, Father." She had sized me up enough to know I would be amused by this. "Immaculate." She said it tentatively at first; then, taking my outstretched hand, she repeated it. " I'm Sister Immaculate."

I was momentarily gob-smacked; then I guffawed. And Immaculate laughed at my laughter, tilting her head apologetically, still holding my hand.

"You know, your story is too much!" I said.

"I'm sorry. But you're an appreciative listener."

"Would you mind my telling it?"

The request didn't register, at first, so I explained: "I would like to write your story. It's perfect for Christmas." The title came to me in a flash. "I'll call it 'Immaculate's conception.'"

She suddenly realised I was serious, and disapproved. My hand was returned.

"Sister," I urged, "have you any idea what an inspiration your story has been to me? You take the myth out of Christmas."

"You don't have the monopoly on cynicism, Father," she said. "Let me think on it more, and I'll let you know."

It was the closest she had let me come to any of her pain, and I was finally consoled. Pocketing my card, Immaculate turned to push the trolley out towards a clutch of similarly clad nuns, excitedly waiting to greet her.

I watched long enough to see her glance over her shoulder, and hear her call back: "You decide the title of the story, Father. I'll look forward to reading it."

I turned in the direction of my connecting flight. "Only in Africa", I decided, was far too cynical an opening for a story about the wonder of Christmas …

On St Valentine's Day 2002, Sister Immaculate gave birth to Emmanuel. She has since returned to Rwanda, where she is raising him in a Roman Catholic orphanage.

(2002)

Incarcerated for the incarnation

David Kirk Beedon reflects on the resonances of St John's
Prologue for prisoners at Christmas

ONE of the highlights during my six years ministering as a prison chaplain
was the annual carol service in the chapel. It was an ecumenical affair,
shared with my Roman Catholic and Free Church colleagues, and with
prison residents from various Christian traditions (and none), as well as
community guests from churches near by.

The format resembled many found in churches during the festive season:
the customary collection of readings from the nativity accounts of St Luke's
Gospel, and carols that would be familiar from primary school. Slightly
self-indulgently (because of my love of Johannine incarnational theology),
we would always have John 1.1-14 as the fourth and final reading.

I was aware that, for many residents, the nativity may have been little
more than a vague memory from school festive events in childhood. So,
throughout Advent each year, a weekly study group would look in turn at
each of the four readings, by way of preparation for Christmas.

In each session, we would co-create a reflection to follow each reading,
that spoke about the meaning of the nativity for them, in that place — a
prison — and at that time, more than 2000 years after the birth of Christ.
Feelings of homesickness would be expressed, alongside regret for past
actions and general frustrations at being in such a place at Christmastime.
Through all this came a reflective expression of faith that — despite all the
difficulties they had experienced previously, and those facing them in the
future — God would be close; this they knew, because of the coming of
Jesus.

During the carol service, each reflection would be read aloud after the
relevant lesson by a member of the Advent group. In their own voice, their
lived experience was related to the story of a family gripped in an unfair
system, separated from their loved ones, and caught in unfavourable circumstances. Many community guests would comment on how the juxtaposition
between the two worlds (incarceration and incarnation), described from
the heart by the reader, was deeply moving, and added a depth to their own
Christmas reflections.

It was always a privilege to accompany the men I served on this Advent
journey. The way in which they brought the incarnation to life was both

humbling and inspiring. In the service, as we concluded the reflections, the reader would declare, "Emmanuel!", and the worshippers would respond, with gusto, "God is with us!" (with a pronounced emphasis on the "is").

LAST year, after a colleague expressed reluctance to use the fourth reading, I began to question whether John's Prologue might be theologically too "high brow" for this context, and came to the conclusion that it was for the men themselves to decide. At the penultimate Advent meeting, the group spent their time looking at the reading, and I asked them, "Do we want this in the carol service?" I suggested that it might be thought too "philosophical" or "theological".

After reading the passage, I let them think about the task in hand, but, immediately, one of the group declared, "No, we've definitely got to have this [reading]," and others nodded vigorously. I gave some background to the reading, and pointed out its deliberate scriptural resonances with the opening of Genesis and God's creative work of bringing the world into existence.

When I asked them which parts of the reading appealed to them, they identified "the power to become children of God"; "in the flesh"; and "the light shines in the darkness." One participant said "I just love 'the Word' bit." I explained that the Greek word *logos* — translated in our Bibles as "Word" — also meant "logic, meaning, or purpose", and described how the reading posits that everything (including us) that has being, and has come into existence, has done so through what we see embodied in Jesus. At this, one participant from the south of England smiled, nodded his head, and declared — in appreciation, if with conflicted understanding — "That's proper mad, that is!"

The Service of Nine Lessons and Carols introduces the Prologue to St John's Gospel in terms of the unfolding of the great "mystery" of the incarnation. A mystery stretches our comprehension almost to breaking-point. In his poem "Christmas", John Betjeman twice asks of "this most tremendous tale of all", "And is it true?"; and I am sure that many of us can relate to the notion — so eloquently expressed by my group member — that the doctrine of the incarnation is "proper mad".

Yet he, with others on that Advent journey and in the subsequent carol service, experienced something profound: a belief that they are "children of God". This band of seekers after something to hope in — a group made up of the abandoned, dysfunctional, neglected, abused, marginalised, dangerous, and unloved — had a faith stirred in them: that the one who became the human face of God provides them with a light to shine in their darkness: a light that cannot be overcome.

PRISONS, and those who are held in them (83,000 people at the time of writing), are going through challenging times. This Christmastide, I invite you to hold close these places and people (including staff) in your prayers. Although there were many harrowing encounters during my time as a priest behind bars, I also frequently experienced the best of days. For it is in such dark places that it is, paradoxically, often easiest to witness the light of God's love transforming lives, and to rediscover that incarnational truth that "God is with us."

Far from turkeys, trees, and tinsel, God is at work in the unlikeliest of places (unlikely, that is, if we take as our reference traditional Christmas-card scenes). To recognise this is to realise — of the incarnation, and in the best of ways — "That's proper mad that is!" Thank God.

(2018)

The Innkeeper's Wife
by Kenneth Steven

I reckon it was the girl,
not more than fourteen. Those eyes.

Something made him stop his talk,
hoist down the lantern and mutter out with them.

And that was one sour night —
dust and wind, things banging;

folk still wandering the town like ghosts
and hammering the doors.

Our place was loud with coins and drink,
and this was long past midnight.

It wasn't him that came back somehow;
that's all I'll say, I can't explain.

As though he'd seen something;
as though his eyes were somewhere else.

The first spear of light next day and he was out
with that fresh pail of milk —

and he would not say where he was going.

(2020)

Now you see him ...

A relationship with Jesus involves the interplay of presence and absence, says **Paula Gooder**

WHEN I was a student, I remember listening to a sermon about Christmas. The preacher was talking about the theme of Emmanuel — God with us. He, as so many of us love to, was playing with words, and, in this instance, the aural similarity between "presents" and "presence". Reaching the climax of what he wanted to say, he left a dramatic pause, and said: "So you see, Christmas is all about presence." At this point, his rather flamboyant daughter jumped up, threw her arms to the ceiling, and yelled: "Yes, lots and lots of lovely presents." In an odd way, her unasked-for contribution made that sermon for me. Christmas is about exactly that: "lots and lots of presence".

The season of Christmas is, in so many ways, the season of presence. The season when we celebrate the presence of God — Emmanuel — in our midst. On one level, this understanding of God's presence in the midst of the people of God finds its roots deep in the Old Testament. One of the vital strands of Old Testament tradition is that God established a home for himself (in the tabernacle and then the Temple), placed his name there, and did, from time to time, descend to the holy of holies.

The important words there, however, are "from time to time". This was no permanent presence. It could never be guaranteed. In contrast, as the well-loved Prologue of John's Gospel reminds us, Jesus not only dwelt in the midst of the people, but did so permanently. In John 1.14, the author plays with this idea. In the NRSV, John 1.14 is translated as "the Word became flesh and lived among us, and we have seen his glory".

Unfortunately, this translation, though accurate, does not quite communicate the significance of what John is saying here. The Greek word used for "lived" here has more of a resonance of setting up camp. In the Septuagint (the Greek translation of the Hebrew Scriptures), it is sometimes used to translate the verb "*shakan*" or "dwell" (and hence is the root of the word "*Shekinah*", the Hebrew word associated with God's presence). Thus, just as God was present among the people by setting up camp in the tabernacle with his people in the wilderness, so Jesus did the same here.

The crucial difference, however, is that Jesus did this by becoming flesh, not by descending from time to time in an ephemeral cloud. Not only that, but "we have seen his glory": God's presence in the tabernacle (and then the

Temple) was a rare occurrence, and beholding his glory was an exclusive and somewhat dangerous privilege. The story of the announcement of John the Baptist's birth to Zechariah in Luke 1.5-22 illustrates this tradition well. Zechariah was alone in the Temple when he was met by Gabriel, and was struck dumb as a result of the encounter. Zechariah's meeting with the angel happened alone, and resulted in an injury, albeit a temporary one.

In contrast to this, the Prologue to John's Gospel declares that Jesus not only became flesh (and hence did not come and go), but that "we" have seen his glory. Many people, not just a rare few, encountered and were transformed by Jesus's glory. The Prologue of John's Gospel makes it clear that what is being talked about is lots and lots of presence.

TO a certain extent, presence is to Christmas what absence is to Advent. In Advent, we focus on the one who is absent. In Advent, we wait, we expect, we yearn for the one that is to come. At Christmas, we focus on Jesus's presence. We celebrate, we worship, and we cherish God made human before our eyes. Advent leads into Christmas, and lends meaning to it. We cannot truly celebrate Jesus's birth until we have learned to yearn for his presence.

In the same way, however, Christmas also lends meaning to Advent: we cannot wait for Jesus as we should until we have recognised, fully, the wonder and power of his presence. As in all relationships, absence and presence intertwine to remind us how much we value the one we love. When I am away from my husband and children, I miss them deeply and value them even more when I return, but it is my time with them in the first place which causes me to miss them when I am away.

In the same way, our yearning for Jesus's presence in Advent allows us to celebrate Christmas in a deeper and more powerful way, but it is the fact that we have celebrated his presence in our lives at all that makes our yearning for him at Advent so strong. We need the absence of Advent just as much as the presence of Christmas to deepen our awareness of Jesus.

One of the great paradoxes of the Christian faith, however, is that presence and absence are never absolute. Just as, in our Advent waiting, we often discover that the God for whom we wait has been present all along, also at Christmas we encounter a divine presence laced with intimations of absence.

In the stories of Jesus's birth, this finds its expression in many different ways, but two stand out. The first is the way in which the whole story of Jesus, including his death and resurrection, is woven into the stories of his birth. The second is that Jesus constantly and regularly defies all expectations of him. The birth narratives draw our attention to the fact that even the great festival of presence — Christmas — has absence woven within it.

Intimations of absence can be found in the birth narratives of the Gospels of Matthew and of Luke. Barely has Jesus's presence been made permanent in our midst, when his future death is indicated. In Matthew's Gospel, this is famously indicated by the gift of myrrh — burial tomb spices — from the Magi. While two of the threefold gifts point to Jesus's identity as king (gold) and priest (frankincense), the third reminds us that his presence will find its culmination in death. Right from his birth, Jesus's presence as "God with us" finds partial expression in future absence. It is his expected death that shapes the nature of his presence among us.

Luke also weaves a similar theme, not into the birth narratives, but into the stories that form part of the Christmas season. Jesus's dedication at the Temple (celebrated at Candlemas) has within it Simeon's bone-chilling words to Mary: "a sword will pierce your own soul too" (Luke 2.35). Simeon's great hymn in praise of Jesus, as a light both for revelation to the Gentiles and for glory to Israel, is followed by a prediction of his death. His presence, it seems, is defined — at least in part — by his future absence.

JESUS'S absence is not only future absence. Another feature of absence in the birth narratives is that Jesus is not where he is expected to be — nor, indeed, is he who he is expected to be. This finds its clearest expression in the search of the Magi for the location of Jesus's birth. The Magi look for Jesus in the place — the royal palace — where they expect him to be, and find that he is not there. Luke's Gospel has a similar motif in reverse. Luke focuses not on where Jesus might be, but on where he is: wrapped in cloths and laid in a feeding trough.

Jesus continued to be absent from people's expectations for the rest of his life, choosing to be found more among the tax-collectors and prostitutes than among the great and powerful. Jesus continues to be absent in the same kind of way today. It seems to be an essential part of his presence that he is never where we expect him to be.

In my experience, Jesus is constantly surprising. When I expect to feel his presence in prayer, I discover it — much to my surprise — in a chance encounter on the train. When I expect to feel his presence on the train, I discover it in a mundane household task. When I have given up on prayer altogether, I experience Jesus anew in worship. It seems to me that Jesus is constantly defying our expectations, and can be found in the most surprising and least expected of places. At his birth, he defied all expectation of where the saviour of the world was to be found, and has continued to do so ever since.

OF course, this absence-laced presence finds its most acute expression in our own celebration of Christmas. We celebrate Jesus's presence — God with us — in his absence. The manger is, in effect, empty. The baby has grown ... and has died, risen, and ascended into heaven. Jesus is truly present with us, but not any longer wrapped in cloths and laid in a feeding trough.

At Christmas, we celebrate the baby who is no longer present as a baby. Indeed, it is the fact that he is no longer a baby that gives meaning to our celebration. We celebrate the Jesus who, grown into adulthood, lived among us, healing and teaching, and died and rose again.

At Christmas, we celebrate the baby because of all he will be, as much as for all he was as a baby. Without Jesus's absence — risen, ascended, and seated at the right hand of the father — the message of Christmas presence would be greatly impoverished.

Just as in Advent, when we feel desolate and alone, we are reminded that God is never entirely absent, so at Christmas the suggestion of absence, in the times when we feel God's presence most strongly, challenges us. This challenge reminds us that we cannot control Jesus's presence among us. Christmas, one of the most joyful of the Christian festivals, is celebrated under the shadow of the cross. Similarly, just when we become confident that we know and comprehend Jesus, we discover that, once again, he defies our expectations, and can be found where we least expect him to be. Probably most importantly of all, Christmas challenges us to recognise that we can truly comprehend Jesus's presence only when we embrace his absence, and discover how great is our need of him.

Christmas is indeed the festival of "lots and lots of presence", but this presence is mediated through absence. Christmas draws us deeper into the mystery of God, where absence and presence are not so much opposites as necessary constituents of each other. It is only when we encounter Jesus's absence in all its forms that we can fully comprehend his abundant presence in our midst — God with us.

(2008)

Saint Nicolas

A short story for Christmas by **Elizabeth Goudge**
(originally published in the *Church Times* in 1951)

IT was Christmas Eve, in a century long ago, and the old country town had robed itself in magic. The first snow had fallen, a light fall, but enough to powder the steep gabled roofs and cobbled streets with virgin whiteness. The frost fires sparkled upon it, and, overhead, the stars were a weight of glory in the sky. From sheer good will, doors had been left ajar and windows uncurtained, so that bright beams of light lay across the snow.

Delicious festive smells floated out from the doors, scents of baked meats and roasting apples, ale and wine, spices and perfumes, and the fragrant smoke of innumerable fires of apple-wood and beech logs and resinous pine branches. The bells rang out, and all the children of the town seemed to be laughing. They were glad it was a fine night, for the Players had come. Their stage was set up even now in the yard of the White Hart Inn, and decorated with lanterns and mistletoe and great boughs of fir and yew and holly.

In another hour, the trumpet would sound, and all the people would come streaming into the inn yard, and up the steps into the galleries, packing themselves into every inch of space; and then the pealing of the trumpet would come again; then, upon that stage, that seemed set up at the heart of the world, the Players would show forth once again the story of Christ's birth.

How dared they do it? wondered the actor who played the devil, as he sat repairing his tail in the disused inn stable, where the Players would live and sleep and eat, until they took the road again. The stable was too derelict to be used any longer for the horses of the quality; but the Players were used to discomfort, and it opened on the yard just behind their stage, and so was convenient for them. No doubt, thought old Nick, it was a lot more comfortable than the one where Christ was born.

"Lord have mercy on us!" he murmured. "Such a set of scoundrels as we are!"

He always felt this shame, when the time came round to play again the story of Christ's birth. Such a good-for-nothing lot, as men — and as actors, not much better. Yet, each year, he hoped that this time, just this once, they would give a perfect performance. But, of course, they never did, least of all himself. Not that it mattered about him, for he was only the devil. Perhaps this year, just this last time while he was with them —

He caught himself up. Why did he keep thinking that this year, for him, it was the last time? Master Roper, of course, had only yesterday threatened to kick him out for reasons of age, infirmity and general incompetence; but then he had been doing that for the past five years. In reality, he found old Nick uncommonly useful. Ugly as the old poor devil was, and full of eccentricities, he was the butt of the company and kept them all good-humoured.

He was good with the children, and any who had fallen sick. And he was a useful scapegoat. Master Roper was accustomed to visit the sins of the whole lot of them upon old Nick, for it drove them mad to have the old devil kicked and abused; and he kept the whip-hand of them that way. Proud man though he was, old Nick did not mind, because he was glad to be of use. Especially to the children.

Laying down his mended tail, he looked at the two little boys where they lay beside him, asleep on a pile of hay, warmly covered by the Lady's cloak. It would break his heart to part from the children. What would they do without him? He was father and mother to them both. He pushed the thought aside and reached for Gabriel's robe, that needed a patch behind. He had learned to sew after a fashion.

Indeed, he had had to learn to do most things after a fashion, because he was always too proud to ask for help, and such people must do everything for themselves or perish. He very nearly had perished, time and again, because he was not very bright and did things only after a fashion, and never very well. He had been born a failure, and, as life went on, had sunk always a little lower; but he had never accepted charity on that account. Nor sympathy either. "Proud as the devil." He'd always been proud, and they said it was a sin.

"God be merciful to me a sinner," he prayed. He knew he needed mercy, for he was getting old, and, so far as he could see, was for all his striving no nearer heaven than when he started out. The fact was, he thought gloomily, that he only followed his Lord after a fashion.

To cheer himself up, he looked again at the cloak. It was made of warm, black cloth and lined with lambswool; the Lady had pulled it off her own shoulders to give it to the children. It had been only three days ago, and he remembered the scene as vividly as though he were reliving it.

Her coach came round the corner of the narrow lane rather unexpectedly, and somehow the Players' poor old cart, piled high with stage properties and costumes and the children, got upset into the ditch. Old Nick was driving it, and he only drove after a fashion. Although her coachman was in no way to blame, the Lady stopped the coach and got out, and made her serving man help the Players pull the boxes and bags out of the ditch, and haul out the cart and bony horse.

Old Nick, as soon as he scrambled out himself, got the children out; and then, oblivious of everyone else, sat down on a big boulder at the side of the lane to comfort them. He took the little golden-haired Tom Thumb on his knee and blew his nose, and then he opened his pack and dived into it for a bit of gingerbread to comfort Benjie.

Tom Thumb did not care for gingerbread. He liked hot bread and milk, but he did not get it very often. Knowing he wasn't going to get it now, he burrowed into the crook of old Nick's arm and tried to get warm that way. Benjie, a dark-haired, grave-faced little boy, was past the burrowing age, but he leaned against old Nick's knee on the other side, and looked up at the Lady out of his great dark, sad eyes, as he munched his gingerbread. Absorbed in the children, old Nick did not even know that the Lady was there until she spoke to him.

"Are they your own children, good sir?"

He looked up and he saw her, and with Tom Thumb still in the crook of his arm, got up and bowed to her.

"No, Lady. I have no children."

The cold wind blew keenly down the lane and the sky was heavy with grey and desolate, and the Lady shivered and drew her cloak more closely about her. Old Nick did not permit himself to shiver. He stood straight and tall and gaunt, and his scarecrow garments flapped about him in the wind. She thought she had never seen an uglier man. His sallow face was pock-marked, and his dark eyebrows had an upward tilt at the corners, such as one see in pictures of the devil. His eyes squinted to such an extent that she did not think that either of them were looking at her, until an amused quirk, at the corners of his mouth, told her that he knew quite well what she was thinking.

There was a kindly mockery in his face now, and pride in his stiff figure. From habit, her hand had moved toward the purse in her pocket; but now she quickly withdrew it, and did not insult him with her pity. But in her heart, she offered him her sympathy, even as he was offering his to her. She, too, was childless, and she was always glad when Christmas was over. Yes, glad, even though it was that season when the thought of the Child in the manger broke hard hearts, and bent stiff wills, and queer flowers of under-standing bloomed and flourished in unexpected places, and between unlikely people; as now, on a wind-swept road, between unlikely people; as now, on a wind-swept road, between a proud great Lady and a proud poor man, who had never seen each other before, and had nothing in common except their pride, the children and the Child.

For they both worshipped the Child, and the children in him and for him. Suddenly they knew that of each other.

She swept the cloak off her shoulders and gave it to him. "For the children," she said. "To keep them warm. For Christ's sake."

He bowed and smiled, and took it and did not mind at all, for there was suddenly no pride left in him. And she got into her coach and drove away, and though she had no cloak now, and knew her servants mocked at her, she did not mind, because there was, for the moment, no pride left in her either.

HE thought much of her as he sat patching Gabriel's robe. He had these two adopted waifs to care for, the child actors of the company; but he pictured her living in some great house, widowed and barren and no longer young, and perhaps now unloving and unloved by human kind. If that was the case, he was the wealthier of the two; for really all the Players were his children, not only Tom Thumb and Benjie.

He kept an anxious eye on the stable door as he sewed, for very soon now they would be coming in to dress for the play, and tonight of all nights he was desperately anxious that they should be in good shape … To play the story of Christ's birth …

It would, he thought, be ridiculous presumption for even the best of men to attempt to set forth such great matters, but when it came to a rapscallion company of vagabond good-for-nothings — he pulled himself up sharply. It was for good-for-nothings that Christ had died. And at least he and Herod were God-fearing men, who could be relied upon to keep sober — he pulled himself up again, for there were worse sins than a mug of ale too much now and again. Pride, for instance. And, in any case, in his experience, it was always the same in the theatrical profession. Your noble blue-eyed hero was always a proper scoundrel, and your villain an honest fellow, on the whole.

The stable door was flung open, and Gabriel came in on a gust of wind. His battered cap with its peacock's feather was clapped on the side of his curly red head at a riotous angle, and the condition of his torn cherry-coloured doublet suggested that, during the course of an argument, someone had flung a bucket of pigwash at him. But he looked cheerful, his rosy cheeks distended by the apple he was munching, and his gait was only slightly unsteady.

He'd be all right, old Nick decided thankfully, after he'd stuck his flaming head in a bucket of cold water. And so would the two young shepherds, who came in a few moments after; merry, but not more so than boys should be at Christmas time. Poor old Kit, the old shepherd, could always be relied on to keep out of mischief, because he was too decrepit to do anything else. He'd not been out like the young fellows. He had spent the day huddled by the little fire of glowing coals that old Nick had lit for him in the brazier, trying to keep warm. That was four of them safe.

Herod was not here yet, but he, good, humble, selfless fellow, had never let anyone down. St Joseph could be relied on, too, though at the thought of him old Nick's face tightened grimly. For Master Roper himself played Joseph. The great benign beard he put on for the occasion was a most admirable disguise, and it was a torment to old Nick that such a whited sepulchre should play the part of the foster-father of the Lord. It was almost impossible to remember that for him, too, the Lord had died.

But where was Mary? There were no women in the company; and Will, who played Mary, was a perpetual anxiety. He was, on the whole, a good boy, and certainly a beautiful boy, with his clear treble voice that remained so long unbroken, his mild, dark eyes and pale, oval face; but he was an inveterate and indomitable fighter. His fragile appearance was entirely deceptive, and so was the mildness of his eyes. He would go on fighting until he was beaten to a jelly; and he still would go on fighting.

The gutters of every town they played in ran with his blood; but it would boil up again by the time they reached the next one. Old Nick took great care of Will, giving him most of his own food to build up his anaemic condition, and sitting with him night after night putting goose-grease on his bruises. And Will loved old Nick, and had promised not to go out tonight … Yet he was not here.

The Magi came in, and Herod and the Innkeeper, but still no Mary.

With a sense of disaster growing upon him, old Nick woke up Benjie and Tom Thumb and dressed them. They were the cherubs who worshipped at the crib, and they wore white tunics, small gold haloes and little feather wings. Old Nick had these heavenly garments in his special care, and kept them as clean as he could wish, because he only laundered after a fashion.

In his care, too was the crude little figure that he had carved from a bit of wood (he carved only after a fashion) and wrapped in swaddling bands. He kept it in a box by the children's bed, and felt for it such reverence that his feeling had communicated itself to the rest of the Players, good-for-nothings though they were. The corner of the various outhouses where the children slept, and where the Babe lay, seemed to them always a place apart. Old Nick was mostly to be found there, too, and so it was their refuge in all times of trouble, perplexity or downright disaster.

The stable door opened again, and, to the corner where old Nick was washing the children's faces, Will came stumbling in his tribulation. He was speechless, because his upper lip had been badly cut; and it was a wonder he had been able to see his way to the corner, because both his eyes were closed up. His nose was bleeding and he was shaking as though he had the ague. But it was not because of his physical misfortunes that he was so miserable. It was because he had broken his promise. He would not be able to play Mary. And his sins would be visited by Master Roper, not upon him, but upon old Nick. Will could not speak or look his penitence; but he stood before old Nick with his head hanging, and, when there was no word of reproach, he began to sob.

Old Nick took the boy in his arms, and laid him down on the straw where the children had been sleeping, and washed his face and covered him up with the Lady's cloak. Then he turned and looked bleakly at the rest of the company, who had gathered round in consternation. Not a single one of them could play Mary. Gabriel must play Gabriel. Of the two young shepherds, one was round and fat, and the other was wizened and hunch-backed, and the voices of both of them were already broken.

"Look after Will," old Nick said to the others. "Now then, Tom Thumb, don't cry. I'll go and tell Master Roper."

He went outside, where the stage was waiting, garlanded and gay with the lighted lanterns swinging at the four corners. The audience was already streaming in, happy and laughing in their bright clothes, gathering about the stage and climbing up the stairs to the outside galleries. Light streamed out from the inn, and overhead the stars were sparkling.

Master Roper always had his own room at the inns, and never shared the draughty barns and stables that housed his Players. Old Nick turned into the panelled hall of the White Hart to ask where he might find him. It was a good inn, that sometimes housed the quality; and, coming down the stairs, wearing now a blue cloak and holding up her sweeping blue gown, was the Lady. When she saw old Nick, she smiled without surprise, as though he were an old friend, whom she had expected to see there.

"St Nicolas, how are the children?" she asked. And then she went on companionably: "A wheel has come off my coach, and I am waiting here in the warm while they put it on again … St Nicolas, are you in any trouble?"

As companionably as she had told him about the coach wheel, he told her about Will. She stood thinking for a moment, and then asked: "Could I play Mary? It would not take you long, would it, to tell me what I must do?"

"But, Lady, your reputation!" he gasped.

"I do not live in the town," she said, "and I do not think there would be anyone who would recognise me." Then she lifted her head proudly. "Nor should I mind if they did."

He looked at her. She had a slender figure and a clear, treble voice. The blue veil over her head would hide her greying hair. She might very well pass for a boy, and she would play the part with grace.

"Thank you, Lady," he said. " I had wanted this performance to be very perfect."

At the stable door, standing beside him as he fumbled for the latch, she said: "I hope I shall not fail you. I know by heart all the words that Mary speaks. Sometimes I have felt that I understand her a little." She paused, as though she had a little difficulty breathing. "I had a son once, but they killed him in the wars."

He could think of nothing to say, and so said nothing; but he was grateful for the honour done him.

IT was, as old Nick had hoped it would be, a perfect performance. The presence of the Lady, moving among them with such loving dignity, as though she were the mother of them all, drew from each actor the best that he had to give. Even Master Roper gave of his best, and reserved what he said about the events of the evening until the performance should be safely over. Old Nick had not to appear until the end, when he would leap upon the stage with a flash and a bang to fetch Herod away where he belonged. Hidden among the greenery, he watched spellbound.

How could he ever have thought of this woman as barren? She might have borne one son only, and he, taken from her and killed, while still in his young manhood. But once a mother, always a mother, through life and death and through eternity. She seemed to him not only the Mother of the figures who moved about her on the stage, but the Mother of the entranced audience of men and women and children who packed the courtyard, the stairs and galleries, the Mother of the whole world, the Mother of heaven, the Mother of God.

Mary had borne only the one Son, the Child she held in her arms. He held in love all that was, heaven and earth, angels and archangels, men and women and children, because he had made them and was their God; and so she, holding him, held them, too. The hushed audience worshipped him by their reverent silence; the actors, those good-for-nothings, worshipped him by their movements; and his Mother worshipped him as she

31

sat there with him in her arms, on the stage that is set up on Christmas Eve at the heart of the world.

IN this life, one can fall very quickly from heaven to a sort of hell. Old Nick was scarcely aware of any passage between the sounding of the trumpet that told the audience the play was finished, and the moment when he came back from seeing the Lady to her coach, and found Master Roper in the stable most cruelly belabouring Will before the horrified eyes of all the Players.

Hitherto, except for a few kicks here and there, Master Roper had not been accustomed to use physical violence upon the boys; he had chosen the more subtle method of visiting their delinquencies upon old Nick, which hurt them infinitely more. But now something or other, perhaps the fall from the heights to which he had attained on the stage to what he was, the realisation of the contrast between St Joseph and Will Roper, had driven him quite mad.

He had pulled poor Will to his feet and was beating him about the head, so that his nose had started to bleed again, and the cuts on his face reopened. And the Players, so recently in heaven, were all too shocked and sickened to do anything at all about it.

For a moment, old Nick could do nothing either, until he saw the children, still in their angels' wings and haloes — Benjie clasping the wooden Babe in his arms — looking on with great wondering eyes of astonishment. Master Roper's great hand, swinging back for a fresh blow, caught Tom Thumb on the side of his golden head, and he fell headlong with tears and lamentations.

That sent old Nick mad, too. With all the force that still remained in his spent old body, he hit Master Roper a crack on the jaw that sent him staggering. Then he picked up the unconscious Will, and laid him back on the straw beneath the Lady's cloak, grabbed Benjie and the wooden Babe under one arm and Tom Thumb under the other, shouted to Herod to open the stable door, and vanished like a flash of lightning.

Would she be gone? No, the coach was moving only very slowly along the street, over the ruts of frozen snow. Gaping and staggering, he caught up with it and shouted to the coachman to stop. Then he wrenched open the door, and flung the children inside.

"Take them!" he cried to her.

"Why?" she asked. "What has happened?" But even while she spoke, her arms, holding the folds of her cloak, lifted like wings and the children were gathered in. Then her arms fell, and there was nothing to be seen of them except the top of Tom Thumb's golden head, where she held him in the crook of her arm.

Still gasping for breath, old Nick told her as well as he could. "Take them and keep them," he commanded her. "Do you want them to grow up grey-faced and wizened like the hunchback boy? Or drunken and dissolute while in their teens, like the boy who played Gabriel? Or to lie in their blood on a stable floor like Will? Or to be as I am? Take them and keep them, and the Child, too, for his sake." And he banged the coach door, turned away and left her.

"Stop!" she cried. "Stop! Come back!"

She knew by the proud way that his head jerked up that he had heard her; but he did not stop and he did not come back. She would have saved him, if she could, from what lay before him now. She was weeping as the coach drove on. Yet, in his place, she would have done the same. She would have preferred to die forsaken in a ditch than live the pensioner of a rich woman. She, too, had often been described as "proud as the devil".

The fate she had envisaged for him fell upon old Nick almost immediately. Kicked out at last by Master Roper, Christmas Day found him tramping along the road, a homeless vagabond. He did not mind much; for it was what he had always expected. Failure that he was, doing things only after a fashion, and sinking as life went on always a little lower, he had known he would come to this.

Death was always a difficult act of penance, he thought; and to die of hunger and exhaustion in a snowy ditch was no worse an end than many a rich man had to face. He missed the children, of course, but on this day, of all the days of the year, he had the Child, and the glow of possession warmed him through. Nevertheless, as he toiled along, he murmured often: "God be merciful to me, a sinner," for he was tramping now to the end of the way, and (as far as he could see) was for all his striving no nearer heaven than when he started out.

(1951 & 2003)

33

Be swept along by the drama

From fear to hope, the Christmas story has it all,
says **Helen-Ann Hartley**

WE spend a good deal of our lives waiting: for everything from buses (which tend, of course, to come all at once) to news of loved ones, test results, or the outcome of job applications. In W. H. Auden's "Christmas oratorio", *For the Time Being*, the Third Shepherd comments: "What is real About us all is that each of us is waiting."

Advent provides a holding space for the period of waiting which has its end on Christmas Day. It embraces the possibility that the coming presence of God is an answer to an absence. In its context, of course, the absence was unknown, but was filled with imaginative and visionary wonderings about who the Messiah might be, and when he would arrive.

For us, the question "Who are we waiting for?" seems to lead to an obvious answer: Christ. So why begin with what we already know? The answer lies deep within the question; we do indeed wait for Christ, but the certainty is balanced by an uncertainty about what lies ahead. The incarnation invites us to delve deeper into the mystery of God's love, about which we cannot know everything — not yet, anyway.

OUR Gospel authors crafted their narratives in order to tell a story and to proclaim its good news. If we follow the suggestion of the New Testament scholar Richard Bauckham that the Evangelists are working from eyewitness testimony (which, in Bauckham's definition, is both the narrating of events and the interpretation of their meaning), there is an immediacy to the words of those Gospel texts, a closeness to the abiding presence of the one they write about.

But Matthew, Mark, Luke, and John did not write in a vacuum. They wrote because they needed to make sense of what seemed like an impossibility to their communities. Their writing is rooted in the life of people whose identity was being crafted into that of Christ, and who wanted to make sense of impossibilities at both ends of the story: birth, and death and resurrection. As a friend of mine once said to me (paraphrasing an idea from C. S. Lewis): "Sometimes important things become real only when they seem impossible." At the heart of both the incarnation and the resurrection lie events that could have appeared to be impossible. Yet, as it turned out, they were not impossible, and our Gospel writers tell us that.

In Luke 1.34, Mary asks the angel: "How can this be?", and the angel responds in the next verse with the certainty that what might have seemed impossible will be made possible. The sense of mystery remains, however. In order to gain a sense of what these events of birth, death, and resurrection meant, and still mean today, we need to put ourselves in a place of unknowing; facing anew the full impact of the knowledge that, in Christ, God was doing something utterly new and profoundly transformative.

The unknowing persists: it does not end with Christmas Day; for mystery is part and parcel of the pilgrimage. "Who are we waiting for?" Let me tell you; come and see; share in the amazement that unfurls before our eyes. Let us wonder together; for, if we do, we shall surely realise that the wonder and awe at the manger make the apparent impossibility of the incarnation suddenly real in our lives.

One Advent, an encounter with the arresting life-size nativity scene outside Canterbury Cathedral startled me out of my usual relationship to crib scenes, as I imaginatively entered the story and played my part alongside the crowds of visitors who were likewise mesmerised by its vividness.

SOME years ago, when I was an undergraduate in Scotland studying theology, I was occasionally asked (somewhat tongue in cheek): "Are you a Christmas Christian, or an Easter Christian?" This reached dizzy heights one year when Holy Week fell during term, and the events of Christ's Passion, death, and resurrection were played out in between lectures, seminars, and everything else that makes up an undergraduate's week.

Easter Day was a typically blustery day on the Fife coast. I was given the task of leading a group standing "confused" (and certainly shivering) by the "unexpectedly empty tomb", situated in the ruins of the cathedral, as another group headed towards us carrying lit torches of fire (their walk more of an urgent and determined push into the wild winds). I was aware that I had to respond to words that were being shouted at me, but were disappearing out towards the sea. The dialogue went something like this.

"Hello."

"Pardon?"

"Who are you waiting for?"

"What?"

"WHO ARE YOU WAITING FOR?"

("What are they saying?")

"Sorry!"

At which point, my script, which in any case was folded in two by the gales, was blown out of my hands; a flimsy bit of paper carried away by the forces of nature that were gaining in strength.

When I reflect on those events now, they present a refreshing framework through which to view not just Easter, but the Nativity. Often, we need a new lens through which to view familiar stories. Looking back at that blowy Easter morning, there we were, imagining ourselves at the tomb, trying to make sense of an absence, not realising that the presence of the one who had been laid there dead now walked in the light of the resurrection.

BACK at the very start of the story, the presence in the manger is part of the journey towards the absence in the tomb, which itself creates the eternal presence of Christ in the resurrection. Both parts of the story matter: the manger and the tomb tell of the dynamic forces at work. Both stories contain the fear of unknowing, and the awe-filled response to the divine presence at work.

Many artists have, of course, captured the annunciation in varying ways. Dante Gabriel Rossetti's *Ecce Ancilla Domini!,* first exhibited in 1850, in particular captures more of a sense of fear in Mary than joy, something that has always challenged my thinking about this important episode.

The Lukan account presents Mary "pondering" what she has been told by the angel, and responding with words of praise. The women at the tomb in Mark's account apparently say nothing to anyone, yet are in awe at what they have encountered (not quite "shivering in their sandals" as some would have it, although they perhaps do model fear in a positive way).

All of this should be an encouragement to us that we have a part to play in the story if we only allow ourselves to be swept along with the drama, and think ourselves into the places of the characters. How would you respond?

MARK's Gospel is often cast aside at Christmas. This is perhaps understandable, given the lack of stable-and-manger action. Mark also leaves us unsatisfied with the ending of the story, concluding with a "for" (the literal final word in Greek, if we favour the ending at Mark 16.8). Likewise, John is distinctly lacking in Wise Men, angels, and shepherds, although of course the Prologue is usually offered as part of the Christmas morning readings.

Both Mark and John, however, provide strong clues about "Who are we waiting for?" through the cross. It is on the cross, and in the events that follow, that the true depths of Jesus's identity are revealed, but it becomes real only if, when we reach the end of the story, we reconnect with the beginning: seeing beyond the incarnate God lying in the manger, reading and listening to the events of that child's life as his public ministry ushered forth the Kingdom that turned everything upside down.

In that sense, Christmas Day is not just about a birth, it is also about a life lived, experienced, betrayed, destroyed, and lived again, for all time, through the power of the resurrection. But still, the question that we began with — "Who are we waiting for?" — needs constantly to be asked. For all our certainty, our knowing that we wake on Christmas morning to the dawning of a new reality, we cannot and should not be lulled into a complacency about the one for whom we wait. Mystery, wondering, and pondering are essential elements of our faith.

ADVENT has been filled with visionary readings that prepare us for Christmas Day. Visions in the Bible tend to take the form of divine messages communicated to human beings by direct voice — by angelic presence or by the exercising of the imagination in tune with God's direction. The result is often a process of wondering and pondering. Visions are held by the relationship of trust that must be in place; the possibility that God can give us difficult tasks to do because God believes that we can manage.

Part of the challenge of any visionary encounter is the creating of space within which object and mystery might come together to experience God's eternity: the point of encounter creates the opportunity for change. Having a vision allows us to dare to hope with courage. The incarnation offers that hope, because it encourages us to be part of the sharing of that wondrous event with others. As recounted in the biblical narrative, it is not a flat, distant story; it is rooted, yet timeless. The gospel is meant to be shared, and the difference that the incarnation makes to our world is something that ought to be celebrated.

In many homes, the Holy Family begins, on Advent Sunday, its journey from room to room towards the crib scene. It is significant, however, that we do not spend the whole of Advent slowly reading our way through the birth narratives. Rather, Sunday by Sunday, and day by day, we approach Christmas Day from the perspective of other biblical passages.

As we have listened to these texts, our reflections on their meaning have given them new colour and texture in our here and now. The question "Who are we waiting for?" has been enriched with a pondering at the very heart of the big-picture narrative of Scripture itself. Story, context, and conversation have become part of our experience of this season.

We tell about what happened; we watch it unfold in nativity plays that can take place in many different contexts; we talk about what we have seen and what Christmas means for us (for some, negatives as well as positives). Yet this is not without its challenges. One year, my local city council decided to hold a "Winter Light Festival" rather than celebrate Christmas. The result was a blend of traditional carols, accompanied by a brass band; illuminated symbols of the sun, moon, and stars; and inflatable Santa Claus balloons.

The meaning of the narrative became interrupted, and I suspect that that is part of the challenge of proclaiming the mystery of the incarnation. Stories are not isolated from the context in which they are told, and this is where interpretation can help us to appreciate the time and distance between us and the story that we are encountering. Stories mark time — both the time in which they were told and eventually written down, and our own time.

But, if the sense of the story gets lost in the midst of commercialism and other so-called secularising agendas, how can we hope that the vision of God's love that lies rooted in that story may find the light of day? It is as if the Holy Family en route to the crib scene has been held back from making progress, waiting for an opportunity to continue on its journey.

ONE of the consequences of recognising a relationship between deeper meanings that may reside within the texts, and the ways in which we may be able to tell our stories as part of the larger story of God's dealings with our world, may be most helpfully described as a theology of reading. The stories we tell ourselves and the stories we tell each other can (if we allow them to) constitute a redemptive endeavour.

In his work on narrative theology, the English Literature scholar Alan Jacobs reflects on us becoming consciously aware of telling our own stories and of thinking about our lives narratively so as to impart wisdom. In his book *Looking Before and After: Testimony and the Christian life* (Eerdmans, 2008), Jacobs reflects that telling a story well without simply veering into sentimentality or forcing a happy ending is key in Christian witness.

Our task — mandated, one might say, in the Gospels — is to bear witness to the truth, including the difficult parts, and the details that do not seem to make sense, at least at the outset. I wonder whether this is what John is doing in his Prologue, which interprets the wonder of the incarnation in a way that allows us to be bathed by the light of its wisdom. The incarnation is a story full of the unexpected delights, fears, and hopes of a new life. John, and for that matter Mark, too, hint that there is yet more for God to do.

Both these Gospels end with events "off the page", as if to open the door ever wider to a sense of "what happens next?" They artfully craft their narratives in a way that is echoed by the words of the French philosopher Jacques Maritain, who muses that "things are more than they are", and "give more than they have".

As we approach the dazzling light of Christmas Day, we know that it is only the beginning of the story.

"Who are we waiting for?"

Emmanuel, God with us!

If God is indeed with us, then that relationship of encounter invites us to respond in word and action. The incarnation creates discipleship, an opportunity to participate in the story.

"Who are we waiting for?"

Christ.

"Who is that?" the next question might be. Our response: "Let me tell you; come and see."

(2011)

Descent
by Malcolm Guite

They sought to soar into the skies,
Those classic gods of high renown,
For lofty pride aspires to rise,
But you came down.

You dropped down from the mountains sheer,
Forsook the eagle for the dove,
The other Gods demanded fear,
But you gave love.

Where chiseled marble seemed to freeze
Their abstract and perfected form,
Compassion brought you to your knees,
Your blood was warm.

They called for blood in sacrifice,
Their victims on an altar bled,
When no one else could pay the price,
You died instead.

They towered above our mortal plain,
Dismissed this restless flesh with scorn,
Aloof from birth and death and pain,
But you were born.

Born to these burdens, borne by all
Born with us all 'astride the grave,'
Weak, to be with us when we fall,
And strong to save.

(2013)

Eternity wrapped in a span

Catherine Fox finds it a struggle to grasp the magnitude
of what happened in the Bethlehem stable

Here is the little door, lift up the latch, oh lift!
We need not wander more but enter with our gift.

BEFORE I received my musical education in the English cathedral tradition,
I had never come across this carol (words by Frances Chesterton, music by
Herbert Howells). Springing as I do from good Nonconformist stock, I
knew the carol section of the Baptist hymn book. I also waited eagerly each
year for the new Bethlehem carol sheet to be distributed at primary school.
There was considerable overlap between the two publications, but the carol
sheet always included more pagan nonsense than we Baptists had any truck
with (three ships, holly and ivy, etc.).

These carols were a jolly good sing, of course, but we were aware they
weren't *biblical*. I dare say we were encouraged in this by our father, who
mischievously made up extra verses: "The holly bears a branch as tall as a
pylon. And Mary bore sweet Jesus Christ, who was wrapped up in nylon."

Nylon. You tell that to young people nowadays, and they just look at
you. What even *is* nylon? Ah, a whole generation has grown up not knowing
the pleasure of creating a static storm in the privacy of your own nightdress!
Much has changed since the Christmases of my youth, but traditional
Christmas carols are still a staple. Like family, a *proper* tree, and Brussels
sprouts, carols crop up on the list of Christmas *sine qua nons*. (Or perhaps
— bearing in mind my erudite readership — I should say *sine quibus non*.)

Carols are everywhere: in churches and cathedrals; on the radio; on your
doorstep; in schools, hospitals, and old folks' homes. They are also on the
high street, where they are promiscuously mixed with secular schmaltz,
and poured like Bailey's over our festive retail experience. We slog through
the shopping mall with Mommy kissing Santa cheek by jowl with the
incarnate deity. I find this disorientating.

But perhaps that's the point? The deity did not become incarnate in
some rarefied space, hermetically sealed off from the slog of daily life. The
Magi discovered this. They started with the obvious. Where is he who is
born King of the Jews? Where kings belong, presumably: in the palace in
Jerusalem. But no. Here is the little door. It's not some vast imposing door

Lift up the latch: a byre door at the Palloza Museum,
Casa do Sesto, Ancares, Spain

found at the end of a sweeping drive, up marble steps, set between pillars on hinges of gold. Just a little door to a humble house.

SOMETIMES, a phrase lodges in my head and I turn it round for months, pondering. I try not to do this aloud in public (though I have caught myself in the car thoughtfully repeating place names — Clatterbridge, Strines Moor — for several minutes). It's a by-product of the writing life, I expect, this obsession with words: the sound and meaning of them, their curious networks of association.

Here is the little door. We have no means of knowing what the door of the house looked like, the one that greeted the Magi when they finally arrived in Bethlehem and found the child with his mother. Did they have to stoop to enter with their gifts?

Our gift of finest gold,
Gold that was never bought nor sold;
Myrrh to be strewn about His Bed;
Incense in clouds about His Head.

I need it to be a little door. It feels right that these travellers — full of knowledge, full of treasure — should have to lower their sights in their quest for the King, and finally bend to get in.

41

OLD houses can be charming, but low doorways are not. ("Duck or Grouse" as pub signs put it.) If you live in an old house, the brute fact is that you will have to adapt. The doorway is not going to change, no matter how many times you clout your head on it. *Here is the little door* — deal with it. In my pondering of that phrase, I begin to sense a spiritual truth I keep clouting my head on. You are overlooking the obvious. It's not that difficult. The door to life is very small and very low. Ditch your dignity and stoop.

This reminds me of Naaman. He travelled in state from Aram to Israel, to be healed of his leprosy. Like the Magi, he started with the king in the palace. Powerful men like to deal with powerful men. Like the Magi, he came laden with gifts and treasure. Like them, he was bounced. He was forced to make a detour and call on the prophet Elisha, who didn't even do him the courtesy of stirring from his house.

Out came the servant instead, with a terse message: "Go, wash yourself seven times in the Jordan, and your flesh will be restored and you will be cleansed." What?! I thought he'd at least come out and wave his hands over me. The *Jordan*? We've got better rivers at home!

Sometimes the path to life is so very small and low, it looks like a deliberate insult. *Here is the little door. Get over yourself.* I smile in recognition at the words of Naaman's servant: "If the prophet had told you to do some great thing, would you not have done it? How much more, then, when he tells you, 'Wash and be cleansed'!" Can it really be that simple? Is there nothing I can contribute to this process? What about my talents of silver, my shekels of gold? Come on, guys. Look at my ten suits of clothing!

THE oddity of the life of faith is that it is simultaneously all too small and all too big. *I* am simultaneously too small and too big. How does it all fit together? How does it work? There is a tiny girl I am longing to meet. She's due to arrive at Epiphany, and the building blocks for her body come partly from me: she is my granddaughter. Or to look at it another way, the building blocks for her body — like the building blocks for everything in our physical universe — were forged in supernovae millions of years ago.

How can I take in the enormity of that? My brain is too puny to accommodate it. (To be honest, half the time it's too puny to keep hold of my car registration, or to recall where I hid those Christmas presents I so brilliantly bought back in August.) And yet my brain — any human brain — is the most complex structure in the known universe.

How does it fit together, this incompatible vastness and tininess? What does it look like? Hail the incarnate Deity! Hail the God programme running on human hardware, on our flesh-and-bloodware; stripped of omniscience and omnipotence, scaled down and down and down, until it's earth-compatible and won't crash our system.

This is what it looks like: it looks like a baby. (*Such tiny hands and Oh such tiny feet.*) Seriously? Can it be that simple? It looks like a child growing, learning, "waxing strong in spirit", as the old translation says. It looks remarkably like one of us. It walks and laughs and weeps like one of us. It speaks our human dialect, drinks our wine, knows our songs. It gazes at us uncalculatingly. Like a friend. "They're hurting. Let me go to them." It looks like faithfulness, unwavering to the bitter end. And then it looks like death.

I THINK a lot about death. I try not to chant it out loud in lifts, as this can be disconcerting for my fellow lift-passengers. Death, that final door I will pass through. Into what? Sometimes it feels like a bottomless abyss, one I stare down into with my atheist friends. They think there's nothing, and I hope there's God. I can't prove my case. I can only talk about what I experience, and what faith feels like. It feels as though there's something like a God programme, downloadable to any human heart.

But how? *Here is the little door. Install now?* How hard it is for the rich to enter the Kingdom of heaven. *Here is the little door.* Here, where the playing field is level. The more you have, the harder it is to get through — or even to believe that the way could be so ridiculous, so low down. You must become like little children to enter. The only requirement is to believe that it's this simple: that grace is a free gift to the undeserving poor. *Then* we can bend and enter with our gift.

I'm guessing it's rather like "Mummy, look, look, I made you a Christmas bell!" To which no loving mother on earth ever replied, "What is this crap? It's just glitter on a yogurt pot! Get out of my sight." That bell will be hung on the tree, and the child scooped up and hugged to bits.

He stooped down first to show us how it works. No more wandering. Get over yourself. Enter. Here is the little door. Here. Here.

(2017)

No room — in the room

Paula Gooder invites us to look again at the detail
of the Christmas story

THE connection of Jesus with Bethlehem is important theologically, since it allows the Gospel writers to make the significant connection between Jesus and David. This connection reminds us of how important place is within the Jewish mindset.

It was important that John the Baptist went out to the wilderness to be in the place where God's people first crossed into the Promised Land, and the place where God promised he would return after the Exile. Being there was as important as being ready.

In the same way, going back to Bethlehem to David's roots is another new beginning — going back this time not to the roots of God's people in the land, but to the roots of kingship and the rule over God's people by David. Jesus's being born in Bethlehem tells us much that therefore does not need spelling out in detail.

The beliefs about a Davidic descendant focus on the Jewish longing for a true return from exile. Although God's people were back in their land after the end of the exile in the Persian period, much was missing. You only have to read the Isaianic prophecies of God's glorious promises of return, peace, prosperity, and unity to realise that the existence in the land was a poor shadow of what God's people hoped for.

One of the striking lacks in the post-exilic world was a descendant of David. The kings went off into exile with the people, but, despite the mention of Sheshbazzar, a descendant of David, in some of the texts (such as Ezra 1.8), no Davidic line was ever re-established. This fact became the focus of future expectation: an expectation that, over time, also became intertwined with one of an anointed figure or Messiah (although priests and prophets were also anointed, the specific Davidic connection became important for the Messiah).

We learn much, therefore, about Jesus from the simple fact that Matthew and Luke take us back to Bethlehem, to the place from which David was called to be King in the first place. It is worth noting that David was first called when he was a shepherd in the fields around Bethlehem — and this is exactly where Luke takes us in the next passage of his story. Again, through subtle detail, Luke communicates a central theological point: that Jesus is indeed the new David, who will emerge as King from the same place as his illustrious ancestor.

ONE of the central details of nearly all nativity plays is that Mary went into labour on the way to Bethlehem, and was so desperate for somewhere to stay that she and Joseph had to settle for a stable — or a cave — in the outhouses of a local inn.

Enter the spoilsport New Testament scholar. Let us be clear that the traditional version is far to be preferred in terms of drama, but is not really what the text suggests. There is no timescale given for Joseph and Mary's stay in Bethlehem. The assumption that the baby was born as they arrived comes solely from the statement that there was "no room at the inn". This small phrase — with its translation "inn" — has shaped almost the entirety of popular imaginations of what went on at Jesus's birth, and is disputed by the majority of New Testament interpreters.

There is little evidence to support the translation "inn" here. Inns were to be found almost exclusively on trade routes where there were no other houses in the vicinity. Indeed, in Luke's telling of the parable of the Good Samaritan, there is an "inn" exactly where you might expect one to be. The Samaritan took the wounded man to an inn on the deserted road between Jerusalem and Jericho. The isolation of the route and the inherent danger of travelling on it made it an ideal place for an inn.

The important thing to notice, however, is that when referring to the inn in Luke 10.34, Luke uses an entirely different word from the one used here in 2.7. There, the word used is *pandocheion*; here, it is *kataluma*. This word is used elsewhere in Luke: somewhat fascinatingly, at the Last Supper (Luke 22.11), to describe the guest room where Jesus and his disciples met to eat their last meal together. Luke uses the word in 2.7 not for an inn, but for a guest room in a house.

It is highly unlikely that a place such as Bethlehem would have had an inn at all. Rules of hospitality dictated that people — even complete strangers — should be welcomed into your home and cared for. There would have been no need for an inn in a place such as Bethlehem.

In Jerusalem, the "guest room" would probably have been a whole room, as it appears to have been in Luke 22.11 (though it might have been a "room" on the roof of the house). In smaller rural villages, such as Bethlehem, it is more likely to have been a corner of the one-roomed abode where the whole of the family dwelt. In such houses, what normally happened was that the family lived "upstairs" on a kind of mezzanine level, with the animals on a lower level in the same space. What Luke probably envisioned was that

Jesus was laid in the feeding trough of the lower level, as the upper level was so crammed with people.

There is little in the text to suggest that Mary and Joseph arrived with urgent need of accommodation; little to suggest the presence of an inn or innkeeper; nothing to suggest a search through multiple inns before finding a kind-hearted innkeeper who allowed them to stay in a stable. All of this is extraneous detail, added to make the story more engaging and dramatic.

As far as I'm concerned, that is fine, so long as we are clear that it is the result of an imaginative rereading of the story, and not the story itself. Much has been made, over the years, of there being no room for Jesus at his birth. There was even a carol based on the theme by Hilda M. Jarvis ("No room for the baby at Bethlehem's inn ... No home on this earth for the dear Son of God ... Will you still say to him 'no room'?"). In other words, there was a deliberate refusal of room to Jesus at his birth.

The visual reason why people are reluctant to accept that the *kataluma* might have been a guest room, not an inn, is because all of our nativity plays would look different; but there is a theological reason, too. If there was an inn, someone refused Jesus room; if it was just a guest room, no one refused him room — he just didn't quite fit in.

Surely this is a profound theological statement itself, and maybe even closer to the truth. So often we assume that people's lack of acceptance of Jesus, and all he came to be, is deliberate, thought through, and clearly stated. The reality is that, more often than not, a refusal of Jesus is not thought through — he just doesn't quite fit into our lives.

When we are busy, when so many other concerns press in all around us, it is not so much that we make a decision about what to accept or not, but that things slip by unnoticed. The lack of room for Jesus in our modern world is sometimes a deliberate refusal, but, it seems to me, it is most often, now as then, that there simply isn't quite space for him.

PART of the power of Luke's birth narratives are the sparse details he provides. There is much more he doesn't tell us than he does. Where do Mary and Joseph stay in Bethlehem? How did the shepherds find them? How many shepherds were there — two, or more than two? What was the response of the visitors in the overcrowded house to these odd nocturnal visitors? Other than Mary, did anyone else remember these events, and wonder what they might mean? How did Joseph react?

It is the sparseness of Luke's account that requires us to enter the story imaginatively, and to supply some of the missing characters. The problem we face today is that the supplied details have taken the status of canonical text, and it is very difficult indeed to suggest alternative imaginative details.

Luke himself, however, suggests how we should respond to "these words": we should follow the example of Mary, preserving the stories in our hearts, pondering the stories in our hearts, and wondering what they might mean for us.

It may be that if we do this, and carry on doing it, our imaginative tellings and retellings of the story might become richer; we might imagine new characters into the tableau — characters excluded by traditional renderings of the tale. We might linger a little to feel the terror of shepherds, the joy of the angels, the wonder of the villagers. We might sit for a while with Mary, as she pondered what had happened. And, as we do all of this, we might recapture some of the wonder of that very first Christmas, and find ourselves hurrying, like the shepherds, to share the good news that we have seen and heard.

(2015)

Nativity
by Kenneth Steven

When the miracle happened it was not
with bright light or fire —
but a farm door with the thick smell of sheep
and wind tugging at the shutters.

There was no sign the world had changed for ever
or that God had taken place;
just a child crying softly in a corner,
and the door open, for those who came to find.

© Kenneth Steven 2020
(from *Out of the Ordinary*, Canterbury Press)

The gift of John's cosmic retelling

No manger, no baby, but all the drama is here,
says **Barbara Brown Taylor**

In the beginning was the Word, and the Word was with God,
and the Word was God. He was in the beginning with God.
All things came into being through him,
and without him not one thing came into being.
What has come into being in him was life,
and the life was the light of all people. (John 1.1-4)

THIS is John's birth narrative, which explains why there are no Christmas pageants based on it. The stories that Matthew and Luke tell are full of things you can put costumes on: shepherds, angels, wise men, sheep. They are full of things you can paint on the backdrop: a stable, a manger, a guiding star overhead. We love them because they stay put, coming out of storage once a year with their invitation to remember a holy night long ago when all was calm, all was bright. They let us be children again, before putting our heavy coats back on and heading into a world that is going who-knows-where, with a bunch of swollen egos changing the script every 24-hour news cycle.

But there is no Bethlehem in John's Gospel, no holy family, no inn with no room, no manger. There's not even a baby in this story, because John's nativity begins before any of those things existed. It begins "in the beginning", the same way the Bible does. It begins with the Big Bang of God's Word, bringing the world into being one utterance at a time. In the Genesis story there were six days full of words. "God said, 'Let there be light'; and there was light" (Genesis 1.3).

After that came day, night, sky, earth, seas, plants, and planets. After that came living creatures of every kind, including humankind. All God had to do was *say* them and there they *were*: fish, birds, wild animals, creeping things, earthlings. They all came forth on the breath of God, taking shape through the power of God's creative Word.

But if you're thinking of phonics and sound waves, you're thinking too small. You might try thinking of "the Logos" instead, since that's the term John used, and it's not as tame as "the Word". In the world of Genesis, God's Logos is God's agency, God's dynamic intelligence entering the cosmos like a meteor, taking on shape as it passes from the unbounded dimension of eternity into the bounded atmosphere of earth.

God's Logos is God's rocket ship of self-revelation, the manifestation of God's divine reason and creativity in the material realm, where it both brings things into being and then holds them together so they don't fly apart. John didn't invent the term: Greek and Jewish philosophers used it before him, and they weren't referring to Jesus when they did. But John made the connection for his Christian community, and it stuck. From his time to ours, Christians identify the Logos as the Christ, the dynamic agency and intelligence of God that came to earth in the flesh.

His human name was Jesus. He landed in Galilee. It was a whole new beginning, but how was John going to write about that? A manger was too small to contain the divine Logos. Shepherds were a dime a dozen. Even Mary, God bless her, was so *provincial*. So John did not include any of that in his story. He wrote a cosmic story instead — a second Genesis — about the pre-existent Logos who was with God in the beginning, long before there was a Bethlehem, a Caesar, or a single star in the sky.

In John's birth story, the Logos is singular, and it does not come out of God's mouth — at least, not at first. The Logos is *with* God. The Logos *is* God. It both is and isn't God, which may be why it doesn't have a name in the beginning — because it is not yet separate from God. God is bound to put breath behind the Word soon, because, for some unknown reason, God does not love being alone.

GOD loves company. God loves "being with". How else did God know that Adam needed a partner, that it was not good for him to be alone? But there is no Adam in John's origin story yet. There is no Jesus. There is not even a world. There is just this primordial intimacy between God and God's Logos — God's dynamic energy, wanting to *become* something, even if that means leaving the divine womb and entering a too-bright cosmos full of loud noises, hard surfaces, and the smell of blood.

Before that happens, however, John wants to make sure we understand several crucial things. The first is the Logos's relationship to darkness ("The light shines in the darkness, and the darkness did not overcome it," verse 5). The second is the Logos's relationship to John the Baptiser ("He himself was not the light, but he came to testify to the light," verse 8). The third is the nature of the Logos's birth ("not of blood or of the will of the flesh or of the will of man, but of God," verse 13).

There is no need for a gender reveal. The Logos has been "he" from the start, since John already knows whom he is talking about, but he still takes his time getting to the verse that passes for a birth in his story: "And the Word became flesh and lived among us," he says at last, "and we have seen his glory, the glory as of a father's only son, full of grace and truth" (verse 14).

That's when God finally exhales and changes everything, releasing the Logos into the world like an only child, although not to remain one. Paradoxically, the twofold mission of this only child is to make his Father known and to make more children for him. All who receive the Logos, John says — all who breathe in what God has breathed out — will receive the power to become God's children, too.

I know we put all kinds of conditions around that — yes, sure, we're all God's children, too, but not like Jesus. He alone is the only. He alone is our clear window into the heart of God. Yet there it is, right on the page: this only child does not love being alone any more than his Father does.

He means to enlarge the family, filling the world with more brothers and sisters who are willing to become God's Logos made flesh. He has high expectations of his siblings, too. When it is time for him to go back to where he came from, the Logos will turn to them and say: "Truly, I tell you, the one who believes in me will also do the works that I do and, in fact, will do greater works than these, because I am going to the Father" (John 14.12).

The good news is that this transmission is built into the grand scheme of things, beginning in creation and stretching into the future further than any of us can see. If evolution isn't a bad word for you, you might think of it as divine evolution — the way the Logos keeps coming into the world in different forms at different times, showing us as much of God as we can take in until the next time, when the form may be different but the Logos is the same.

When Jesus goes to the Father, he says, God will send another Comforter to be with them — the Holy Spirit, the Spirit of truth, who will go forth from God as Jesus did. The Spirit will not act the same way Jesus did. It won't have a human body, for one thing (unless you're a fan of *The Shack*), but it, too, was with God in the beginning, moving over the waters at the genesis of creation — one more life-giving expression of God's energy and purpose.

CHRISTIANS traditionally draw the line there. The Logos has one name, and that name is Jesus. Along with God the Father and God the Holy Spirit, he completes the Trinity that has been part of baseline Christian belief from the earliest centuries of the Church.

Yet the same Scripture that informed the Trinity contains intriguing glimpses of other Logos-like energies coming forth from the mouth of God. In Jewish tradition, Torah is God's energetic word, given to God's people that they might choose life and not death. In one old story, the Torah rested in God's bosom before the creation of the world. Another says that, when it came time to start making things, God looked into the Torah the way an architect looks into a blueprint, creating the world for the purpose of revealing the Torah. Only later did God spell the whole thing out for Moses so that he could write it down.

Proverbs 8 introduces another Logos-like energy, named Wisdom, sometimes known by her Greek name, Sophia. "Ages ago I was set up," she says, "at the first, before the beginning of the earth" (verse 23). When God established the heavens, she was there. "When he marked out the foundations of the earth, then I was beside him, like a master worker," she says, "and I was daily his delight, rejoicing before him always, rejoicing in his inhabited world and delighting in the human race" (verses 29b–31).

Statue of Sophia/Wisdom at Ephesus

She appears again in the book of Sirach, which was written too late for inclusion in the Jewish Bible, but which shows up in a set of books between the First and Second Testaments in some Christian Bibles. Sirach is approved for use in worship on occasion — as on the second Sunday after Christmas Day, when Sophia is on the list of potential speakers along with Jeremiah, Solomon, and John. The preacher gets to choose whose voices will be heard, but, as far as I recall, I have never heard Lady Wisdom's voice in church. Have you?

The book of Sirach comes right after the Wisdom of Solomon and right before the book of Baruch. It might be called Ecclesiasticus in your Bible. Sirach, chapter 24, beginning at the first verse:

Wisdom praises herself,
and tells of her glory in the midst of her people.
In the assembly of the Most High she opens her mouth,
and in the presence of his hosts she tells of her glory:
"I came forth from the mouth of the Most High,
and covered the earth like a mist.

I dwelt in the highest heavens,
and my throne was in a pillar of cloud.
Alone I compassed the vault of heaven
and traversed the depths of the abyss.
Over waves of the sea, over all the earth,
and over every people and nation I have held sway.
Among all these I sought a resting place;
in whose territory should I abide?
Then the Creator of all things gave me a command,
and my Creator chose the place for my tent.
He said, 'Make your dwelling in Jacob,
and in Israel receive your inheritance.'
Before the ages, in the beginning, he created me,
and for all the ages I shall not cease to be.
In the holy tent I ministered before him,
and so I was established in Zion.
Thus in the beloved city he gave me a resting place,
and in Jerusalem was my domain.
I took root in an honoured people,
in the portion of the Lord, his heritage." (Sirach 24.1-12)

Did any of that sound familiar to you? It sounded familiar to me. Wisdom came forth from the mouth of the Most High. She dwelt in the highest heavens, her throne in a pillar of cloud. She could have stayed there, but she wanted a resting place on earth. How Logos-like of her ...

She didn't want to cover the earth like mist any more; she wanted a zip code, a place to pitch her tent — the same word John used when he said that the Logos became flesh and pitched his tent among us. Wisdom wanted to move into the neighbourhood, and God was happy to oblige. Looking down at the map, God said, "There: 'Make your dwelling in Jacob, and in Israel receive your inheritance.'" So she took root there, hoping for as many new children as her tent could hold.

It's a pattern you can see over and over again in the sacred story: God's eternal energy for sending the Logos to take up residence in the world, bringing the creation close enough to the creator to be kissed — by Torah, by Wisdom, by Jesus Christ, by Holy Spirit — all of them offering us direct access to the fierce love and creative intelligence that is always looking for a new place to call home.

TOO often, I think, religious people want to restrict that divine access: the Logos comes only by this name, not that name, to this people only, not that. The last lines of John's Prologue certainly sounds like that. "No one has ever seen God. It is God the only Son, who is close to the Father's heart, who has made him known" (verse 18). What John *doesn't* say is that the only Son is the only one who has ever made God known. Make of that what you will, but I think it's why we need to keep John's Christmas story in the mix.

Matthew and Luke have captured our hearts with their stories of Jesus's birth in Bethlehem a long time ago. We can see the baby; we can hear him. The script is familiar, and the costumes have a lot of wear on them. That's part of why we love it: because we know the ropes. John alone reminds us that the Logos is eternally being born. His story isn't set in the time of King Herod in a town six miles south of Jerusalem: it's set in the cosmos, where the Logos has no beginning or end.

This is much more difficult to imagine: that the Logos has been coming into the world for ever, spoken by the God whom no one has ever seen, to make the divine energy and purpose known on earth. What kind of costume do you put on that? Is one outfit enough?

During the Christmas season, we recognise the one that is definitive for us — the Logos made Jesus, the Logos made flesh — even as we affirm his coming again in a form we may not recognise next time, and the coming of the Holy Spirit between now and then. The creativity of the Logos is never spent.

You may feel bound to point out Jesus's famous saying in John's Gospel, that "'No one comes to the Father except through me'" (14.6). Yet this is also the Gospel in which he says, "'Whoever believes in me believes not in me but in him who sent me'" (12.44). *What a Logos-like thing to say!* John couldn't see the Sender; no one can. But he couldn't take his eyes off the One the Sender sent, whose story John was given to tell. That made John the Logos for the Logos, the one who got to put his own breath behind God's Word as it landed in his own time and place.

I hate to press the point, but it's your turn now. Jesus said so. Those who believe in him will do the works he did — greater, in fact — now that he has returned to the Source. It is our turn to put our breath behind God's Word so that it lands in our own time and place.

However well or poorly things seem to be working out for us, there is something else at work here that has been pouring itself out for us *for ever*, which the darkness does not overcome. Light from light. Fullness from which we have all received, grace upon grace. Christmas every day.

(2020)

Christmas in 28 verses

The birth narratives are poor grounds for theology,
argues **Tom Wright**, which might be why
theologians ignore them

TWO frequently asked questions at the back of Westminster Abbey are: "Is this a Catholic church?" and "Why is Charles Darwin buried here?" I leave it to your imagination which visitors ask which question — and, for that matter, what we who greet them say in response. But in the first week of December another question was asked even more frequently: "Why is the baby already in the crib?"

There are many demands made on the Abbey at this time of the year, and the Holy Family has to join the rest of the staff in trying to satisfy them. The baby appears in the crib for the two children's events in early December, the Christingle and the Children of Courage. He then disappears to return (we hope) on Christmas Eve.

Of course, if we're being strictly chronological, not only would you not have a baby, you wouldn't have a shepherd, nor Mary, nor Joseph, until the last minute … And during the day the animals wouldn't be there, anyway. An empty shed, with the manger stocked with fodder: not a great aid to devotion, that. But, of course, the real question is: why do we go to such trouble for something that is, after all, marginal to the New Testament, and to early Christianity in general?

The entire birth story occupies eight verses in Matthew's Gospel. The wise men take another 12; 11 more describe the flight into Egypt, the slaughter of the innocents, and the return to Nazareth. Important, but not that important: they haven't made it into Christmas-card mythology. In Luke's Gospel, the actual birth story, shepherds and all, takes 20 verses, preceded by the annunciation, which is a further 12, woven into the story of Zachariah and Elizabeth.

Notoriously, there is nothing about Jesus's conception or birth in Mark or John. Even supposing (as some of us do) that the opening of Mark is lost, it's a long stretch to suggest that it contained something like the narratives we have elsewhere.

Quantity isn't everything. After all, Matthew's resurrection chapter is only 20 verses long; Mark's is shorter; Luke's and John's longer. But whereas the shadow of the cross and the light of Easter are already falling across the page in the birth narratives (Herod, the flight into Egypt, the sword piercing Mary's soul), the reverse is not the case. Nowhere in the long, vivid and theologically charged crucifixion narratives are we reminded of Jesus's conception and birth. At Easter, the only echo of the beginning is the angel saying: "Don't be afraid."

The mode of Jesus's conception, and the place and circumstances of his birth, play no role whatever in the theology of Matthew 3–28, or Luke 3–24, let alone Mark or John (apart from the intriguing 8.41).

Or Paul. Paul could have said in Galatians 4.4: "God sent forth his son, born of a virgin, born under the law," but he didn't. He echoed Genesis 3.15, not Isaiah 7.14. Think of Paul's great resurrection chapter, 1 Corinthians 15. Think what it would have sounded like if he had written a similar one about Jesus's conception: "Now if our gospel declares that Christ was born of a virgin, how can some of you say that there is no virgin birth? If there is no virgin birth, then Christ wasn't born of a virgin; in which case, he isn't the son of God: your faith is empty, you are still in your sins. But in fact Christ was born of a virgin ..."

Doesn't have the same ring, somehow, does it? Perhaps the truth of the matter is that we, heirs of the science-versus-religion debates of the past 200 years, have allowed ourselves to imagine that the virginal conception and the bodily resurrection, the womb-story and the tomb-story, are the two equal and vital pillars of our faith.

Of course, that's not to say Paul hadn't heard of it, or didn't believe it. If we didn't have 1 Corinthians, we wouldn't know he'd ever heard of the eucharist. But he has plenty of opportunity to use Jesus's birth theologically, and never takes it. Philippians 2.6-11, a great Christological statement to rank alongside John 1.1-18 (why do carol services stop at verse 14, by the way?), never mentions it. Nor does the spectacular Christological poem in Colossians 1.15-20.

Despite recent arguments, Paul certainly believed that Jesus was God's son in the full sense: equal with God from all eternity. But the details about Jesus's birth play no part in that belief or its exposition. The same is true for Hebrews, the other great New Testament exposition of the divine glory of Jesus Christ.

In case it isn't clear, this is not an argument against the truth of Matthew's and Luke's stories. It is a plea that in our thinking, our liturgies, our symbols, and our preaching, we should avoid reinforcing the impression that Christmas is the centre of Christianity, and that everything Christians believe is somehow concentrated here. It isn't.

Listen to the words of half the carols, and see how hopeless is their attempt to derive a full theology of redemption from the birth stories. Observe how easily baby-sentimentality sneaks in and takes over from real devotion. See how the Christian year gets pulled out of shape if we make Easter an appendage to Christmas instead of vice versa.

(2001)

The first Christian assembly?

Perhaps Christmas, not Pentecost, is the sign of the birth
of the Church, says **James Jones**

*This will be a sign for you: you will find a child wrapped in bands of
cloth, and lying in a manger.* (Luke 2.12)

AN infant wrapped in baby clothes was hardly a distinctive sign. You would
have thought that any newborn child would have been wrapped up well
after leaving the warmth of the womb. A baby clad in bands of cloth would
have been of little help to the shepherds in their search through the streets
of Bethlehem for this special child.

The mark of distinction was not the infant's clothing, but, rather, the cot
in which he lay. A trough. A manger for feeding livestock. A risky place to
put a baby with animals about.

Such a sign would have caught the attention of shepherds. They knew
only too well that nature was "red in tooth and claw". That is why they spent
cold nights on the hills, to protect their sheep from wolves savagely
descending upon their folds. A newborn baby lying safely in a manger
suggested that his promised uniqueness heralded a new world, in which
there would be a very different relationship between all God's creatures.

The shepherds might have known that picture of the new world from
the prophet Isaiah, where "the wolf shall lie down with the lamb". Rogues
though many of them were, they would have warmed to a vision that took
much of the danger out of their work. The new world that was coming,
Isaiah said, would have a child in the lead, and see a radically new relationship
between the calf and the lion, the cow and the bear, the nursing child and
the adder.

This child in a manger, in an animal's feeding trough, in all its unusual-
ness, spoke of harmony between all God's creatures. It was nothing less
than a sign of the coming Kingdom. This clue was given to shepherds who
knew first-hand the wildness of nature. In other ways, they were a surprising
choice for this message. They were disreputable characters, forbidden to act
as witnesses in court. It may be why Jesus never called himself "the shepherd".
He always qualified it. He styled himself "The Good Shepherd", as if it could
not be taken for granted that a shepherd was always good.

IT is one of the reasons that I have always been sceptical of the view that the birth narratives have no basis in history. Why would you make it up, or include it, if, as St Luke was doing, you were trying to convince others of the veracity of your accounts of Jesus's life? Shepherds had no gravitas, or authority, to lend to the gospel to persuade others.

Not only were these outsiders the early witnesses of the Good News: they, together with Mary, Joseph, and the Wise Men, gave expression to the first Christian assembly. The manger was the first altar to bear the body of Christ, and Mary was the first person to minister to the body of Christ. The Wise Men, shepherds, Joseph, and Mary were the first to hear, and give voice to the worship of Christ. So perhaps it was Christmas rather than Pentecost that made the beginnings of the Christian Church. The birth of Christ giving birth to the Church.

This fragile congregation was missionary from the start. Mary treasured all that she had experienced for future disclosure. The Wise Men bore witness to Herod, but, with dove-like innocence, cloaked in serpentine wisdom, they soon learnt not to cast their pearls before swine, and gave him a wide berth on their return from the manger. The shepherds went on their way with a contagion of enthusiasm.

But no sooner had this first celebration of Christmas lost its starlit wonder than this infant Church began to learn the paradox of the life of a faith centred on Christ. The nativity is a story of intervention. Mary, Joseph, the shepherds, and the Wise Men all experienced it differently. God invaded their worlds. This microcosm of humanity found the course of their lives altered for ever, a symbol of God's predictable commitment to his creation, and of his unpredictable moments of intervention.

THE question that might have bothered them, and that lingers today, is why God intervened to save the world, but stood back from staying the hand of Herod's murderous soldiers as they took the sword to innocent children. This is the question that people of Christian faith have wrestled with constantly.

Faith is like a piece of string that disappears up into the clouds and tugs occasionally. There are times of spiritual intimacy when, through silence or sacrament, through nature or fellowship, we sense the presence of God. Then there can follow long periods of alienation, when spiritual intimacy gives way to distance, doubt, and even despair, not least when cries for God to intervene go unheeded.

There is new despair in the air at what is unfolding in the Middle East, once such a theatre of God's intervention. The place where the Church was born is rapidly becoming the graveyard of Christianity. We look on as helpless as the mothers of the Innocents. As Islamic State holds a knife to the throats of humanitarian workers, and rapes and slaughters Christians, people have pleaded and prayed, but to no avail.

But this is not a new scenario in the history of Christianity. One of the first to put Christians to the sword was Saul. In case we skate over the brutality of his aggression, we should remember that his acts were as violent and as merciless as those of the Islamic State.

After his conversion to Christ, and years later, at the end of a letter he wrote to Christians in Rome, Paul gave a clue to his change of heart. He wrote of two relatives "who were in Christ before I was". Presumably Junias and Andronicus, when they saw their cousin murdering their Christian brothers and sisters, sought to love him and pray for him. It is what our Lord told us to do to terrorists.

PERHAPS it is too uncomfortable a thought for Christmas, but a universal campaign to pray for Jihadi John and his comrades, that love would conquer their hearts, would be in the spirit of the Early Church. It is the only intervention I can think of which would obviate escalation. Such an intervention would be consonant with the example of Paul, who did more than any other to establish the Church in the Mediterranean world.

Those angels who sent shepherds searching for a sign sang them on their way, "Glory to God in the highest heaven, and on earth peace". This was the theme that the Christ-child would one day take up, and make the centrepiece of his universal prayer: "Your will be done on earth as it is in heaven." It is a petition for the earthing of heaven: a new world, where the relationships between all God's creatures will be transformed towards peace in the reunification of earth and heaven.

In Bethlehem, "The House of Bread", the first Church turned a feeding stall into an altar, on which was laid the body of Christ. It was a sign for their times, and for ours. In our Christmas eucharist, we feed on him in our hearts by faith with thanksgiving.

(2014)

Where Christmas came from

Elements of the Christmas story cannot be found in the Gospels;
Margaret Barker tracks down their ancient origins

MANY of the words and images we use at Christmas can seem to be just an elaboration of the simple Gospel story. Some of the well-known details are certainly later additions: St Matthew does not say there were only three Magi, nor does he name them; and there is nothing about midwinter, bleak or otherwise. But many additional details are as old as the New Testament, and can be found in early materials.

The New Testament gives only an outline of nativity stories, but the value of other sources is now being recognised. Embedded in art, liturgy, and stories are important details that preserve earlier traditions: what happened, and how it was understood.

The non-canonical early texts are now a significant area of study: English translations are available from such languages as Ethiopic and Old Irish, as well as Latin, Greek, and Syriac.

Take, for example, the ox and the ass. These are not mentioned by Matthew or Luke, but are present in the earliest depictions of the nativity. The earliest reference is about 155 CE, when Justin in Rome told the Emperor Antoninus Pius that Christianity fulfilled ancient prophecies, even though many Jews did not recognise Jesus. He quoted Isaiah 1.3: "The ox knows its owner and the ass its master's crib; but Israel does not know, my people does not understand" (*Apology*, 1.63).

We cannot know when this prophecy was first used of the nativity, but Justin shows that fulfilment of prophecy influenced what details were preserved. By the time a Latin Infancy Gospel known as *Pseudo-Matthew* was compiled in eighth- or ninth-century Europe, the prophecy of Habakkuk 3.2 had been added to the scene.

This is not what we have in English Bibles, which are based on the Masoretic Hebrew text, compiled in the seventh to tenth centuries CE, printed by Daniel Bomberg in 1524. Instead, it comes from the Septuagint Greek, compiled from the third to first centuries BCE: "In the midst of two living creatures you will be known, in the drawing near of the years you will be recognised, and when the right time comes you will be shown forth" (*Pseudo-Matthew*, 14).

This is not in the Latin Vulgate, translated by Jerome about 400 CE, and so *Pseudo-Matthew* drew on material from the Greek East. The verses before and after the Habakkuk prophecy are still woven though the Christmas Eve services in Orthodox churches.

When *Pseudo-Matthew* was written, the earliest surviving nativity scene had been painted in Egypt. This is an encaustic icon now in St Catherine's Monastery, in Sinai, from the seventh century CE or even earlier. The nativity scene is almost a diagram, with the manger, the ox, and the ass at the centre, Mary lying on a red rug across the mouth of a cave, the star on a beam of light from heaven, Magi and shepherds, Joseph looking anxious, and two midwives bathing the newborn Child.

Most of these details are not in the New Testament, and yet they formed the nativity icon which has remained unchanged in the Orthodox churches. When the Western Church began to develop a different style, the nativity icon was still the template, and the fundamentals remain unchanged to this day.

ALL the details in the nativity icon come from texts outside the New Testament. Matthew's story of the Magi gives no detail of how many Magi came to Bethlehem, or where they came from. They were astronomers looking for the prophesied King of the Jews. The idea that they were three Gentile kings from the Orient is unlikely to be accurate, but lesser-known early texts have preserved details that Matthew did not record: things which seem strange because our picture of the Magi has been shaped by later elaborations.

Two of these early texts are the *Protoevangelium* (Infancy Gospel of James), a Greek text known to Origen in the early third century which has never been lost, and *The Revelation to the Magi* (*RMagi*), an early Christian text in Syriac, possibly from the third century CE, which has been neglected but is now available for the first time in English (B. C. Landau, *The Sages and the Star Child,* www.academia.edu).

The basic story in *RMagi* is also in a fifth-century Latin commentary on St Matthew's Gospel, the *Opus Imperfectum*, and was known in 15th-century Flanders. Three Magi, their holy mountain, a sacred spring, and a great star enclosing the Child appear in a painting from the workshop of Rogier van der Weyden.

The *Protoevangelium* has some of the details in the icon — the birth in a cave, the goats drinking, and two women helping after the birth — but it says little about the Magi. The *RMagi* has more, since it describes the nativity cave being at the top of a mountain, two women washing the newborn at the foot of the mountain, the star on a beam of light coming from heaven into the cave, and the Magi as kings or philosophers of different ages — old, middle-aged, and young — ascending the mountain to see the Mother and Child. None of these details is in the New Testament.

The *RMagi* tells the story of 12 Magi living near a holy mountain in the East, in the land of Shir. They were sons of Seth, descended from ancient kings, and they were known as the silent ones, because they prayed in silence and knew that the truths of God were beyond words.

At the top of their mountain was a cave: "The Cave of Treasures of the Hidden Mysteries of the Life of Silence". The hidden mysteries are mentioned 21 times, and must be the key to the text and to the identity of the Magi. They were guarding some ancient holy books in which Seth, the third son of Adam, had recorded his father's teaching.

These were the mysteries handed down from father to son for many generations, which explains the three ages of the wise men in the icon. Jewish tradition remembered Adam as the first high priest, and Eden as his lost temple; so the Magi were priests as well as kings, guarding mysteries older than Moses. They were also astronomers. They used to ascend to the cave and look for the great star which Adam had seen over the tree of life in Eden.

One year, when they were purifying themselves in their sacred spring at the foot of the mountain, they saw a pillar of light. They went up to the cave and received a vision of the heavens opening, a pillar of light, and angels bringing a great star enclosing the Child. Led by the star, the 12 Magi and their entourage went to Bethlehem and found a similar cave, where they saw the Child and offered their gifts.

The silence, the great star that dwarfed all others, and the human form within it, were known to Bishop Ignatius of Antioch, who wrote in about 100 CE of the three mysteries of the great silence: the Virgin, her child-bearing, and the death of our Lord. They were made known by a great star which shone with a light beyond words. God was appearing in human form (Ignatius, *To the Ephesians*, 19).

None of this is in the New Testament.

The mountain of the Magi in the land of Shir was Mount Seir, whose people were cursed by Ezekiel (35.1- 9); yet the Lord was expected to come from Seir with blessings (Deuteronomy 33.2), and the Magi of Mount Seir were guarding books from Adam and waiting for the Messiah. They must have been of Hebrew heritage. Who were they?

M. R. JAMES, best known for his ghost stories, was a scholar of the apocryphal texts. In 1927, he published a book on two medieval Latin texts (alas, with no English translation): one from the Arundel collection now in the British Library, and one from Hereford Cathedral Library (*Latin Infancy Gospels*, Wipf and Stock, reprinted 2009). These show another version of the Magi story: related to the *RMagi*, but saying that they found their prophecies about Christ in Scriptures older than the Old Testament: *apud nos sunt antiquiores scripture* ("We have older writings").

James, writing 20 years before the Dead Sea Scrolls were discovered, assumed that these ancient writings in a cave were the works of the Gentile philosophers; but now there is more evidence. What were these older holy writings?

He discovered the same story of the older Scriptures in an Old Irish text, found copied in the *Leabhar Breac* (*c.*1410), which is now in the Royal Irish Academy in Dublin. This version has only three Magi, and they brought many gifts, including a length of fine white linen. This story and several other Old Irish apocryphal texts are now available in English (M. Herbert and M. McNamara, *Irish Biblical Apocrypha*, T&T Clark, 1989).

The Grey Friars of Hereford and the Carthusians of Mainz, who copied out those Latin Infancy Gospels, the unknown scribe of the *Leabhar Breac*, and the painters of 15th-century Flanders knew stories about the Magi that we have largely forgotten.

When the Magi had the vision of the Child in the cave, and when they saw him in Bethlehem, he addressed them as "the sons of my mysteries". Early Christian texts often mention secret teachings with a temple context — the liturgy and its meaning — and the early Christians claimed that Jesus was their great high priest (Hebrews 4.14), who had learned these mysteries and taught them to his disciples.

Bishop Ignatius wrote of Jesus: "The priests were worthy men, but the high priest is greater, the one to whom the most holy things were entrusted, for to him alone were the secret things of God committed" (*To the Philadelphians*, 9).

Clement of Alexandria wrote in about 200 CE of a tradition of blessed doctrine "which has descended by transmission to a few, having been imparted unwritten by the apostles ... The teachers of truth are those who enter in, through the tradition of the Lord, by drawing aside the curtain" (*Miscellanies*, 6.7, 7.17).

Origen (d. 251 CE), perhaps a pupil of Clement, said that the tabernacle furnishings were wrapped before the Levites were allowed to carry them (Numbers 4.1-15), because only priests were permitted to see and understand them. So, too, certain Christian practices and teachings "were handed down and entrusted to us by the high priest and his sons" (*On Numbers*, Homily 5).

A century later, Basil of Caesarea wrote of practices that had no basis in the New Testament but came from unwritten tradition: liturgical customs such as the sign of the cross and facing east to pray; and prayers such as the *epiklesis*.

"Does not this come from that unpublished and secret teaching which our fathers guarded in silence out of the reach of curious meddling and inquisitive investigation?" They "guarded the awful dignities of the mysteries in secrecy and silence". They were matters beyond words, and so should not be spoken. They were the mysteries (*On the Holy Spirit*, 66).

ORIGEN's "high priest and his sons" points to a widely quoted saying of Jesus that is not in the New Testament: "My mystery is for me and for the sons of my house." Clement of Alexandria said that it came from "a certain Gospel", but did not name it, (*Miscellanies*, 5.10). A work attributed to Clement, Bishop of Rome in the 90s, has Peter say: "Our Lord and teacher said 'Keep the mysteries for me and the sons of my house' wherefore he explained to his disciples privately the mysteries of the kingdom of heaven" (*Homilies*, 19.20). In an early hymn, Jesus says: "Keep my mystery, you who are kept by it" (*Odes of Solomon*, 8.10). There are several other examples.

The mysteries are mentioned in the New Testament, but little is said of their content. Jesus told his disciples that he taught in parables to conceal the mysteries: "To you it has been given to know the secrets [literally 'mysteries'] of the kingdom of heaven, but to them it has not been given" (Matthew 13.11 and parallels).

St Paul wrote of "the revelation of the mystery which was kept secret for long years but is now disclosed" (Romans 16.25), and of "the mystery hidden for ages and generations but now made manifest to his saints" (Colossians 1.26). He said that Christians were "servants of Christ and stewards of the mysteries of God" (1 Corinthians 4.1); and "Great indeed is the mystery of our religion: he was manifested in the flesh, vindicated in the Spirit, seen by angels, preached among the nations, believed on in the world, taken up in glory" (1 Timothy 3.16).

Were the Christian mysteries the teachings preserved by the Magi? Increased knowledge of biblical Hebrew means that the saying attributed to Jesus, "My mystery is for me and for the sons of my house," can now be identified as Isaiah 24.16, when the prophet announced the coming of the Righteous One.

St John saw this in the vision of the mighty angel coming from heaven bringing a little book that he gave to John. He said that when the seventh angel sounded his trumpet, the "mystery of God as he announced to his servants the prophets, would be fulfilled" (Revelation 10.7).

The Magi on Mount Shir had been guarding the mysteries until the Righteous One appeared, and then they went to find him in Bethlehem.

The following texts mentioned above can be found online: Justin Martyr, *Apology, Pseudo-Matthew, Protoevangelium, The Revelation to the Magi*; Ignatius, *To the Ephesians, To the Philadelphians*; Clement of Alexandria, *Miscellanies*; Basil of Caesarea, *On the Holy Spirit*; Clement, *Homilies, Odes of Solomon*.

(2020)

Bring on more of the mystery

We should approach the birth narratives with greater imagination, says **Nick Jowett**

YOU finally sit down to write that nativity play, or sermon on the incarnation, and the chances are that you will feel some pressure to present the birth of Jesus as something relevant today. As a result, the people sitting on the school chairs, or in the pews, are highly likely to get variations on the "gritty realism" scenario. There will be: Jesus's birth in poverty; his lack of a proper shelter; his welcome by outsiders, and foreigners; or his threatened murder by political power.

Now, all these political and social themes are perfectly justifiable. But have we noticed what a strong this-worldly emphasis they have? Christian tradition down the ages has often preferred to focus on the wonder and mystery of the theological paradox of God's becoming human. For example:

> *Hark, hark, the wise eternal Word,*
> *Like a weak infant cries!*
> *In form of servant is the Lord,*
> *And God in cradle lies.*

"Behold the Great Creator Makes", Thomas Pestel, 1584–1659

Or else we have:

> *Welcome, all wonders in one sight!*
> *Eternity shut in a span.*
> *Summer in winter, day in night,*
> *Heaven in earth, and God in man.*

"A Hymn of the Nativity", Richard Crashaw, c.1613–1649

Such formulations take their cue from the theologically imaginative birth narratives in Matthew and Luke, and, of course from John's Prologue, reflecting on the eternal Word's becoming flesh and dwelling with us.

But, for me, the question arises: are we still willing and able to explore, in narrative and symbol, the mystery of God becoming human? Are we seeking, in fact, to capture the numinosity of that moment? Surely we do not need to be limited to ever more literalistic or sociological versions of what originally were imaginative, theological narratives, created by Luke and Matthew.

NOW we know that the process of creating narrative around the birth and childhood of Jesus continued after the canonical Gospels were written. We have the *Protoevangelia* of James and Thomas — both probably appearing in the second century, but always regarded as apocryphal.

The *Protoevangelium* of James, which was clearly very popular, tells us about Mary's miraculous birth to Anna and Joachim, Mary's upbringing in the Temple, and about her continuing virginity, which it repeatedly emphasises — even to the point of having a midwife examine her after Jesus's birth. In this text, Joseph is explicitly an old man with grown sons of his own. His horror at finding that Mary is pregnant is increased, and both he and Mary have to undergo tests by drinking water in the Temple to prove that they have not had intercourse.

This Gospel of James includes versions of the annunciation, and the visit of Mary to Elizabeth; it places the birth of Jesus in a cave, describes the visit of the astrologers, and has Jesus hidden in a cows' feeding trough to escape the violence of Herod. Already, in these passages, there is material which could inform and expand modern presentations of the nativity.

But, for me, the high point of this narrative comes in chapter 18, when we suddenly get a first-person narrative by Joseph. He has left Mary, who has not yet given birth, in a cave near Bethlehem, with one of his sons guarding her, and he is looking for a midwife. And then, in an extraordinary way, time seems to stand still:

> Now I, Joseph, was walking along and yet not going anywhere.
> I looked up at the vault of the sky and saw it standing still,
> and then the clouds and saw them paused in amazement,
> and at the birds of the sky suspended in midair. As I looked on
> the earth, I saw a bowl lying there and workers reclining
> around it with their hands in the bowl; some were chewing
> and yet did not chew; some were picking up something to eat
> and yet did not pick it up; and some were putting food in their
> mouths and yet did not do so. Instead, they were all looking
> upward. I saw sheep being driven along and yet the sheep
> stood still; the shepherd was lifting his hand to strike them,
> and yet his hand remained raised. And I observed the current
> of the river and saw goats with their mouths in the water and
> yet they were not drinking. Then all of a sudden everything
> and everybody went on with what they had been doing.

WHEN Joseph returns to the cave with the midwife, he finds the place over-shadowed by a dark cloud. As the cloud withdraws, an intense light shines from inside the cave. They cannot bear to look at it. But when the light fades, they see the baby taking the breast of his mother, Mary.

The Gospel of James gives us an astonishingly imaginative way of experiencing what T. S. Eliot calls "the point of intersection of the timeless with time". At the moment when Jesus is born, time stands still. There may be, in this passage, a memory of Luke's scene of the annunciation to the shepherds, but it works entirely in its own right, subtly suggesting the unique moment when God stepped into the human story.

A passage such as this could encourage us to write spiritually imaginative narratives around the characters of Mary and Joseph, Elizabeth and Zechariah, and others who might be involved. They could reflect on, and sensitively present, the moment when the divine became human, when the eternal became bound by time and space.

One such numinous moment comes in Elizabeth Jennings's poem "The Annunciation":

> *Nothing will ease the pain to come*
> *Though now she sits in ecstasy*
> *And lets it have its way with her.*
> *The angel's shadow in the room*
> *Is lightly lifted as if he*
> *Had never terrified her there.*
>
> *The furniture again returns*
> *To its old simple state. She can*
> *Take comfort from the things she knows*
> *Though in her heart new loving burns*
> *Something she never gave to man*
> *Or god before, and this god grows*
>
> *Most like a man.*

There is still the shadow of an angel here. But I wonder whether we are now grown up enough to decide that angel messengers, or some of the other symbols, no longer really work for us. Perhaps they are now overworked and, positively, there are fresher ways of expressing wonder. If so, there is surely a need for writers — perhaps inspired by the strange James's Infancy Gospel — to express the mystery of the incarnation in new-minted narratives.

(2012)

God's gift of goodwill

The incarnation means that Christmas isn't just about the faithful,
says **Angela Tilby**

AS we groan yet again at the sentimentality and commercialism that mark our annual winter festival, we might be inclined to downplay the magic of Christmas. We would be wrong to do so, though. There is real magic, though it is not in the tinsel, but in the theology.

Christmas is magic because it is miracle: singular, unique, and inexplicable. It is the feast of the incarnation, the great mystery of the Word becoming flesh, which is spelt out in the Prologue of the fourth Gospel. In Christian understanding, the incarnation is a once-and-for-all event. God becomes human, and, by doing so, changes the meaning of human history. What is achieved is summed up in the famous phrase of Athanasius: "He became human so that we might become divine," or, more literally: "He was humanised so we could be divinised."

In the writings of the early Christian Fathers, Jesus does not come merely to die for our sins. He comes to work a divine alchemy of healing which transforms the whole human race. His death on the cross is the final breakthrough in restoring lost humanity to God. But the central miracle is the incarnation. Gregory of Nyssa says: "The Word, in taking flesh, was mingled with humanity ... so that the human might be deified by this mingling with God."

The implication of such statements is that God in Christ does not come just for those who respond to the gospel message or for those who receive him in the sacraments of the Church. The humanity he assumes is shared by every human being who has ever walked the planet, and every human being is potentially healed by his taking of our nature.

So Christmas is the most universal of festivals. Carols, hymns and liturgies follow patristic thinking by expressing this universality in terms of the great exchange between God and man. Charles Wesley echoes Athanasius and Gregory: "Veiled in flesh the Godhead see, Hail the incarnate Deity! Pleased as man with man to dwell, Jesus, our Emmanuel."

The problem is that in our time, it is a struggle to say anything universal about the human race. Even the term "man" is thought by many to be no longer usable as a generic noun, as it no longer includes women (many would say it never did) as part of its meaning. So we struggle for a suitable word to describe what the word once implied, that is, the human race taken as a theological reality, created by God in his image and yet fallen. Words like humanity and humankind do not quite deliver what the stark and simple "man" once did.

But, even if we found a word that would do, it would only bring us up sharply against another form of the same stumbling-block about universality: that it is beginning to seem arrogant for followers of any particular faith to speak theologically at all about the whole of humanity. Respect for cultural diversity makes the incarnation difficult to articulate: if God in Christ has come for everyone, why is it that only Christians recognise him? And if Christians claim that others, by their holy lives and virtuous aspirations, do, in some hidden sense, recognise him, are they being patronising?

The cultural changes of our time are driving a wedge between Christmas and the secular winter festival, which becomes deeper year by year. As if in commentary, Bible scholars and liturgists make the problem worse by narrowing the scope of the Christmas story. An example: the King James Bible translated the song of the angels to the shepherds with a wonderful generosity: "Glory to God in the highest, and on earth peace, good will towards men." That is not what Luke's Greek says, but it made sense in the context of the way Christian nationhood was understood at the time.

It also made sense in the liturgy of holy communion, which is where the words were most frequently encountered. There, as the hope of Christendom waned, Luke's words became an impetus to mission, urging the faithful to recognise that the glory of God cannot be contained within the bounds of the Church. The more correct contemporary version found in the NRSV sounds, by contrast, hideously smug: "Peace to those whom he favours." Even the liturgical: "Peace to his people on earth," suggests that it is only "his people" in the restricted sense who receive God's peace at Christmas.

BY such wooden biblicism the world is sold short. It is left with the tinsel of Christmas, but robbed of the magic. It is the Church itself that seems to want to limit the universal Christian promise to churchy insiders, with their privatised convictions of sin and salvation. Yet it is important for those of us who wish Christmas to retain its universal meaning to give some account of what God really has done for all of us in the incarnation. Why is it that our human condition calls forth such divine alchemy as the birth of the Son of God? In the light of Christmas, what is human sin?

Christmas carols answer this by taking us back to our first parents, that is, in biblical mythology, to Adam and Eve. "Adam lay ybounden, bounden in a bond": biblical mythology presents the primeval sin as disobedience, the taking of the forbidden apple in response to the tempting of the serpent.

Salvation in the form of a newborn baby: part of The Nativity *(c.1420),
by the Master of Flémalle, Robert Campin, in the Musée des Beaux-Arts, Dijon*

This does not help us much. The story is neither history nor explanation. It does, however, express the age-long frustration that human beings experience as we contemplate the futility of our actions. There is something wrong with us, a dissonance between our hopes and their outcome; a fatal rift between our sense of what we could be and our bitter knowledge of what we are.

The fact that our salvation comes in the form of a newborn baby is astonishing. A new baby melts our cynicism by its total need and dependence. We realise once again that we are all older and more experienced than the just-born. Christmas, then, reminds us that, theologically speaking, the human race is marked by age. Compared with the freshness of God, we are all old and hard and withered.

Biology supports theology: we know now that our life on this planet goes back far beyond the "four thousand winter" which the Adam of the carols had suffered. The Bible pictures our beginnings in Eden; but the story revealed by Darwinian science is one of a slow evolution that is still going on.

Science tells us that our future lies in dialogue with the technologies we have ourselves created. But common sense, and theology, tell us that these technologies, no matter how sophisticated, will not free us from what is wrong with us. We already know that the benefits of new discovery will be shadowed by new evils. Not only are we old, in terms of the life of the world; we are also caught up in bad habits which we have learnt from one another and pass on, from generation to generation.

Again, the birth of the Christ-child, in poverty and vulnerability, reveals what these habits might be. Because of our need to survive long enough to pass on our genes, we have developed habits of aggression that are excessive. We are greedy for experience, for power, for security. We cannot bear to be restrained or contained.

Something of this is well conveyed in the Garden of Eden story. Adam and Eve were attracted by the forbidden fruit simply because it was forbidden. The fruit held potential secrets for them, a fact that the serpent exploited. Adam and Eve were not prepared to be simply who they were; they wanted to be what they were not. The apple drew out their fantasy of what it would be like to be God, to be omnipotent, to know that every fantasy could be instantaneously realised.

What we call the Fall, the bond in which Adam lay ybounden, is, then, a problem of human desire. We want to be God, not the selves we are. Of course, in one sense, this desire is not wide of the mark. Both the Bible and tradition insist that we are made in God's image and likeness, and it is precisely that divine image to which the incarnation restores us. God becomes human so that we might be divine. But, in our natural state, we imagine we can be God simply by an act of will; by imposing ourselves on ourselves, on others and on our world. If we are to be divinised, as God intends, we cannot grasp equality with God for ourselves. To do so is to become slaves to the serpent, endlessly hungry and needy, consuming all that lies in our path to assuage our inner emptiness.

The great sin is grandiosity, the attempt to incorporate the other into ourselves. This is what God will not do. He delights in our otherness, and is not afraid or ashamed to stoop to our level. Paul's hymn on humility in the second chapter of Philippians contrasts our aggressive neediness with the humility of the Son of God. The Son does not "count equality with God a thing to be grasped, but emptied himself, taking the form of a servant, being born in human likeness".

So, when we look at the Christ-child, we see what God intends for us. Christmas is a gift to the world, and I believe it can be offered to the world in humility simply because the image of the newborn baby and his mother is already a universal symbol.

A baby does not threaten. It makes no imperialistic claims or demands, but it reveals a truth that all may recognise. We have to learn what it is to be human in order to become, by God's grace, divine. And only God can show us what being truly human means.

(2003)

His nativity is our own origin

At the moment of Christ's birth, we touch eternity,
says **Robin Ward**

Of the Father's heart begotten,
Ere the world from chaos rose …

THE great Christmas hymn by Prudentius begins not at the crib, nor in the fields, with the shepherds: it begins with the eternal and mysterious birth of the Son, begotten of his Father before all worlds. In the Western tradition, it is the midnight mass of Christmas which celebrates this most profound of mysteries: in the obscurity of the darkest moment of the longest night, a fitting setting for announcing the truth most hidden from the ingenuity of human wisdom, the Church proclaims: "In the beginning was the Word."

God is Father: he does not become a father, or earn the title of father because of his paternal care for what he has created. He is Father from all eternity, and it is from his fatherhood that every family in heaven and on earth is named (Ephesians 3.15). We learn what fatherhood is from our human experience, and indeed human fatherhood is an example of how we manifest the divine image in a way the angels do not. But God is Father before creation began, because from all eternity he actively communicates his very nature to the Son.

So that we should understand this communication of nature, this begetting of the eternal Son, in a way that preserves God's nature as spirit, St John calls the Son of God "the Word". There is no physical process of generation by which the Father brings forth the Son, no bodily act. If we are to look for an analogy in human experience to understand how the Father gives his nature to the Son, then we find it in our spiritual acts as intellectual creatures, not our bodily acts as physical creatures. The Son is called "Word" by the apostle, because his eternal begetting is most like the formation of a concept in the mind: indeed, the mind forming a concept of itself.

Because there is never a time when God lacks this self-understanding, the generation of the Word is eternal: the Father is God Understanding; the Son, God Understood. The Scriptures demonstrate this mental analogy by the way in which the Son is described: the wisdom of God (1 Corinthians 1.24); the image of the invisible God (Colossians 1.15); he who bears the very stamp of God's nature (Hebrews 1.3).

This eternal Fatherhood of God was unknown to the holy men and women of the old covenant, and to the philosophers and sages of antiquity; it is revealed only in the incarnation of the Son of God. By this means, as St Leo the Great writes: "The Incomprehensible willed to be comprehended." So, too, the eternal sonship of the Word is not altered or added to by his birth from the Virgin Mary; as St Germanus sings: "The Word becomes incarnate And yet remains on high."

The incarnation is no necessity for the Son, no completion of his sonship. It is a purely gracious act, undertaking our humble state without diminution of his majesty, so that the union of our nature with himself might accomplish the work of our salvation. It is at the crib that we realise, in the words of Charles Coffin's hymn, the paradox and the glory of the incarnation: "Art thou the eternal Son, The eternal Father's ray? Whose little hand, thou infant one, Doth lift the world alway?"

THE birth in time of the eternal Son is accompanied by signs that point to the awesome mystery of what has been revealed. The most profound sign is the virginity of his mother. St Thomas Aquinas writes: "Since Christ is the true and natural Son of God, it was not fitting for him to have any other Father than God, lest the dignity of God be transferred to another." Jesus Christ has God as his Father exclusively: his conception in the womb of the Virgin Mary is spiritual, because his eternal begetting by the Father is spiritual; when he assumes human nature, he does not also acquire a new father.

The virginal conception of the Word testifies to Christ's status as the New Adam. His human nature is in solidarity with ours, but it is also a new creation, a reformation of what has been tainted by sin, and a new beginning. The virginal conception points to our own incorporation into Christ as adopted sons and daughters of God. Just as, through an exemplary loving faith, the Blessed Virgin conceives the eternal Son of God in her womb, so we, through that same loving faith, are reborn in him, not of blood, nor of the will of the flesh, nor of the will of man, but of God (John 1.13).

If the principal sign that reveals the unique character of Christ's birth is the virginity of his mother, then the place, time and circumstances of his nativity likewise illuminate the mystery of the incarnation of the Son of God. Already in the account of the visitation given by St Luke, the child conceived in the Virgin's womb is identified with the presence of the most high: Elizabeth greets Mary, and the infant John dances in her womb, just as King David greets the Ark of the Covenant and dances before it as it is brought up to Jerusalem (2 Samuel 6).

Born a Jew in Judaea, Jesus fulfils the prophetic election of the Jewish people: "of their race, according to the flesh, is the Christ, who is God over all, blessed for ever" (Romans 9.5). The precarious but enduring lodging of

God's people in the Promised Land anticipates the hazardous obscurity of the infant Messiah among those whom he has come to redeem: "the sceptre shall not depart from Judah, nor the ruler's staff from between his feet, until he comes to whom it belongs; and to him shall be the obedience of the peoples" (Genesis 49.10).

Jesus is born in Bethlehem: at once the royal city of David (Luke 2.4), and the least of the cities of Judah (Micah 5.2). The Son of God comes into the world not where human power waxes its strongest, but where the promise of God given to the house of David in the Old Testament is to be fulfilled, and where the utter obscurity of his circumstances will demonstrate the sovereign power of God in accomplishing the work of salvation. So, too, the incarnate Christ is not revealed to all humankind at the time of his birth. It is through the assumption of our human nature that the Word purposes to redeem us, and the reality of that human nature must be credible.

So the Word made flesh is made manifest not through his own power, but by the witness of his creatures: hence the fittingness of the shepherds' faithful testimony. St John Chrysostom calls them "simple men, living in the ancient practices of Moses and the Patriarchs". It is to these first of the poor in spirit that the truth of Christ's humanity is made known, even while the summoning angels testify to the hidden Godhead.

Here, too, we find confirmation of the fitting moment of the incarnation in the course of human history, its coming "in the fullness of time" (Galatians 4.4). Just as Virgil, the great Roman poet of the Augustan peace, was hymning the pastoral life as the model for virtuous living and contemplation, so the incarnate Word, humbly submitting to enrolment in the census of Caesar, is first hailed by shepherds whose hastening is a sign of the impetus of the spiritual life.

SO Christ is born eternally from the Father's heart, and temporally from the womb of the Virgin, from whom he assumes our nature. His third birth is a spiritual one, in the hearts of believers. The events of Christ's nativity and infancy are in the past. However, just as his glorified body bears the marks of his Passion, so his glorified human soul perpetuates the virtue of every mystery of his earthly life for the good of his Church.

These mysteries of Christ's life are not simply beneficial to us as examples, they are effective in us as transforming grace. The virtue of the Christmas mystery is divine adoption, participation in Christ's sonship, renovation of the old Adam. As the collect for Christmas Day prays: "Grant that we being regenerate, and made thy children by adoption and grace, may daily be renewed by thy Holy Spirit."

At first hearing, this sounds as if it were an Easter collect, but it is through the grace of baptism that we are reborn into the divine life. As St Leo the

Great says: "As we worship the birth of our Saviour, we discover that we are celebrating our own origin." The divine sonship that Christ possesses by nature, we possess by the adoption of grace. Again, Charles Coffin makes the point in his Christmas hymn: "So shall thy birthday morn, Lord Christ, our birthday be, Then greet we all, ourselves new-born, Our King's nativity."

But the Christmas mystery is not only baptismal, it is eucharistic. The poverty, the speechlessness, the humble dependency, the mortal peril of the Son of God at Bethlehem — all point eloquently towards the Cross. Many of the greatest proponents of devotion to the infancy of Christ have been most conscious of this: Pierre de Bérulle calls infancy, with a startling lack of sentimentality, "the lowest and most abject state of human nature after death". It is for revealing his divine sonship, the heart of the Christmas mystery, that Jesus suffers death: "This was why the Jews sought all the more to kill him, because he … called God his own Father, making himself equal with God" (John 5.18).

St Gregory the Great reminds us that Bethlehem means "House of Bread"; here the Word incarnate finds his first earthly throne in the manger, a place of feeding. The infant Christ has already begun his work as priest and victim, offering to the Father the perfect worship of his sinless humanity spent for our sake, and offering himself to us as the "Living Bread which came down from heaven". Just as he begins this work by assuming our human nature from his mother, so he wonderfully completes it by uniting us to himself in the sacrament of the altar.

St Thomas Aquinas writes of the Christmas mystery: "Of all the works of God … this surpasses reason more than any other, since one cannot conceive of God doing anything more wonderful than that the true God, the Son of God, should be made true man."

As we contemplate the Christmas mystery, we adore the eternal birth of the Word in the bosom of the Father; we adore the incarnate Son, whose deity is worshipped by angels, and whose humanity makes shepherds hasten to wonder; and we rejoice at the birth of Christ in our own hearts. We have been adopted at our baptism; fed at the altar by the one whose cradle was a manger and whose birthplace was the House of Bread; and imbued by the virtue of his divine infancy with the spirit of humility, innocence, and the new youth of eternal life.

The Word in the bliss of the Godhead remains,
Yet in flesh comes to suffer the keenest of pains;
He is that he was, and for ever shall be,
But becomes that he was not, for you and for me.

(2005)

Tears and smiles like us he knew

Both the Early Church and Mrs Alexander wrestled
with Christology; so must all Christian children,
argues **Jane Williams**

"But little Lord Jesus, no crying he makes"

AS a teacher of doctrine, I have sometimes set students the task of sorting out the best and the worst Christmas carols. They do not have to assess the poetry or the tune, just the doctrinal content. They assure me that the exercise ruins the Christmas spirit only a little bit, and that, after a few years, they are able to start enjoying the season again.

Take, for example, "Away in a manger". When we sing "The cattle are lowing, the baby awakes, But little Lord Jesus, no crying he makes", what exactly is being implied about the baby? Normally, we would worry about a baby that did not respond to stimuli, and did not cry to express hunger or fear, rage or weariness. The carol is clearly implying that this particular baby is not normal, and that his passivity is some sign of divine calm and control. This both subtly undermines the real humanity of this baby, and makes some very questionable assumptions about what divinity is like.

There is a similar undercurrent to "Once in royal David's city", as we sing about Jesus's "wondrous childhood" of honour and obedience to his mother, although Mrs Alexander does concede that "Tears and smiles like us he knew". The phrase "Christian children all must be Mild, obedient, good as he" suggests that the hymn is less interested in teaching us about the incarnation, and more interested in subduing unruly Sunday-school children.

"Christian children" might be pleased to know that there is very little biblical warrant for this annoyingly perfect baby Jesus. Only Matthew and Luke tell us directly about the birth of Jesus, and they say remarkably little about the baby himself. We see the reactions of Mary, Joseph, the shepherds, the Wise Men, Herod, and the angels, but, like any other baby, this baby is dependent upon the adult world to interpret his needs.

LUKE'S is the only Gospel to give us a snapshot of the child Jesus, and what he shows us is much stranger and harder than the "childhood's pattern" of the carol. We see the 12-year-old Jesus in the Temple, completely at home, talking and listening, having forgotten entirely to tell Mary and Joseph where he was. Dear Christian children, please do not copy Jesus in this respect.

The boy Jesus visits Jerusalem: his mother finds him among the doctors in the Temple, from Jésus parmi les docteurs *(1804) by Ingres (Musée Ingres, Montauban)*

After this, all that Luke tells us about the rest of Jesus's childhood is that Jesus "increased in wisdom and in years, and in divine and human favour" (Luke 2.52). That is a sentence that has caused problems ever since, especially for those whose idea of the incarnation is that a miniature god came down fully formed and inhabited a human body. Luke seems to suggest that Jesus grew and changed, and learned more about himself and about God as he did so, which is what you might expect of any child. But is it what you expect of this one?

Some of the non-canonical Gospels give in to the temptation to embroider Jesus's childhood with the kind of stories that you would expect to gather around a divine child. So they imagine him making little images of birds, and, when he releases them, they really fly; they also imagine him striking dead a disagreeable teacher — the religious impulse in the latter story may be hard to find, but it does help to demonstrate that what is going on here is someone imagining what they would do if they had divine power.

The biblical Gospels, on the other hand, know only one unusual thing about Jesus as a child, and that is that he felt drawn to the Temple, the home of God.

IN his adult ministry, Jesus constantly provoked people to ask who he was. Some asked in anger, some in bewilderment, and some in awe. That question was exacerbated by the crucifixion and resurrection, and by the preaching of Jesus's followers.

So, everywhere they went, the earliest Christians had to answer the question of who Jesus was and how he related to God. They had to answer it in a way that made sense of the witness of those who had known Jesus, who knew that he was really born, that he ate, slept, wept, and died. In other words, they could not pretend that he was not really human, even if they wanted to.

But, equally, they testified to his intimacy with God, to his miraculous powers, to his extraordinary teaching, and to the claims of authority he made for himself, both implicitly and explicitly — such as the claim to be able to forgive sins. And they testified to his resurrection from the dead and his continuing presence with them, though no longer in human, physical form.

Gradually, over the first few Christian centuries, Christian teachers tried out one theory or another of the relation between God and Jesus. Some suggested that Jesus was really only God in disguise, and that his humanity was just an appearance, not really like ours at all. Others suggested that Jesus was really just a human being, with a particularly close relationship with God, but not actually God living with humanity. Still others suggested that perhaps Jesus was some kind of a hybrid — a god-human — with characteristics of both, but not fully either one or the other.

After a good deal of arguing, praying, consulting, and insulting each other — the usual Christian mode of decision-making — the Christian Church came to a common mind at the Council of Chalcedon in 451. It said that Jesus is exactly like us *and* exactly like God, and that that does not make his humanity less human or his divinity less divine. In Jesus, humanity and divinity exist together "without confusion, without change, without separation and without division".

IT may sound as though this definition has strayed rather a long way from the Gospel picture of Jesus, and that I have strayed rather a long way from the theme of Christmas, but that would be a mistake. What we are celebrating at Christmas is exactly what Chalcedon describes. We are celebrating the presence and power of God, fully at work in the reality of our own human life. We are celebrating God's respectful, compassionate, joyful, uncoercive yet transformative love for creation.

Those Christians of the fifth century who came up with the abstract definition of Jesus as "fully God and fully human" thought that this was the only way to describe what they actually experienced through the incarnation. Salvation in Christ is not salvation *from* the world, but salvation *in and for* the world. We are not saved from ourselves, but enabled to be ourselves.

So, at Christmas, we do not have to search for the likeness of God somewhere behind the baby, or above it, instead, we can look with attention and love at this real baby. Where Jesus is, there is the presence and power of God, and God chooses to be here, completely with us, living life as we do. That is why Christmas is a celebration. We are celebrating reality — the world that God made and loves, the people that God comes to live with — all of us, and our real lives.

JESUS is really human and really God, so he holds together, in his own being, our real lives and the transforming, creative life of God. That is why Paul says, in Romans, that nothing can separate us from the love of God in Jesus Christ. That love is now part of our lives and our world because God the Son came to live with us. That means that every single aspect of life — and death — is potentially one where the life-giving, resourceful power of God is at work. It does not override our reality, but lives in it, and so transforms its possibilities.

That is why it is quite right to eat and drink and give presents at Christmas, and celebrate the material world. The challenge of Christmas is to make it possible for more and more people to enjoy God's world as we do. Babies living and dying in hunger and poverty, women and children trafficked like objects, people living by violence, thousands believing themselves worthless — how can we who celebrate Emmanuel, God with us, help them, too, to know God's joyful presence in the world?

The baby Jesus comes at Christmas, without power, without protection, dependent on the people around him. The only power he chooses is simply to draw out of people what is in them, the longing to love and care for the vulnerable. That is the Christmas present that he gives to us: this picture of how much God trusts us, how much God sees in us — God's belief that we will share ourselves with this baby. The baby needs us, and we respond. But because this baby is also God, our tiny, half-hearted response is taken into the life of God and unimaginably transformed. All we have to do, as Christina Rossetti's carol tells us, is "give our hearts".

At its simplest, that is what Christmas celebrates — people who are prepared to give their hearts in response to the God who seeks them out. The community that Jesus creates is one that challenges the barriers that prevent us from responding to each other.

It is a community based not on race, class, or gender, but simply on our common willingness to respond to God and to each other. It is still a human community, because the God who becomes incarnate in Jesus Christ clearly likes human beings.

But it is also one that carries, almost despite itself, however little it recognises it, God's own vision for the world and humanity. This is our world and it is God's world, and the two cannot be torn apart, any more than humanity and divinity can be torn apart in Jesus. These are tidings of comfort and joy.

(2008)

God takes on the human family tree

The creeds — particularly the one we rarely use any more — provide a challenging insight into the meaning of the incarnation, argues **Andrew Davison**

"LOVE came down at Christmas," we sing. To this, each of the three great creeds of the Church bears witness. This is the story of God born of God, *and* born of Mary, of the Son's journey from the Father to the dereliction of the cross, while still remaining in the Father's bosom. It also tells the story of cavemen, and the General Synod.

The earliest of the three, the Apostles' Creed, is the simplest. It covers the incarnation with the words "who was conceived by the Holy Spirit, [and] born of the Virgin Mary". In the next one, the "Nicene" Creed, we find a fuller discussion. Most lavish of all is the longest and latest text, which we call the Athanasian Creed (although its attribution to St Athanasius is certainly wrong).

Each creed has the incarnation at its centre, set within the logic of a Trinitarian faith. This is clearest in the Athanasian Creed, where the section on the incarnation follows an extended and lyrical discussion of the doctrine of the Trinity. Even the short Apostles' Creed follows a Trinitarian structure: Father, Son, and Spirit.

If we wish to explore the creeds from a Christmas perspective, we might consider the Greek word *ek*, meaning "from". With this word, the Nicene Creed spells out the divinity of Christ: he is begotten eternally "of [literally 'from' — *ek*] the Father"; he is "God from [*ek*] God, light from light, true God from true God."

The word *ek* is taken up again in the section on the incarnation, pointing, subtly, to the link between Christ's birth in time and his eternal coming forth from the Father. Just as the Son is begotten "from" the Father, God from God, he comes "down from [*ek*] heaven", and is conceived "of [again, literally 'from' — *ek*] the Holy Spirit and the Virgin Mary".

THE "mission" or "sending" of the Son in the incarnation rests on his "mission" (or eternal sending forth) in the Trinity. The Son is sent into the world because God is always, and already, concerned with "sending" in the eternal sending of the Son from — *ek* — the Father.

With the word *ek*, the creeds establish the divinity of Christ. In the earliest days of the Church, it had also been necessary to emphasise his humanity. The early theologians took that position against the Docetists — those who held that Christ only seemed (the Greek is dokein) to be human.

By the time the Nicene Creed was written, and expanded at the Council of Constantinople, the divinity of Christ, not his humanity, was under attack. An emphasis on the humanity remains in the creed, all the same. We might not notice it at first, but we will find it once again in that small Greek word *ek*.

When the liturgies of *Common Worship* were in the last stages of preparation, the General Synod faced few disputes fiercer than the debate over this single word, at the centre of the Nicene Creed. With *Common Worship*, the Church of England decided to translate into English the original Greek of the Nicene Creed rather than the Latin (itself a translation) familiar to many from musical settings of the mass: *Credo in unum Deum*, etc. This shift also gave us a creed that begins with the "We believe" of the Greek rather than the "I believe" of the Latin.

Previous English translations had followed the Latin, and recounted the incarnation with the words "was incarnate by the Holy Spirit, of the Virgin Mary" (the Latin words are *de* and *ex*). That, however, makes a distinction not present in the Greek, which has the Son incarnate both from the Holy Spirit and from the Virgin Mary: *ek … kai* — from … and from. Christ is as fully human as he is fully divine. He is as much "from" Mary (as to his humanity) as he is from the Father (adding the caveat, however, that ultimately everything, including his human descent, comes by the gift of God).

IN the contemporary Church, we pass over the Athanasian Creed. It is long and complicated, and its beginning and end are tough, even harsh, on heretics, who, we are told, "without doubt" will "perish everlastingly". All the same, it deserves our attention, since there are points of theology, especially concerning the incarnation, that find no more perfect expression than they do in this creed.

One of them makes the point just recounted, that Christ is from Mary, as well as being from God. He is "God, of the Substance of the Father, begotten before the worlds, and Man, of the Substance of his Mother, born in the world."

When it comes to being divine, Christ takes his "substance" (or nature, or being) from his Father, in the eternal gift that we call his "begetting". When it comes to being human, Christ takes his "substance" from his mother, born in time. Jesus really is one of us, as human as any human being ever born of a woman. This opposes the subtle heresy, still encountered today, that everything about Christ — his humanity as well as his divinity — was introduced directly into the world by God, Mary functioning (as this position sometimes puts it) as no more than a viaduct.

The Athanasian Creed may seem abstract, but the point it is making here could not be more earthy, physical and human. With the incarnation, God takes on a human family tree. What we are is determined by where we come from, especially when it comes to being born or begotten. Our new favourite word — *ek* — explains where Christ "comes from" in this sense: that he has natures both human and divine. As much as we use the word "from" to describe closeness and continuity, we use the word to describe distance and departure. If I have travelled from London, then I am no longer in that city.

Statements of faith: an icon of St Athanasius, whose name is lent to one of the creeds

WE naturally describe the incarnation as a journey, with this sense of "from". The tradition that Christ was born in the middle of Christmas night comes from a passage in the book of Wisdom, describing a journey. Or, rather, it describes a leap: "For while gentle silence enveloped all things, and night in its swift course was now half gone, your all-powerful word leapt from heaven."

There is a truth and a falsehood in treating the word "from" — "came down from [*ek*] heaven" — like this, as a journey. The Son comes to be one among us, and one of us. This, we might say, is quite some departure. Yet, in another way, it is not: he comes to be human, without ceasing to be what he was before. He comes from heaven, while remaining in heaven.

"Heaven", here, does not primarily mean a place, but Christ's relationship with the Father and with his own perfect divinity. On this front, he departs without leaving: "The heavenly Word proceeding forth, yet leaving not the Father's side", wrote Thomas Aquinas in a hymn. "Remaining in the bosom of the Father," Augustine preached, "he made pregnant the womb of the Mother."

Our Christology is at its most compelling when we hold to both the humanity and the divinity in their fullness: to both departing and to remaining. Christ's divinity makes his humanity all the more extraordinary and significant. It is difficult to imagine why we should think that the suffering of a Palestinian peasant in AD 33 urges us to defend the poor at every turn, were this peasant not also Almighty God.

SIMILARLY, it is only in Christ's humanity that we encounter God with the directness of one who can be "seen with our eyes ... looked at and touched with our hands". What is revealed there shows God to be more extraordinary than we could ever have imagined. The incarnation gives us a window on to God as three and one: we see not only "God made visible", but also this God living in the power of the Holy Spirit, and addressing God as his Father. It is from here that Trinitarian theology begins.

The Son of God was not changed by the incarnation. As Augustine, again, put it, the incarnation has him "remaining what He was in Himself, and receiving from us and for us what He was not". This is another point where the Athanasian Creed gets to the heart of the matter, with pithy directness. In Christ, we see a union "not by conversion of the Godhead into flesh: but by taking of the Manhood into God". The incarnation was no "conversion" of God, which is to say that it was no truncation of God.

On this, a great deal rests. If the incarnation was a truncation of God, then Jesus is not really Emmanuel, not really "God with us", but "God-reduced with us", or "a-sliver-of God with us". Only because the fullness of God was incarnate in Christ ("in him the whole fullness of deity dwells bodily," (Colossians 2.9) can we say with Karl Barth and his followers (and, on this front, that means a great cloud of witnesses in the 20th century), that God is as he is in Christ.

IN *The Everlasting Man*, G. K. Chesterton takes great delight in the particular destination of the Son's "journey": tradition has it that the stable in which Christ was born was a cave. The Church of the Nativity, in Bethlehem, was built in the early fourth century over the cave that was held to be the site of the stable. Archaeology confirms that caves often served this purpose. "The human story began in a cave," Chesterton wrote, at least in as much as our imagination is captured by the figure of the "caveman" drawing animals on the walls. Caves with paintings, such as those in Lascaux in France, stand at the beginning of human history.

At Christmas, we remember that the "second half of human history", as Chesterton writes, "also begins in a cave. Animals were again present; for it was a cave used as a stable by the mountaineers of the uplands about Bethlehem". And, whatever Pope Benedict XVI might write in *Jesus of*

Nazareth, if there was a manger, there were probably also animals. At the nativity, God, too, became a "caveman".

The Son "came down from heaven", as the Nicene Creed puts it, not to be born on the surface of the earth, but under the earth, in a cave: a cave that Chesterton calls "a hole or corner into which the outcasts are swept like rubbish", such that Jesus was "born like an outcast or even an outlaw". From the first moments of his nativity, we see where the Son's journey is to take him: to a cross between two bandits. After this birth in poverty, writes Chesterton, who is always a "political" theologian, our sense of our duties to the poor and outcast can never be the same again.

The word "from" presents us with a journey, and, at Christmas, that journey-while-remaining of the Son of God has only just begun. Ahead lie infancy and childhood, adolescence and adulthood, death and resurrection; ahead lie Egypt and Nazareth, Capernaum and Jerusalem, Hades and Heaven. The Church will follow this story in the coming months, to Holy Week and beyond. Its missionary challenge at Christmas is to encourage others to follow the journey with us. Perhaps the very fact that we are concerned with the infancy of Christ can be a spur, because with every birth comes the fascination of a story begun. Again, Augustine makes this point: "We have the infant Christ, let us grow with him."

The Apostles' Creed is the creed of baptisms, and of the personal confession of the faith. The Nicene Creed is the creed of the eucharist, and being one body together. At Christmas—more than at any other time — the Church can expand its "I believe" to a "we believe", which others can say alongside us.

We do this in the hope that, in time, they will be able to take this "we believe" and make it an "I believe" of their own: an "I believe" that can grow into the theological maturity of the Creed of St Athanasius, that poetic, profound and underappreciated exploration of Christian faith.

(2012)

Stars of wonder, stars of grace

Amid all the new scientific discoveries, the birth of Jesus
is still key, argues **David Wilkinson**

IT is tempting for someone like me, with an interest in science, to approach the Christmas story and quickly be transfixed by discussions about whether the star of the Magi was a comet, or about the genetic challenges of a virgin birth. But the central Christian belief of the incarnation of Jesus has far more profound things to say about science and current apologetics. In particular, it might help Christians to think about the latest big scientific questions — such as the origin of the universe, and the search for extra-terrestrial intelligence — and the legacy of new atheism, besides what it means to be human.

When carol services end with a reading of the opening of John's Gospel, its ancient author would surely be surprised by today's context of candlelight and children dressed as donkeys. Yet this context is not too far away from this overture, which highlights themes in the Gospel such as glory, life, light, witness, truth, and the nature of the world, and how they relate to Jesus.

John subtly picks up many strands of the human thought of his time. Those from a Hebrew background would note the reference to Genesis 1.1: "In the beginning". The first cause of creation was God's personal creative activity through his self-expression, his word. Thus, in Genesis 1, God speaks, and things come into existence. In a creative synthesis, however, those from a Greek background would also recognise the word *logos*, which represents the rationality behind and inherent in the universe. Those who put emphasis on life, the symbol of light, or the eventual triumph of light over darkness would find something that resonated with their thought, too. In addition, those who saw the importance of the witness of others, or spiritual experience, would feel affirmed by John.

Through all of this, however, John is beginning to work out his central theme. It is about someone who underlies all of this, and is greater than all of these approaches. If the listener does not pick up the clues, John offers it boldly and dramatically in verse 14: "the Word became flesh."

Although rationalism or mysticism may provide pointers to God, you cannot know the true nature of God simply through these means. Even the witness of John the Baptist, or of the Old Testament Scriptures, is not enough. All these things have to be understood in relation to Jesus Christ. So what might this baby of Bethlehem mean for some of the key scientific insights of today?

THE extraordinary ability of cosmology to describe the history of the universe through 13.8 billion years, back to a small fraction of a second after its beginning, is astonishing. Exactly a century ago, Einstein produced an understanding of gravity in his general theory of relativity, which allowed predictions of an expanding universe. A few years later, observations of the redshift of galaxies were the first indication of a rapid expansion of space-time, evidence of what Sir Fred Hoyle nicknamed "the Big Bang".

Currently, our laws of physics are not capable of describing the very first moments of the universe, but it would be unwise to use this as an argument for a "god of the gaps" who simply sets off the firework of the Big Bang. Stephen Hawking and others are hard at work to unify general relativity with quantum theory in order to understand that first moment, and I am excited to see the success of this quest. Indeed, the indications are that in this we may see that our universe is one in a multiverse.

Some Christians see this as a threat. For many centuries, theologians laid a great deal of emphasis on logical arguments that would prove the existence of God. The cosmological argument tried to prove that the universe needed a first cause, and that this first cause was God. The design argument pointed to apparent design in the natural world, and argued that such design needed a designer. These arguments became key to theology and evangelism up to the 19th century.

The trouble was that they did not work. Philosophers such as Kant and Hume pointed out the flaws in the logic, and Charles Darwin demolished the design argument by showing that the design in the biological world was the result of natural selection. Today, quantum gravity and the multiverse caution against a return to these kinds of arguments, used by some of those who advocate Intelligent Design.

YET there is an even more important problem with these attempted proofs of God. That is: what kind of God do you end up with at the end of the process? At most, you could claim the existence of some sort of cosmic architect, but nothing more than that. A God who is personal, and whose nature is one of love and justice, is a long way beyond such proofs. How can a finite mind, functioning within a finite universe, ever know anything about an infinite God?

The Christian approach is to contemplate the possibility that the infinite God decided to reveal truth to our finite minds in a way that would be understandable. This is central to what John is saying about Jesus. God has become a human being in Jesus, and lived among us.

In answer to the question of what God is like, Christians respond that he is like Jesus. This is a surer path to the nature of God. The vastness of the universe, and the beauty and simplicity of the laws of physics underlying it might point, through a sense of awe, to a good and extravagant God.

But what about Stephen Fry's much-publicised example of insects that burrow out of the eyes of children; or, on a larger scale, the recent discovery that the universe is destined to futility in heat-death? These things might lead people to another conclusion altogether.

In a fallen universe of mixed messages, Jesus is the baseline by which we calibrate our understanding of God, the evidence on which our theological models are constructed, and the assurance of the personal at the heart of impersonal mathematical theory. Christian faith ultimately rests on the borrowed barn rather than the Big Bang.

This has much to say to mission in a culture that lives with the legacy of new atheism. The popularity of Professor Richard Dawkins may be past its peak, but its legacy has perpetuated the idea of conflict between science and Christian faith. This is far too simplistic, both in its reading of history and its understanding of the nature of science today. Against a background of such a conflict, however, there is a need to be positive when offering the evidence of the Word made flesh.

IF cosmology dominated much of the science–religion dialogue of the second half of the previous century, the question of what it means to be human is the question of the first part of the 21st century.

Advances in medical technology have reawakened questions about the beginning and end of life, and they are now joined by some new challenges. As artificial intelligence and situated robotics surpass human processing power, and come ever closer to mimicking human decision-making, might a conscious machine emerge among us? And, if the majority of my genetic code is shared with a cauliflower, never mind an ape, what distinguishes me from the rest of the created order? It is a question also raised by human evolution, and in the tightening relation of brain and mind in neuroscience, which squeezes out any distinct place for a spiritual soul.

One new and unexpected challenge is the extraordinary rate of discoveries of planets outside our solar system. An app on my smartphone informs me daily of yet another confirmation of one of some 2000 such planets, some of which are not too dissimilar to earth, and located in a "habitable" zone in relation to their central star.

For example, in July 2015, NASA announced the discovery of Kepler 452b, a planet 60-per-cent larger than the earth, and located in the habitable zone of a sunlike star. So the argument goes that, as extrasolar planets seem plentiful in a universe of 100 billion stars in each of 100 billion galaxies, then surely there must be other life out there. Some people fear that this could undercut the Christian belief in the uniqueness of human beings.

The science is, of course, a little more complicated than this argument assumes. A habitable planet does not necessarily imply the existence of life, and it certainly does not imply intelligent life. It is a long way from an amoeba to an accountant. But would alien accountants be a difficulty for the Christian faith?

Some years ago, the historian of chemistry Professor Colin Russell pointed out that Christians had been at the forefront of the search for other worlds. There were two theological convictions that provided the reason for this. First, because God was the free creator of the universe, then God could create whatever God wanted to create.

Second, the special nature of human beings was not to be defined by location at the centre of the universe, or by being completely distinct in physical or mental makeup from the rest of creation. Rather, human beings are special because of the gift of intimate relationship with God, given in creation and seen in Jesus.

So, we see in the manger a God who loves human beings as they are; and also we see what human beings can be, and are meant to be.

With such a view of what it means to be human, the Christian can be more relaxed about many of these scientific questions. Of course, many questions will remain. Not least, perhaps, is the relevance of the cross and resurrection to the whole of the universe. As the hymn-writer Sydney Carter speculated many years ago: "Who can tell what other cradle, High above the Milky Way, Still may rock the King of Heaven On another Christmas Day?"

WHILE science dominates the modern world, it is, at the same time, under threat. Blamed by some for the environmental crisis, it is feared by others, who see its power as uncontrollable, and is laughed off or ignored by many who struggle to understand it. Such attitudes exist outside and within the Church, not least by those who have bought into the conflict model of science and faith.

Yet the word made flesh is not just about God's becoming a human being, but God's becoming part of his created order of cells, molecules, atoms, protons, and Higgs bosons. It is a God who pitches his tent in the very physicality of this world, both affirming it and showing a commitment to redeeming it.

This Jesus will not only save us from our sins, but will inaugurate a kingdom that will lead to a new heaven and a new earth. The revelation of the Creator God in Jesus is not simply a divine escape plan from this world. It is God saying that this world of time and space, of quantum theory and the human genome, and of supernovae and structural engineering is important.

So, in the midst of the light of Christmas candles, and surrounded by the desperation of teachers trying to find enough animals in the stable to give a part to every child, the opening of John's Gospel affirms the interpretation of light from distant galaxies through telescopes and the study of biodiversity of which this Christ-child is a part.

The physical world is not so evil that it has to be avoided in preference for the purity of the spiritual world. The fact that "through him all things were made" affirms the work of scientists and technologists; for at the heart of the physical order is the Jesus whom we worship and follow as disciples.

Perhaps the most effective contribution to mission in a world dominated by science would be if the Church saw science as a gift, and gave confidence in witness to those scientists who see their work and thinking as a Christian vocation.

(2015)

Christmas on the edge
by Malcolm Guite

Christmas sets the centre on the edge;
The edge of town, out-buildings of an inn,
The fringe of empire, far from privilege
And power, on the edge and outer spin
Of turning worlds, a margin of small stars
That edge a galaxy itself light years
From some unguessed-at cosmic origin.
Christmas sets the centre at the edge.

And from this day our world is re-aligned;
A tiny seed unfolding in the womb
Becomes the source from which we all unfold
And flower into being. We are healed,
The End begins, the tomb becomes a womb,
For now in him all things are re-aligned.

(2013)

God or merely Godlike?
A walk on the incarnation tightrope

The arguments about Christ in the fourth century matter today,
argues **John Saxbee**

A SHEPHERD peers into the crib in which Jesus Christ, Son of God, lies sleeping.

"He's the spitting image of his father," the shepherd observes.

"No," says one of the Magi, just arrived from the East, "he's a chip off the old block."

"Aren't they just two ways of saying the same thing?" asks a bystander.

"By no means," retorts the theologian in residence, "they are totally different … " — and so begins one of the most fiercely contested debates in the history of the Christian Church.

In what sense is Jesus the Son of God? Is he the Son of God because he is, as it were, genetically the same as God — one substance with the Father, as we say in our creeds. Is he, in that sense, "a chip off the old block"? Or is he the Son of God in the sense that he is the closest any human being can or ever will get to being like God — "the spitting image of his father"?

Who cares? Does it matter? Why trouble ourselves with such apparently trivial theological debating points? In the fourth century, it boiled down to whether the word *homoousion* (of one substance) or *homoiousion* (of like substance) best described the relationship between divine and human nature in Jesus. Do battle over an iota? Ridiculous!

Well, it does matter. It matters to such an extent that making sense of a tsunami, a devastating cyclone, or a terrorist atrocity depends upon how we answer. If Jesus is "the spitting image of his father", there is a likeness between him and God which is as close a likeness as any human being has ever revealed before or since. And that is good news, because, on the one hand, he becomes the means whereby we can glimpse something of what God is like: in the words of Bishop David Jenkins, "God is as he is in Jesus, and therefore there is hope".

On the other hand, we can glimpse something of our own capacity to grow in the likeness of God in so far as we fashion our lives after the example of Christ. Day by day like us he grew, so that day by day we might grow like him.

Yet a likeness is not a sameness. If Jesus is no more than "the spitting image of his father", then human beings are left still dependent on our own human resources to make sense of life's joys and sorrows, tragedies and triumphs. Faced with natural disasters and terrorist atrocities, we now have in Jesus an example of divine courage, compassion, self-giving, and sacrifice which combine to help us cope.

But there is nothing here to help us comprehend what all this might mean. If this baby born in Bethlehem is going to make not only a difference to the way we live in the world, but a difference to how we make sense of the world in which we live, then he has to be "a chip off the old block".

What we see in the crib at Christmas is none other than God born into the world. As Mary carried God in her womb, so the world now carries God in its history, its lifeblood, its corporate DNA. This means that making sense of our life on earth does not depend only on our own finite resources for making things add up. Making sense of our life on earth is now resourced by the very being of God, born into the world and around in the world.

If we have only our human resources available to make sense of things, then we find the biggest questions of all totally beyond our comprehension. If we have only human resources available to come to terms with evil and suffering, then the best we can do is project on to God our human understanding of love and power — and then realise that, in the face of such disaster, God may be all-loving or all-powerful, but he clearly cannot be both.

But what if our resources for making sense of such things now include the very being of one in whom "God in all his fullness chose to dwell, through him to reconcile all things to himself, making peace through the shedding of his blood on the cross — all things, whether on earth or in heaven" (Colossians 1.19-20)?

Left to ourselves, we are so constrained by the limited horizons of our fragile humanity that the questions that matter most are the ones we are least able to answer. That is why atheism and humanism struggle to make headway in our so-called secular society.

When, however, we see in the face of the Christ-child, lit by the light of a shepherd's lantern and a distant star, the very reality of God beckoning us beyond the horizons of our own humanity to a place where the Light of the World shines full of grace and truth — ah! then, we have a glimpse of eternity overarching the tragedies and traumas of life on earth; then we see sense in what seems senseless, meaning in what defies human understanding.

God's sense makes sense of non-sense, and all because (as Betjeman wrote):

God was man in Palestine
And lives today in Bread and Wine.

BUT now heed a warning from no less a luminary than Ludwig Wittgenstein: "An honest religious thinker is like a tightrope walker. He almost looks as though he were walking on nothing but air. His support is the slenderest imaginable. And yet it really is possible to walk on it."

When it comes to the doctrine of the incarnation — the claim that God became human in Jesus Christ — then honest religious thinkers may indeed look as though they are walking on nothing but air. The tightrope that supports them stretches between time and eternity, imminence and transcendence, the known and the unknowable.

God, who by definition is not human, is born into the world as a human being. This doctrinal tightrope walk across an apparently unbridgeable abyss separating divine and human nature is as foolhardy as it is fulfilling, as nerve-wracking as it is necessary.

For Christians, this perilous venture of faith and theological exploration *is* absolutely necessary. Even those who are inclined to be a bit picky when it comes to the doctrines and dogmas they choose to embrace will eventually come upon this unfathomable abyss, and there either retreat into mystery or entrust themselves to Wittgenstein's slenderest imaginable support, and find that it really is possible to walk on it.

Of course, the mechanics of the incarnation have to be separated from its meaning if we are going to keep our theological balance as we embark upon this venture of faith. For example, for some the virgin birth is proof-positive that Jesus was God, because only a divine being could be born that way. For others, it is belief in his divinity which comes first, so that the virgin birth is a corollary rather than a condition of his being God.

Either way, the virgin birth is a second-order issue, because what really matters when it comes to us and our salvation is that the theological tightrope does indeed support us across this chasm of conceptual contradictions, even if we never quite get to stand on that firm ground denied to religious thinkers who are truly honest.

Now, as we set out on this perilous adventure, we survey the scene from this tightrope well-trodden but never totally traversed.

First of all, we observe that the scene is indeed a familiar one at this time of year. The incarnation is predicated on humility as a Servant King is born into a subject people as a stranger far from home.

This confirms that, whatever we mean by God as a human being, we cannot rely on our human categories of power, prestige, and prosperity to reassure us that the divine order mirrors our ordering of society and its priorities. At least, that is St Luke's take on it all, because for him the Holy Family clearly lived in Nazareth but travelled to Bethlehem for a royal birth thoroughly counter-cultural in its pathos and banality.

For St Matthew, however, it is Bethlehem that appears to be home to the Holy Family, who then journey to Nazareth via Egypt to escape the perils of Herod's persecution. It is Magi bearing gifts, rather than lowly shepherds, who visit the infant Jesus, so that Matthew's account sits far more easily with our sense of what the arrival of a royal prince should be like in a well-ordered society.

Luke's Prince of Peace in poverty is for Matthew a man born to be King, and the scenes are set for some of the classic skirmishes that have threatened to destabilise the Christological tightrope ever since.

Yet, wherever we position ourselves in relation to the fourth-century controversies centred on the Person of Christ, and determined by the Council of Nicaea, we cannot ignore the extent to which our human relationships, and the power struggles that characterise them, have a bearing on how we see the relationship between humanity and divinity incarnated in Christ.

Both Luke and Matthew have their own agendas in this respect, and so we need both Luke and Matthew if we are to keep our balance and our nerve.

SO is this Christ-child the "spitting image of his father" or "a chip off the old block"? Cyril Connolly professed a belief in

> *God the Either*
> *God the Or*
> *And God the Wholly Both.*

Yet, while there is surely sense in the appeal to Jesus as an exemplar of godly living, this is of little worth unless it is as God that he shows us the Way.

(2007)

Hail! Thou unexpected Jesus

The birth of Christ was by prophets long foretold.
Not exactly, says **John Barton**

AT Christmas, we encounter traditional Christian thinking about Messianic prophecy and its fulfilment. According to Christian tradition, the Old Testament contains a number of predictions of the Messiah. The story of Jesus in the Gospels shows that he corresponds to these predictions. They occur mainly in the books of the prophets, and a number of them are read at Christmas carol services: Isaiah's Immanuel prophecy; Micah's promotion of the status of "little Bethlehem"; Jeremiah's foreseeing the new king, who will be called "The Lord is our righteousness". The fact that Jesus fulfils them, point by point, shows, in the traditional view, that he is, indeed, the promised one.

Problems arise as soon as biblical scholars get their hands on this tidy scheme. We point out that many of the predictions were not originally Messianic prophecies at all. That is true, for example, of the evocative passage in Isaiah 52–53 that we read on Good Friday about the suffering servant of the Lord who was "despised and rejected, yet he never opened his mouth": in Judaism in the first century, few people thought that was a prophecy of the Messiah.

SOME of the prophecies that are Messianic do not, in fact, correspond to Jesus, anyway. Isaiah foretold that the child to be born would be called Immanuel — "God with us" in Hebrew — but in fact he was called Jesus or Yeshua, a version of the Old Testament name Joshua. And some of the alleged prophecies are very far-fetched, or even non-existent: Matthew's Gospel tells us that Joseph settled in Nazareth to fulfil the prophecy "He shall be called a Nazarene", but no such prophecy can be found anywhere in the Old Testament.

So, it is not at all surprising that Jews reject the so-called "argument from prophecy", saying that the texts have many other possible applications, and that Jesus falls far short of fulfilling them. Biblical scholars tend to agree, and to think many had a more immediate application.

Immanuel, for example, was probably meant to be the name given to a child of one of the kings during whose reign Isaiah was prophesying. In any case, prophecy in ancient Israel was not to do with predicting the remote future, but with foretelling imminent events. Even the messianic oracles that there are — and they are few — are normally grounded in the belief that the Messiah, the new great King, will come very soon, not that he will do so in several centuries' time, as the prophets would have to have meant if they were predicting the coming of Jesus.

IF Jesus was the Messiah, he was, as the title of a book by the Dutch Dominican Lucas Grollenberg puts it, an Unexpected Messiah. With hindsight, his followers were able to find passages in the Old Testament which seemed, often to an uncanny degree, to fit his case. The "suffering servant" passage is an extraordinary example, and it's open to Christians to believe that its presence in the Old Testament is providential.

The same may be said of Psalm 22, which Jesus quoted on the cross: "My God, my God, why have you forsaken me?", which goes on to say, "They parted my garments among them, and cast lots for my clothing," though some scholars think the corresponding incident in John's Passion story was made up to fulfil the prophecy — a possibility that injects an uneasy note into our discussion, but one that can't be ignored.

But it is, in any case, hindsight that discovers the passages in question. No one before Jesus thought that these passages added up to create a coherent profile of what the Messiah would be like. They are passages culled from here and there by Christians who already believed that Jesus was the promised one. They are not a syllabus of texts that were already perceived beforehand as a prescription for who the Messiah would be.

WHERE there are clear outlines to what the Messiah would be, Jesus mostly seems to have been the opposite. One absolutely clear feature of most expectations of the Messiah was that he would be a new King David — the person to whom, in the Old Testament, the term "anointed one" (in Hebrew, mashiach; in English, "Messiah") originally applied. But Jesus was not a king. To recognise him none the less as the Messiah is to change the meaning of "Messiah". Jesus was not the Messiah anyone was expecting.

But once we have encountered him, we can say, as Christians, that he is the Messiah people ought to have expected: the person God sent because he knew better than we did what it was that we actually needed. Once we have him, we can look back and see dim prefigurements within the Old Testament — and perhaps elsewhere in the history of human culture — of the kind of person he was; and Isaiah's servant is probably a better candidate for that than is the Messianic king of some of the other prophetic texts.

But no one predicted Jesus. If he pulls threads together, they aren't threads anyone could have foreseen being pulled together in that way.

As Jesus, according to John's Gospel, told Pilate, he was not the kind of king whose servants would fight to establish his kingdom. He was a wholly

*Ecce Homo
(1871) by
Antonio Ciseri:
Pontius Pilate
presents the
scourged Jesus
to the crowd*

new kind of king who, to all external appearances, did not look or behave like a king at all.

It's no wonder that few of his contemporaries recognised in him the Messiah whom they were looking for. They can hardly be blamed — though that didn't stop many early Christians from blaming them, and the subsequent Church from falling into vile anti-Semitism.

Jesus systematically disappointed more or less all the expectations that people had of the Messiah: he didn't get involved in an armed struggle to defeat the Romans; he didn't have followers who could plausibly administer a new kingdom; and he didn't claim royal power or privileges.

In fact, if a traditional Messiah was what you were expecting, Jesus was about the last person you would identify as that Messiah: an artisan living very modestly (though not in actual poverty), associating with highly unsuitable people, and finally being executed as a criminal.

People in the Roman Empire often regarded Christianity as a religion fit only for slaves, and that, of course, is exactly what it was: it was a religion that in principle turned the world upside down, which (as the Magnificat puts it) "cast down the mighty from their thrones, and exalted the humble and meek".

If we define the Messiah by the expectations that many people had at the time, then it would be fair to say that Jesus was not the Messiah. From a Christian perspective, we might, rather, put it by saying that Jesus redefined what the Messiah was. He is the answer to the question that we didn't have the wit to ask. He is something so new that it doesn't fit the old categories. He is what in the history of science is now often called a paradigm shift, where the old interpretative framework will no longer contain the new data.

WHAT does it mean in practical terms to recognise, in Jesus, the Messiah? It means accepting that the values that Jesus stood for are those that are truly crucial in the world as God sees it. If we read the Gospels, we see all our expectations of what constitutes power being overturned, as we recognise in the teaching and life of this man a new set of values — congruent with the Hebrew Bible and with first-century Judaism, and yet developing them further.

The Christian gospel as proclaimed by Jesus reverses normal social pressures and offers us a redefinition of how life ought to be lived. This was put well more than 35 years ago by Gerd Theissen in his book *Biblical Faith*: "Social pressure means internalising family, people and state as authorities imposing obligations. But Jesus requires of his followers that they should break with their families; he presents foreigners ... as exemplary models and makes a sharp distinction between the demands of the emperor and those of God.

"Social pressure means internalising tradition and its rules governing conduct. But Jesus measures tradition by his insight into God's will, and disregards social norms if they go against elementary ethical demands.

"Social pressure means sanctions to the point of exterminating those whose conduct deviates from the norm. But Jesus calls for facing up to social pressure to the point of sacrificing one's own life — and he himself was an example of that."

IF we recognise Jesus as humanity's Messiah, we are accepting that these values are to be our values, and that we will work to try to see them implemented in our world. That involves personal dedication, and it may also require political action. But in no way may we seek to implement these values by methods that contradict the values themselves; for that is to drop back into the kind of activity from which Jesus came to set the human race free. So the fulfilment of prophecy turns out to mean the way in which Jesus — and we as his followers — remain true to the pattern of living which God wills for humankind, "for the Jew first, but also for the Gentile", as Paul puts it.

For Christians, to call Jesus the Messiah is to say that for us he is the perfect example of this pattern, combining the best of the teaching of the law and the prophets, which he did not seek to abrogate, as well as the best insights of the human race in its other Scriptures and wise teachings.

He provides the guiding thread with which we can trace the hand of God in all that went before him, giving us knowledge of the real questions to which we need God's answers.

(2020)

Find the fun in profundity

How do we reconcile the human side of Christmas
with the divine? The stocking and the stable?
Gillian Evans ponders a seasonal paradox

IN one of his Christmas sermons, the 12th-century Cistercian abbot Bernard of Clairvaux lays before his monks the tender notion of the "little Word", the *verbum abbreviatum* (Romans 9.28, Vulgate), which has shrunk himself to a size we can cope with. The idea that God could have come down to our level was by far the hardest thing for the early Christian world to grasp.

Today, we find it easier to think in terms of a human Jesus who set a good example than to accept that he was also God. But, at first, it was the other way round. How could the kind of God whom the intelligentsia of the day respected, who would never get his hands dirty, who was so far above the ordinary goings-on of life that it was disputed whether even "being" might be beneath his dignity, really become one of us? Surely he was just wearing a cloak of human appearance, a kind of mask?

Leo I became Pope in 440, and presided over the Western Church through a period that included the Council of Chalcedon of 451, which agreed that Christ was two natures in one person: a divine nature and a human one. This was the end of a century-and-a-half of claim and counter-claim, a regrettable mutual mudslinging between divided Christians, which resulted in an official clarification of the way the incarnation was to be understood. The crowds of protesters subsided a little. It remains open to question how much most of them understood of the recondite debates they had been cheering on.

Leo did not forget that this was, at best, even for those who thought they understood it, a mechanical explanation of a mystery, which did not cease to be mysterious when the celestial "genome" had been mapped. What mattered perhaps was not the technical formulation, but the fact that to gaze at that child and see him as a pretence, a mere seeming appearance, was to misunderstand what he was.

Once it was grasped and accepted officially that the Word of God had come to earth as a real human being, and a helpless infant at that, explaining what he had come for became all-important. In one of his sermons, Leo says that Christ entered into battle for us in his human nature so that Satan might be overcome in the very nature that he had conquered when he persuaded Adam and Eve to sin. This had symmetry, a supreme fairness, to his way of thinking. In a much-altered climate of thought, John Locke was still insisting on the underlying principle as crucial in the 17th century at the beginning of *The Reasonableness of Christianity*.

"It is obvious to anyone who reads the New Testament, that the doctrine of redemption, and consequently of the gospel, is founded upon the supposition of Adam's fall. To understand, therefore, what we are restored to by Jesus Christ, we must consider what the Scripture shows we lost by Adam."

THE core principle of belief in a God who was willing to do something about our plight has turned out to be capable of being told at many levels, in many ways, and in many media. The nativity comes early in the liturgical year, and the worship of the year goes on to tell the story that ends with the crucifixion of this baby, the resurrection, and new hope.

The medieval Mystery plays also represent the nativity as part of a narrative, beginning with the doings of Abraham, Isaac, Jacob, and other Old Testament preliminaries, and moving on to the annunciation, the salutation of Elizabeth, a shepherd's play or two, the Magi, the flight into Egypt, Herod, and onward to the teaching of Jesus and his death and resurrection.

In many nativity scenes, angels look at the child in delighted amazement. Why should the angels be so pleased? Because this infant is a cosmic challenge, as well as a human-and-divine paradox. In nativity scenes, the infant Jesus, the "little Word", is almost always shown with his mother, who holds him in her lap, and shows him to the world, and invites it to gaze and to wonder. Alessandro Allori (1535–1607) produced a series of Renaissance compositions to please his Florentine patrons, in which the child Jesus is placing a crown of flowers on his mother's head. Yet, in his other hand, he holds a crown of thorns. The *Mystic Nativity* by Botticelli (shown opposite), painted in about 1501, which hangs in the National Gallery in London, includes some of the apocalyptic symbolism of the passage in Revelation 12 in which a woman "clothed with the sun" cries out in labour pains. These are not comfortable Christmas pictures.

Should we allow ourselves to feel uncomfortable at Christmas, then? Christmas is a celebration of something huge; something accomplished; something that transforms the world — achieved by a modest downgrading of the divine to fit our creaturely limitations.

AN event of both staggering cosmic importance and gentle intimacy is to be celebrated. And what happens? Ten days of disappointed expectations: not the presents I wanted; too much rich food to eat; too much money spent; too many dark midwinter days with ordinary occupations unavailable; too much solitude for those who do not have a family; too many quarrels for those who do. Does this matter? In one way, it does not. There is an

The Mystic Nativity
by Botticelli (1501)

accommodating generosity in Jesus's approach to human frailty. But he is also severely uncompromising in the deep expectations he has of us.

It all began with good intentions. The present-giving was originally almsgiving, the Good King Wenceslas approach. This has given way for most of us in the West to an activity whose main challenge is to ensure we have hit the right level of expenditure for presents for friends and relations, who are expected to give presents to us in return. In Louisa M. Alcott's American novel *Little Women* (1869), there is a reminder of the older expectation. "Some poor creature came abeggin', and your ma went straight off to see what was needed. There never was such a woman for givin' away vittles and drink, clothes and firin'," exclaims Hannah, the family servant, on Christmas morning.

Yet the urge to give to the needy at Christmas had already become overlaid in 19th-century England with a certain sentimentality, which allowed one to keep one's distance from the discomforts of the disadvantaged. Charles Dickens "had a surprising fondness for wandering about in poor neighbourhoods on Christmas-day, past the areas of shabby genteel houses in Somers or Kentish Town, and watching the dinners preparing or coming in", remarked John Forster in his *Life of Charles Dickens* (1872).

HOW, then, to balance current social expectations without losing sight of the paradox and the challenge? In one of Dickens's *Christmas Stories*, written in 1850, he festoons the narrative, "A Christmas Tree", with so many ideas about Christmas that the branches sag. The Christmas tree was then a novelty, a German Christmas tradition encouraged by Prince Albert. Dickens calls it "that pretty German Toy". He heaps it with "bright objects", which turn out to be images of the meaning of Christmas. He remembers the toys he was given as a small child, and how, as he grew older, he began to associate Christmas with a sense of wonder, when "common things become uncommon and enchanted".

This happened on his first encounter with *The Arabian Nights*. For Dickens's Christmas is a rich jumble of magic and theatre and ghost-stories; holidays from school; time at home with the family — alongside "an angel, speaking to a group of shepherds in a field; some travellers, with eyes uplifted, following a star; a baby in a manger".

Dickens was not inventing this "mixed Christmas". It is much older. We do not know at what time of year Jesus was born. But the eventual (probably third-century) choice of 25 December set the feast in midwinter, when people had long been in the habit of cheering themselves up with feasting, drinking, and games around the fire. They saw no reason to give all that up to celebrate the nativity. They simply joined the two kinds of celebration together, as we do today. The Christmas "Wassail" ("Good health") is a drinking toast (probably Viking) by origin.

A HINT of the spirit in which Christmas has shaped itself is to be found perhaps in carols, essentially non-liturgical and informal, sometimes danger-ously theologically inventive, partly secular. They resemble the medieval Mystery plays in making Christmas accessible, supremely the Christian people's festival, in which joy is merriment, too. In Chaucer's "The Franklin's Tale":

> *Janus sit by the fyr, with double berd,*
> *And drynketh of his bugle horn the wyn;*
> *Biforn him stant brawen of the tusked swyn,*
> *And 'Nowell' crieth every lusty man.*

In the contemporaneous story *Sir Gawain and the Green Knight*, everyone at King Arthur's court is ready for sport and Christmas games, for they know that the next season is Lent, and a modest diet of fish and self-denial is all they have to look forward to.

Then came episodes of pursed-lipped Puritan anti-Christmas campaigning at the Reformation and after. The Puritans of New England disapproved of Christmas so strongly that it was forbidden to celebrate it in Boston in 1658–81, and, of course, Cromwell banned it in England. But, despite such interruptions, the celebration of Christmas pursued its merry, rackety way through the centuries in much the same mixed style, long before Dickens, though each century had its special flavour.

Samuel Pepys reveals himself as a devout Christmas sinner, cheerfully unapologetic about the way he treats his wife. On 25 December 1664, "Up (my wife's eye being ill still of the blow I did in a passion give her on Monday last) to church alone — where Mr Mills, a good sermon." He relates that he and his wife had a happy Christmas dinner, despite her black eye. Then church again later, where he particularly notes "very great store of fine women" in the congregation. The next day, he mentions the family card-games, "very merry" and blind man's buff and other "Christmas gamballs".

That did not prevent the serious-minded keeping a careful focus on the spiritual mystery at the heart of the festival. John Evelyn, the 17th-century diarist, Pepys's older contemporary, merely made meticulous notes of the main points of the Christmas sermons he heard in his diary (and he heard more than one in the day) and omitted the "gamballs".

Nor did the merry-making that others enjoyed stop people from feeling left out, if the Christmas available to them was less enjoyable for personal reasons. Mary Shelley, for example, records a particularly gloomy occasion in 1814, in her journal entry for 24 December. "Read view of the French Revolution — Walk out with Shelley — and spend a dreary morning waiting for him. . ." Christmas Day "have a very bad side ache in the morning so I rise late".

The balancing exercise is not the same for everyone, and it may present many kinds of dark challenge, such as fighting depression and loneliness.

THE evolving, mixed Christmas of the centuries since has become a commentary on the real humanity of Jesus. He seems to have enjoyed a good meal, for he set sour tongues wagging by "eating and drinking". It is hard to imagine that he would not have enjoyed the games and chatter of innocent family and community enjoyments. (I never understand why the inventor of the sense of humour is so rarely recognised to have one himself.)

The little Word, the *verbum abbreviatum*, made himself "readable" to everyone, theologian or not, by being fully human — not merely in the technical sense, but also in a sense that would surely have made him good company in any age — stimulating, sharing his companions' pleasures, but always the leader who sets the style and expectations.

It remains a challenge to celebrate Christmas with the right kind of birthday party, but, if we get it wrong, the little Word is big enough to forgive, and set us right by example.

(2006)

'Tis the season for us to sign off the world of material power

David Martin finds, in the incarnation, evidence of the most precious part of being human

ONE of the most moving evocations of Christmas a year or two ago was a television advertisement. It juxtaposed a choir singing "For unto us a child is born" from Handel's *Messiah* with pictures of various kinds of human need. Watching it, I realised how, on the one hand, we humans sing, especially in gratitude for birth, and how, on the other hand, we confront universal need. What else is Christmas concerned with other than singing and the ubiquity of human pain? A mysterious fountain of joy emerges in a desert of desolation.

Christmas is a kind of sign language for this extraordinary juxtaposition of joy and desolation, glory and beggary, almighty power and total vulnerability to wind and rain. The extremes are held together so that the light dawns even as the people walk in darkness; universal peace and holy stillness are proclaimed in the midst of clangour and inveterate hostility; the redemptive child is born, even as the principalities and powers hold the world in thrall; the angelic choir bursts out singing, in spite of the realities of destitution and exclusion; an exchange of gifts occurs directly counter to the searing reciprocities of abuse, death and violence.

The renewal of light; the proclamation of peace; the acknowledgement of a birth; the making of music; the exchange of gifts — these are the signs of Christian faith, the true marks of the mass of Christ. In our divine service, we shall make these signs. Since Christmas cannot be argued, but only enacted in sign language, I want to meditate on each sign: on the light, on the peace, on the new life, on the song, and on the exchange of gifts.

Often, we look around, wondering where God is or what he does, expecting better evidence of his existence than he seems disposed to offer. We look for a concrete sign bearing God's certified signature, expressly designed to impose the truth on us. We forget that all the signs of his being there lie in wait for us to recognise. Signs of God are not given as data to be checked, but as actions and embodiments calling out for, and evoking, a response. Every gift is an action and an embodiment — above all, the gift of Christ and our gift of ourselves in response. In both cases, the present signifies a presence: God for us, ourselves before God.

THE first sign of God is light. Nothing precedes light. God is light, and in him is no darkness at all. Each time we re-create light, we act as creatures made in his image. When we light candles, we not only imitate the Creator, but also refer metaphorically to inward light and to enlightenment. Every candle is a visible reminder of invisible light. This kind of light dispels spiritual darkness, and triumphs over the shades of spiritual night. It throws light on the truth, and creates a pool of illumination whereby we can find a better way. God's word is a lamp to our feet.

The primary proclamations of Christmas all have to do with light. The shepherds abiding in the fields are wrapped in darkness, until the glory of the Lord shines round them; the wise men are lost in abstruse calculations, until a great light leads them to an unexpected presence. The people that walked in darkness have seen a great light.

Another sign of God is peace and quietness. Some of the early myths of the birth of Christ imagined a universal moment of stillness greeting his arrival. No other kind of prince is heralded with the miracle of silence. His kingdom is governed by a peace that passes understanding, and one that keeps our hearts and minds in the knowledge and love of God.

Just as in the case of light, which was inward as well as outward, so in the case of peace, it is outward as well as inward. "How beautiful upon the mountains are the feet of him that bringeth good tidings that publisheth peace." "He shall speak peace unto the nations." Christ offers reconciliation for contention. Warfare is not ended, of course, but a space has been cleared in which peace has been proclaimed. The Kingdom of heaven made its peace policy clear in the declaration made by angels to the shepherds. The conditions of citizenship in the Kingdom have also made them clear: "Blessed are the peacemakers."

Singing is a sign of God. Indeed, music, light and silence belong together as the primary signatures of divinity. The imagery of Christmas joins all three signatures in a single statement. As the glory of the Lord shone, "the world" in solemn stillness lay to "hear the angels sing". When we in turn respond by opening our mouths in the shape of a rounded "O", we literally give breath to an affirmation of the angelic message. Everything that has breath is invited to share our human act of praise, and thereby manifest the Kingdom. The rounded "O" of our mouths is the highest expression of every affirmation and every invitation beginning with "O": "O be joyful in the Lord all ye lands."

All music, not just our solemn singing in the temple, "has something of divinity in it" because it is incapable of denial. Music is a manifestation of the Kingdom, through a union of inspiration and human response: being breathed into and then "giving voice" and "giving out". Music is the complete complementing the incomplete; the restful taking up and fulfilling the restless; and so offering the wayfarer an oasis for reflection and refreshment, a fountain in the desert.

The supreme sign of God is embodiment in human form to indicate the loving exchange of gifts between earth and heaven, human and divine. The Word became flesh. Heavenly love expresses itself tangibly in a human body, and we respond with the heart's adoration. Through the incarnation, divinity places itself at our disposal, to cherish or to crucify. In the eucharist, the bread of life is simply placed in our hands, and life is poured out as wine. At Christmas, the gift of a helpless bundle of life in the form of a baby is there, for us to adore or ignore. To ignore it is to close ourselves up in total self-sufficiency. To adore is to open ourselves up to the pattern of redemption realised over and over again in the "unspeakable gift" and the reciprocities of love.

THE gift of an infant king and a powerless Prince of Peace makes a revolution in our ideas that we still find difficult, but it represents just this: fullness and privation; glory and beggary; the source of all, emptied of all but love. This sign language of the incarnation puts a question mark against our notions not only of human honour and glory, but also of divine honour and glory.

Yet the painters of the Renaissance who depicted the nativity in tones of glowing adoration mostly made our Lord larger than life, rather like Christopher Smart's "stupendous stranger", and often vested in imperial power, with the universe still in his hands. In the same way, our Lady appears a fine lady, dressed to match a fine Lord. It is just so difficult to marry eternity to a moment in time, and infinity to a tiny space. The wisdom of men cannot comprehend the foolishness of God. All that wise men and women can do is to offer the heart's oblation.

Yet why, if we have been through this revolution, does it seem to make so little difference? Because, as we pack the decorations away, put out the Christmas lights, and view the wondrous gifts as mere possessions, we must return — as all revolutions do — to power as it is understood in the real world, and make friends with Mammon as the Lord advised. In that world, which we had better come to terms with or else, power is knowledge, the ability to manipulate nature and ourselves; or power is wealth as quoted on the stock exchanges; or power is international reasons of state, where occa-sional massacres of the innocents are the price of peace and justice, or, at any rate, security and survival.

In the paramount reality of every day, where the "wisdom of men" necessarily reigns supreme, what we do now — bowing the knee, bringing gifts, raising the cup of blessing, and sharing bread and wine in peace — is all folly. It is superstition believed beyond the evidence, and a sentimentality remaking the world in our own image and according to our heart's desire. The worship of the infant King is just infantilism: at best, poetic aura; at worst, fanatical mayhem.

To this, we reply that if these words and signs of faith and hope fail, and fall into disuse, it will not, as some think, be our final liberation from falsity, but our last estrangement. We shall lose a most precious element in what forms us as human. We are not only scientists and artificers, politicians or economists, manipulating the natural and social worlds. Faith also includes what is manifest, placed lovingly in the hand, as much as what is manipulated, effected efficiently by hand. It has more to do with personal encounter than with impersonal management. It is communication in kind, offered through our human kind, and not information about a thing.

The sign language of the incarnation is divine body language: word-made-flesh; gestures of love and reconciliation, of release and inclusion, of brokenness made whole again. God suffers from exposure, and the power and the glory have "come down" to this: vulnerable human potential, not raw naked power.

The message of Christmas comes to us in pictograms, not diagrams. Pictures are whole, unique and unrepeatable, and the picture language of Christmas is the bright vision, once-for-all and beyond all measure, of a child shown to benign visitors. The "paramount reality" of the everyday returns soon enough with the mass slaughter of innocent children and the voice of weeping in Rama. For just this moment, though, we are invited on to the holy mountain, where none shall hurt or destroy, and a little child shall lead us to become wiser and younger. If we consent to follow and be born again as children of heaven's Kingdom, we shall see into another world as it really is: whole and entire, here and now, unique and unrepeatable. We shall entertain epiphany in our hearts, in W. H. Auden's words,

> "*Remembering the stable where for once in our lives*
> *Everything became a You and nothing was an It*" ("For the Time Being")

We shall be humanised, made vulnerable to innocence — and experience. And that experience will be divine, because it will enable us to see the works of the Lord as fresh from the hands of the Creator, and look at the sky and the stars all over again "with exceeding great joy".

(2004)

Unfathomable mysteries of the Incarnate

Andrew Davison ponders the infinite and finds it fitting

THIS time last year, I paid a visit to the town of Lambertville, on the banks of the Delaware river, known for its cafés and expensive craft shops. I was on research leave, thinking through the theological implications of life elsewhere in the universe. I went into a church to say a few prayers, and was stopped in my tracks by a statue of the Virgin and Child. As a work of art, the statue was neither offensive nor greatly accomplished, but it arrested me, this depiction of a woman, holding out her son.

The Christmas story shows us something totally beyond our expectations, but, at the same time, marvellously fitting: God with us, as we are. If the universe contains a glorious variety of life, my instinct is that God's dealings with it are correspondingly varied and glorious — and fitting.

FEW scientific discoveries of recent years outshine the detection of planets around other stars. The first confirmed evidence came in 1992 — before that, we had no idea whether planets were common or extraordinarily rare. So far, we have observed about 3800.

It seems that most stars are circled by planets. A decent proportion are somewhat Earth-like, which is to say, rocky, with liquid water. If that applies to only one in 20, that still leaves a remarkably large number of nurseries for life, given that the observable universe contains perhaps 1,000,000,000,000,000,000,000,000 stars: one followed by 24 noughts.

Only a fraction of planets are Earth-like; a small but clearly non-zero proportion harbour life; some of that has probably evolved to sentience — knowing itself, and its creator, and its responsibilities, and perhaps sinning, and being redeemed. That is a fraction of a fraction of a fraction — but of 1^{24} stars.

> With this ambiguous earth
> His dealings have been told us.
> These abide:
> The signal to a maid, the human birth,
> The lesson, and the young Man crucified.
>
> But not a star of all
> The innumerable host of stars has heard
> How He administered this terrestrial ball.
> Our race have kept their Lord's entrusted Word.

The night sky in the Atacama Desert, Chile, site of the European Southern Observatory's Very Large Telescope: the countless stars give a sense of the true scale of the cosmos.

So wrote Alice Meynell (1847–1922), in her poem "Christ in the Universe". Our story is known only to us. Likewise, if there is life elsewhere, God's work there remains hidden from us, wonderful though it surely is:

Nor, in our little day,
May His devices with the heavens be guessed,
His pilgrimage to thread the Milky Way
Or His bestowals there be manifest.

Of those other "bestowals", what can we say? Some theologians tackle the question by asking what might be *possible*. Could the eternal Word, for instance, have been incarnate there, too? Theologians who focus on possibility tend to favour fine doctrinal detail. Others, in contrast, are drawn by the broad sweep of Christian belief. Their starting point is to ask how the incarnation — for instance — fits into the bigger picture. They ask questions about necessity: would other incarnations, for instance, be necessary, to achieve the same ends?

Each of these two approaches yields insights, but there are risks to reducing theology to considerations, either of the possible or the necessary. On the one hand, the human mind can get only so far in thinking about what is possible for God. On the other, God is no passive respondent to necessity — not least because the divine work shows more *art* than that.

ALONGSIDE possibility or necessity, a third category suggests itself, beloved of medieval theologians. They called it *convenientia*. It is the conviction that whatever God does is always truly *fitting*, or *suitable*: suitable both to the situation, and to who God is. It reminds us that God's action is neither necessitated nor an arbitrary choice between possibilities.

Fittingness strikes me as the right way to shape theological thinking about life elsewhere in the universe. I am surprised that, to my knowledge, it has never been invoked explicitly for that purpose. I do not know whether there is any life elsewhere, or whether it is sentient, or sinful. I am sure, however, that God will deal with it entirely *fittingly*.

WITH that in mind, we can return to our story, with our eyes opened to see that God's work among us has that mark of supreme *fittingness* or *suitability*. God deals with us according to the kind of thing we are, all the way to taking up our human life and nature. In doing so, God not only deals with sin, but unites our life to divine life. Neither possibility nor necessity grasps that; only in terms of suitability can we begin to appreciate its majesty.

Exploration of how God's love has so fittingly taken form is an inexhaustible task. Consider, for instance, that we were not given a message from afar. Rather, God, the supreme communicator, came to us as we are — bodily, culturally, historically — and taught us as one human being to another, tangible to our senses. The Christmas preface to the eucharist highlights this:

In this mystery of the Word made flesh
you have caused his light to shine in our hearts …
In him we see our God made visible
and so are caught up in the love of the God we cannot see.

Our story also tells us that God does not wipe things out and start again. It was far more wonderful to have worked in and through creatures — and as a creature — to bring restoration, redemption, and that union beyond imagination. In coming to the Virgin's womb, God did not abhor history or culture, in all its particularity. He endorsed it and redeemed it.

In innumerable ways, God's dealings with humanity have been fitting. Whatever theological story is to be told about life elsewhere, something corresponding could be said. God's dealings will be different in detail, precisely because life will be different, and because God's works are always thoroughly fitting.

How exactly that plays out for life elsewhere — if there is life elsewhere — we do not know. With the idea of fittingness newly impressed on our minds, however, we can rejoice all the more that, for us, God dwelt in a womb, was born, had an infancy, belonged to a culture, learned a trade, ate, drank, danced no doubt, trod a road, lived with friends, and was nailed to a tree. He died — as we do, if we are nailed to a tree — but rose to a transformed life, which is still our life transformed.

That whole story of fittingness is itself perhaps most fittingly summed up in a statue of a young mother, holding out to us her child.

(2017)

Raising up the old Adam in us all

Adam is neglected at the Nativity, but he has a universal significance, says **Rod Garner**

A PIVOTAL character is missing from the vivid nativity landscape painted by Luke and Matthew in their Gospels. His name is Adam — the disobedient figure haunting the opening chapters of Genesis, who, by a solitary act, plunges humankind into darkness and death, and makes necessary the birth of Christ.

In the Christian narrative of our redemption, Adam is a significant player, theologically speaking, but in our Christmas services he is, at best, a shadowy presence, and, at the level of our religious awareness, hardly registers. He appears in the first reading of the traditional service of Nine Lessons and Carols, where he hides in the garden after eating the forbidden fruit. And he is evoked in the medieval theology of the haunting 15th-century poem/carol "Adam lay ybounden", which depicts him bound in limbo until the saving birth and death of Christ.

Adam has something profound to teach us about our human predicament, but at Christmas (and, frankly, most other times, too) we are not tuned in. We are modern people — citizens of a sceptical and scientific culture, where Genesis is routinely interpreted as a story rather than as a factual account of our origins. When evolution offers a more plausible theory of human beginnings, there seems to be no need to fret about a biblical man who never existed.

But some (and here I include myself) do worry, though not for the same reasons. In the United States, millions still cling to the old-time religion that holds the Scriptures to be infallibly and unchangingly true. They consistently tell Gallup pollsters that God created humans less than 10,000 years ago. They believe that the Bible doesn't lie, and, without a historical Adam, there would be no reason for Jesus, or the salvation he brings to a fallen world.

In 2013, a large gathering of Evangelical theologians assembled in Baltimore to debate biblical inerrancy. One creationist speaker declared that "science changes, but the word of God never changes". A packed meeting on Adam turned scholars away at the door. Academic papers bearing his name are circulating, and books on the same subject proliferate. In some instances, Christian universities across the US require teaching staff to sign testimonies

109

declaring that God directly created Adam and Eve, "the historical parents of the entire human race". Jobs have been lost through a failure to comply.

THERE is another way to approach Adam. It pays attention to his great significance for Christianity in a holy season, and avoids the acrimonious debate between arch-conservatives, who regard evolution as a fiendish lie, and scientists, who prefer fossils to faith in an ancient book, as a surer guide to the emergence of human life.

To know ourselves even tolerably well is to be aware of our waywardness: that we frequently get things badly wrong; that, if not actually wretched, we are sometimes cruel and hateful; that, given the choice between evil and good, we can, and occasionally do, choose badly, with calamitous consequences for others.

There is an observable and alarming "human stain": a moral corrosion within us that led the sceptical philosopher Jean-Paul Sartre to conclude that "Man is a being to whom something happened". Theology describes this in terms of the Fall: the venerable and verifiable Christian doctrine of original sin that illuminates the tragic and perverse elements within our nature, after the emergence of *Homo sapiens* millennia ago.

As an archetype or symbol of what it means to be fearfully human, Adam comes to us as the first "theological human". In keeping with his Hebrew name, he stands for all of us: one created from the earth (*adamah*); one to whom something happened, and one who reflects the riddle of our lives since the historical emergence of consciousness and the moral capacity for good or evil.

We shall not find Adam's real existence in archaeology or recorded history. He is no private character, acting in a private capacity. His tale is ours, and his truth lies in the fact that we are all "Adamic" — prone to skewed lives that trail glory but also yield dark fruits.

Adam tells us not to despair. He teaches us to think no worse of others than of ourselves, and to be compassionate, because we have come to recognise our own need for mercy. In so doing, he points us to the second Adam, Jesus Christ, who, in Bethlehem, embraces the same earth, to disinfect us of our pride and egoism and offer us a better way.

THIS is a big story — bigger than the annual recollection of a seasonal goodwill that fades all too easily; bigger even than the innocence and hope that we associate with the Christ-child, and with each new birth. Adam grounds us in the story of our being saved, and in the humbling truth that human frailty can still merit so great a redeemer.

(2014)

God face to face

Christmas is a time to drop the mask, suggests **Mark Oakley**

THERE has been a lot of talk about happiness in recent weeks. It is not a word I like, but the other terms used are even worse — "subjective well-being" is awful, as are "positive emotionality" and "hedonic tone". "Wellness" sounds like a coastal town in Norfolk.

In Aldous Huxley's novel *Brave New World*, unhappiness has been eliminated, and the mantra "Everybody's happy now" is repeated to the young 150 times a night. My guess is, however, that they were no nearer to discovering the meaning of the word than the rest of us. Perhaps the old man interviewed at the Glastonbury Festival got nearest to it when he said that he had discovered the secret of happiness on a bottle of bleach: "Stand upright in a cool place."

It is telling that most people seem to think that happiness lies in what we have, whether that be a Porsche or a loving family. Not a great deal of opinion has been voiced yet about whether it might, instead, be linked to who we are, and what we have become, and how we are resourced internally as human beings.

In the City of London between 1400 and 1560, it was forbidden to wear masks in the streets at Christmastime. As people made their way home from parties, presumably a little the worse for wear, it was too easy for masked villains to take advantage and rob them of their purses. So masks were outlawed throughout the 12 days of the festive season.

We all have our masks, and some fit very comfortably. The problem is that, over time, they can begin to eat into our faces, and we become unsure about how to remove them. One of the reasons we adopt the masks in the first place is the belittling strength of the messages we have received through our personal history, and continue to receive and believe in the present, not least through cultural trends. The voices shout at us from every direction, and are as destructive as they are convincing: "Be beautiful," "Be rich," "Believe this," "You're stupid," "You don't fit in," "You're boring." As we fail to live up to what is expected, and live down to what we are told about ourselves, so we end up beating ourselves up or showing off — the two variations of feeling a failure and unacceptable.

Our fears, though focused on the future, come from our past, disclosing the imprints of all the messages received deep within that we have not been able to control. To hide them, as well as the hurts, and to ensure our internal mess is not seen, we quickly make masks that see us through the day, but which leave us living lives of middle-distance relating, haunted by the life we never had. In his evening reflection, Lancelot Andrewes saw "the old man is bound up in a thousand folds".

One of the disconcerting but liberating things about learning to love someone, and be loved in return, through the years of a relationship, is that we are shown that we are actually lovable beneath all these accumulated defences. We do not choose love: it chooses us.

We cannot heal ourselves; only love received from another can begin the repair work and provide the scaffolding to build again. Love exposes to us the ways in which we have prevented joy. This conventional truth is the incarnation in miniature. As the American writer James Baldwin put it: "Love takes off masks that we fear we cannot live without and know we cannot live within."

CHRISTMAS is a good time to dare to remove these masks; for, instead of listening to what the voices, within and without, are telling us about who we are, we are asked to hear what God is saying to us about ourselves. The birth narratives are full of divine dreams in which God speaks — of heavenly messengers on errands, and of calls from heaven to shepherds, Magi, and many others to re-orientate their journey to the divine compass rather than human signposts.

The constant message from heaven is "Do not be afraid"; do not let the past paralyse you, but come and be surprised by how loved you are. St John tells us in the first chapter of his Gospel that God has put his tent up next to ours. He comes "to set the prisoner free". God has taken off his mask of invisibility in order to defrost us, and to save us from ourselves.

The simplicity of the place the Magi and farmers are drawn to, an animals' outhouse in an insignificant town, begins the distillation of those who come near to it, the star constantly compelling them to look up out of themselves towards God, in whom earth will find itself at peace. The innocent needs of the animals that crowd round the stable remind them of their own yearning — our search for God being like the river seeking the ocean. The ancient Assyrian word for prayer was the same as that for opening a clenched fist.

"JUDGEMENT" is a word that many Christians are uncomfortable with because of the images of hell fire and damnation that it can conjure up. The portrait of God that it can paint is that of a God who is to be feared because of his angry policing of souls. The birth narratives of the Gospels teach us another way of understanding the word.

Divine dreams: The Adoration of the Shepherds *(c.1622)*
by Gerrit van Honthorst

God is not to be feared because he is a tyrant out to get us, but because he is real. Ultimately, the judgement of God is a loving act because it liberates us from our lies, and gives us fresh foundations on which to build a life. St Paul looked forward to that day when he would see "face to face". This judgement, of seeing eye to eye, heart to heart, begins in the crib with the dissolving of our cover-ups by God's opening himself to us, defenceless.

I have often wondered whether, as the word suggests, the Magi were more like magicians than kings. If so, were the gifts of gold, frankincense, and myrrh the apparatus of their show, the ancient dry ice of a "Mystic Meg" performance to baffle and bemuse — and make a living? The laying down of these at the crib, then, would be more than giving symbolic presents. It would mean handing over a profitable but sham lifestyle, with all its smoke and mirrors, and leaving it in the holy house before returning "by another road".

It is with this idea of the birth of Christ giving birth in us somehow, our hard full stops being changed into commas, that the poet Malcolm Guite shapes his Antiphons (*Church Times,* Features, 12 December 2008):

Unfold for us the mystery of grace
And make a womb of all this wounded world.
O heart of heaven beating in the earth,
O tiny hope within our hopelessness,
Come to be born, to bear us to our birth,
To touch a dying world with new-made hands
And make these rags of time our swaddling bands.

God's gift to us is being, and our gift to God is becoming. As St John wrote his Prologue, he kept his eye on the book of Genesis, realising that this Word among us was a birth of births in us, the bringing into life of a new way of being human. As we look at the child in the crib, so we begin afresh the conversion of life which seeks to reflect what we see and encounter in him. The Christmas story invites us into the truth that God loves us just the way we are, but he loves us so much that he doesn't want us to stay like that.

Eugene O'Neill wrote: "None of us can help the things life has done to us. They're done before you realise it. And once they're done, they make you do other things until at last everything comes between you and what you'd like to be, and you've lost your true self for ever."

Wherever we have settled into this staleness, at a distance from our depths, whether in sheep fields or in the company of Herod, we are urged by heaven to be released by divine truth, and to see the being and nature of God in the one named Jesus, recklessly loving his creation at risk to himself.

The Church has used the shepherd's crook through the centuries as a potent symbol. Some have interpreted it as a long hook to discipline and keep people in check. Shepherds will tell you a better use for it: to place it deep into the ground, holding on to it so still that the sheep learn to trust you. To live in this model will mean being a Church that is not infinitely in control, but infinitely resourceful — which is perhaps a more faithful reflection of the incarnation.

Advent is a season in the vocative, calling out to the heavens in the knowledge that we are incomplete in ourselves. The first letter of each of the seven Advent antiphons placed together spells "ero cras", "Tomorrow I shall be there with you."

As our cries go out, so a message comes back, written in the same stuff of which we are made. The Word is made flesh. He comes into the world as poetry enters the poem. No longer travelling incognito, God translates himself into visibility, and asks us to take the same risk. The masks can go now.

(2010)

But what if there had been room at the inn?

Hugh Rayment-Pickard tells a counterfactual history of Christianity after the birth of a bourgeois messiah

JORGE-Louis Borges called history a "garden of forking paths". When time takes us down one fork in the path, it leaves another possibility unexplored. Historians are now calling these alternative scenarios "counterfactual history". This is the history of "what if?". What if Julius Caesar had not named Octavian as his successor? What if Pilate had pardoned Jesus? What if the Great Fire of London had never spread beyond Pudding Lane?

Every counterfactual history begins with a fork in the path or "point of divergence": a historical event with more than one possible outcome. I am taking as my point of divergence the moment Mary and Joseph called at the inn. What if there had been a room to spare? What if Jesus had been born in a guest room rather than a stable?

Although it looks like a quaint narrative detail, the fact that there was no room at the inn has had a tectonic influence on the character of Christian history and theology. A. N. Wilson describes the story of Jesus's birth in the stable as "one of the most powerful myths in human history", and this is no exaggeration. The lowly birth in a stable or cave has been the badge of Jesus's poverty and humility. God's appearance in the muck of the animal quarters rather than the comfort of a hotel room has been crucial to our theology of the incarnation: Jesus not only became human; he became an impoverished human, displaced, homeless, rejected. The image of the stable shows that the incarnation did not mean only "God-made-flesh", but also "God-made-poor". As the liberation theologian Gustavo Gutiérrez has put it, the incarnation is "an irruption that smells of the stable".

Jesus's "poverty" has been vital for his credibility as a Messiah of the underprivileged and downtrodden. It's so much more convincing if the one who preaches good news to the poor is born into poverty himself. It's less convincing altogether — as Peter Mandelson and the other "champagne socialists" found out — when the middle classes try to preach a working-class message.

Here is the interesting thing. If we take away the birth in the stable, there is almost nothing in Jesus's life that indicates his poverty. Jesus chose to undergo hardship in the desert and on the cross; he chose to live the simple life of an itinerant teacher; but the Gospels do not tell us that he was from a poor family nor that he ever suffered from involuntary economic hardship. The Gospels paint a very different picture. We are told that Jesus came "eating and drinking", and that he dined regularly at "middle-class" suppers with the Pharisees and taxcollectors. His father was a blue-collar worker with a sound profession. We know that Jesus could read and write at a time when this must have been an immense privilege. We are never told that Jesus was forced to go without a meal or a bed for the night. The one crucial detail in Jesus's life which indicates his material poverty is the stable. If the birth in the stable never happened, we are left with a well-educated and middle-class Messiah.

St Francis of Assisi saw the stable as "the supreme expression of the Son of God's self-imposed poverty". On Christmas Eve 1223, Francis set up a tableau of the nativity in a cave in Greccio. He gathered there with his friends and celebrated the nativity by candlelight. This was the inspiration for the crib scenes that are now central to our Christmas experience. The crib prompts us to meditate upon the paradoxes of the incarnation: kings and shepherds, grandeur and humility, angels and dirt. It is unlikely that anyone would have bothered to make models of a banal hotel room, without the mystery of the stars and the strangeness of the animals. Even the greatest artist would struggle to produce an inspiring image of the Holy Guest Room.

Let us then imagine this counterfactual history. What would have happened on that first Christmas Day, and what would have been the long-term consequences for Christendom?

THE birth in the hotel was a very different kind of nativity. It was in the middle of the night that the scruffy proletarian shepherds approached the hotel door to be refused admission. They returned grumbling to their flocks. Instead, Jesus was cosseted by the other paying guests, who were all decent folks. The Magi did visit, of course. It is hard to imagine any hotel turning away these wealthy celebrities from the East. They didn't worship Jesus (that would have been rather embarrassing), but they did dandle the Christ-child on their knees. Ensconced in his lodgings and with royal gifts lavished upon him, Jesus was the very model of a bourgeois saviour. It was an incredibly happy affair.

In the fifth century, the Church commemorated the birth by building a basilica on the site of the guest room. Instead of the mysterious and inspiring Church of the Nativity, Bethlehem now boasts the Church of the Holy Hotel. But this shrine to earthly comfort never became an international symbol of sanctuary like the real Church of the Nativity. In April 2002, in real history, the Church of the Nativity provided refuge to 240 people, including school children, fleeing the Israel Defence Forces. The church was under armed

What might have been: the Church of the Nativity, in Bethlehem, reimagined as the Church of the Holy Hotel

siege for 39 days. In our counterfactual universe, the Church of the Holy Hotel did not feel any obligation to show such radical hospitality to non-paying guests: after all, Joseph and Mary had settled their bill like everyone else.

Legends about the innkeeper grew like Topsy. Tertullian speculated that the innkeeper was actually Joseph of Arimathaea. Irenaeus dubbed him "St Joseph of Bethlehem", and he has been celebrated ever since as the patron saint of private health care and cathedral admission charges. Margaret Thatcher cited him during the poll-tax riots. And an international hotel group (The Holy Day Inn) now bears his emblem: a closed door with an open purse.

Jesus's earthly ministry was fraught with unhelpful controversy. His "manifesto" speech — "I have come to bring good news to the poor" — was heckled with taunts about his cushy upbringing. And the political implications of his teaching about the Kingdom were never taken very seriously. In the centuries after the first Christmas, the Church struggled to retain its commitment to social justice. Figures like St Vincent de Paul and St Francis de Sales were in very short supply. Liberation theology never happened. Much to the relief of comfortable Britain, the Church of England never produced a Faith in the City report. St Francis of Assisi thought for a week or two about following Christ, before deciding instead to set up a 13th-century version of Oxfam.

In the developed world, the Church thrived as a pursuit for the respectable, but for some reason Christianity never caught on in developing countries, nor with the working classes. Although his message always seemed to make sense, the oppressed would never come to see Jesus as "one of them". Since Victorian times, the traditional way to celebrate Christmas has been to book the family into a hotel. Families would then re-enact the nativity over breakfast in bed. Presents are given and received — that hasn't changed. And carols are sung, of course: "Away in a chamber", "The first hotel the angel did say", and "O little tavern of Bethlehem".

For all its decency and decorum, this counterfactual Christmas has become prosaic, a matter-of-fact celebration, without wonder or romance. There is little in this Christmas story that would unsettle us; little that would challenge our social orders and hierarchies. Christmas does not touch us with mystery or strangeness. This is a Christmas with many tidings of comfort.

ALL of this never happened, but perhaps it could have done, had it not been for the state of bookings at a certain Middle Eastern guest house 2000 years ago. These flights of counterfactual fancy have a value, argues Niall Ferguson (*Virtual History: Alternatives and counterfactuals*, Pan, 1997), because they deepen our understanding of what really did happen. In particular, we come to appreciate how the actual course of history has depended on innumerable contingent microevents.

Counterfactual history is an antidote to determinism and fatalism: the future is not sealed; so our decisions really do matter. Since the earliest times, Christians have been aware that history could so easily have been otherwise. St Paul posed a counterfactual possibility to the Corinthian Church: "And if Christ has not been raised, your faith is futile and you are still in your sins" (1 Corinthians 15.17). And a medieval lyricist posed a well-known Eden counterfactual: "Ne had the apple taken been, Ne had never our Lady abeen heavene queen." These possibilities remind us that the salvation story was not inevitable: Eve had to choose the apple; Jesus had to choose the cross.

This is why our choices matter, now as much as ever. The decisions we make this Christmas about hospitality and generosity will change the course of history.

(2004)

Going back to baby language

John Inge reflects on the words of love

WHEN I was a youngster, one of my party pieces was to recite the only Russian which my mother had taught me. I can still do it: "*Ya gavarioo parooski*". As a child, I thought it sounded rather impressive. I later learned, when visiting Russia, that it is a singularly useless thing to be able to say if it is the only Russian sentence you know. It means — as connoisseurs of the Russian language will be aware — "I speak Russian". I don't. Neither did my mother, capable though she was. "*Ya gavarioo parooski*" was, for some obscure reason unknown to me, the only Russian sentence that she had learned. She passed it on to me as part of a well-rounded education.

If you are going to communicate with people, you have got to choose the right language. It is an obvious point, but one that is not always easy to adhere to. There are, after all, since Babel, so many languages.

Translation can cause great misunderstandings. As a child, my mother had a French penfriend (you'll have gathered by now that she was a cosmopolitan kind of woman), and this penfriend looked up the English equivalent for "*Dieu vous préserve*." She then carefully inscribed at the end of her letter "God pickle you".

Misunderstandings can cause offence and not just amusement: there was a famous occasion when President Carter was making a speech in the former Soviet Union, and his interpreter had him referring not to our desire for the future, but to our lust for it.

EVEN if you get the right tongue, language is a slippery thing, because it is always changing. In the 17th century, a monarch visiting the newly built St Paul's Cathedral, described it as "awful, amusing, and artificial". Each of those three words has changed its meaning in common parlance: St Paul's was "awful" in the sense that it inspired awe, "amusing" in the sense that it delighted, and "artificial" in the sense that it was a great work of human hands. "Awful, amusing, and artificial" is not a phrase that we would now generally think of as being complimentary when applied to a building or a work of art.

A new layer of possible confusion has arisen since the advent of spelling autochecks. Whole websites are dedicated to the hilarious misunderstandings that they can produce (most could not be repeated in the *Church Times*). If ever you are feeling bored, I recommend looking at such a site — though not surreptitiously, during a sermon, because, if you're anything like me, they will make you laugh out loud. LOL.

LANGUAGE is a particular problem for theologians and preachers. How, for example, can the true meaning and depth of what we celebrate at Christmas be put into words? Language, we are told by philosophers nowadays, is absolutely basic to what being human is all about, but it seems so often to be appallingly inadequate when it comes to communicating anything of real importance.

The problem is not only the theologian's and the preacher's, though; it is God's, too. How can the great and powerful God who is totally "other" communicate to us in a language which we will understand?

The prophet Isaiah speaks of a vision of the Lord "sitting upon a throne, high and lifted up, and his train filled the temple … And the foundations of the threshold shook at the voice of him who called, and the house was filled with smoke" (Isaiah 6). These words speak of the glory, the mighty wonder, the awesome majesty of God. We know that God is powerful — how else could God have created the universe and all that is in it?

But God is *so* powerful that, if he were to be revealed to us in all his glory, we would be totally overwhelmed, and he respects us too much for that.

God is totally "other". God is "beyond" in every sense — beyond knowledge, beyond experience, beyond understanding. As St Augustine says: "What then, brethren, are we to say of God; for, if we have understood, we have understood something other than God." The idols that Richard Dawkins and his like choose to construct and call God — essentially creatures which happen to be very powerful — bear no relation to the true and living God of whom the prophet Isaiah struggles to speak.

SO, God has a problem communicating with us. What language can God use — a language that will speak to all peoples? A language that will communicate to us something of the wonder of God's being, but not overwhelm us? What we celebrate at Christmas is God's glorious solution to that problem. In what Christians refer to as the incarnation, God has chosen a language far deeper than words in which to communicate.

What better language could there be than the birth, life, and death of a human person to speak of God's reality and being? This is stuff with which we are familiar, to which we can relate, whatever our language or nationality, and which will not crush us. God became a human being to show us what God is like. And what do we learn, apart from the fact that God is powerful?

What is the substance of the message contained within that human life — the birth and life of Jesus?

With the birth and life of Jesus, God speaks extraordinarily good news. He tells us that "the All Great is the All-loving, too." It's not just that God approves of love and thinks that it is quite a good thing, but that it is God's very nature, God's essence. God *is* love, St John tells us.

Mother Julian of Norwich, the great medieval mystic and visionary, puts it thus: "Wouldst thou know thy Lord's meaning in this thing? ... Learn it well: love was his meaning. Who shewed it thee? Love. What shewed he thee? Love. Wherefore shewed it he? For love. Hold thee therein and thou shalt learn and know more in the same."

If we "learn well" the Lord's meaning in the incarnation, we shall see that it is love that is the mother tongue of the human race. For love is the essence of the Godhead as shown forth in Christ, and we are made in the image of God. Although it is our mother tongue, it is a language in which, tragically, we have lost our fluency; for we do not "hold ourselves therein". We need to be drawn back to this language by the celebration of the great and glorious event which we remember at Christmas — and, by the grace of God, every day.

AT Christmas, the day when God entered the creation as a baby, we celebrate the beginning of that one perfect life of love which changed the world, and which has allowed us all to rediscover our mother tongue. We are what we speak, and the birth and life and death of Jesus speak the language of love: not in a sentimental or complex philosophical fashion, but in a human life that was the personification of love. From this one life, human and divine, we see that the true language of human life is love.

As Evelyn Underhill puts it:

"He speaks in our language and shows us his secret beauty on our scale. The depth and richness of His being are entirely unknown to us, poor little scraps that we are! And yet the unlimited life who is Love right through — who loves on every plane and at every point — so loved the world as to desire to give his essential thought, the deepest secrets of his heart, to this small, fugitive imperfect creation — to us. That seems immense.

"And then the heavens open and what is disclosed? A baby, God manifest in the flesh. The stable, the manger, the straw; poverty, cold, darkness, these form the setting for the divine gift. In this child God gives His supreme message to the soul — Spirit to spirit — but in a human way."

Further, the language of love which God speaks to us through Jesus is not only a statement about God. It poses a question that invites a response from us. We know enough about love to know that it must be returned if the outcome is to be good and glorious. Unrequited love is tragic. So, the Christ-child invites us to return his great love, to rediscover our mother tongue of love and speak that language fluently in our own lives, just as he spoke it with his. Only when we speak the language of love in our lives do we discover our true humanity. That is why St Augustine writes that "We know in so far as we love."

Our joyful vocation is to become part of this great love story — the greatest love story ever told — and, in so doing, discover our true humanity. We need to stay with the Christ-child and let him grow in us so that he can teach us the language of love and give us grace to speak it fluently with and in our own lives.

Then God will truly be with us, Emmanuel.

(2017)

O little one meek

You have to grow up in order to be able to relate to the baby Jesus, argues **Sara Maitland**

IT IS Christmas again. All around us there are images, words and pictures, of beauty and tenderness — "O little child of Bethlehem"; the young mother with her new-born baby; God humbly in a manger. But in prayer I think we stumble a little. Can we have a real relationship with this baby? Or is it more like seeing the photo album of someone who as an adult has become a friend? Or a nudge towards praising the invisible God who has given us this gift in sacrificial generosity?

In peasant societies, as in all pre-industrial societies, people tended to know each other all their lives. If you were older than someone, you probably knew them from their birth until one of you died. Occasionally, perhaps, a stranger came by, or someone brought home a bride (or in some cultures a groom) from elsewhere. Relationships were long and linear — time was a part of their making. (Perhaps we need genetics and psychoanalytic theory now because we do not usually know people in that way, and need a substitute.)

As far as we can tell, relationships were not one-to-one and "romantic": they were dense webs of social meaning, fabrics in which love, sex, economics and kinship were woven together. Jesus was born into a society in which no one would have asked: "Can you have a relationship with a baby who is not part of your biological family?"

But now we do need to ask that question. I'm with Teresa of Ávila here: "Until we are very proficient, we can only know the creator through the creatures." What relationship can we have with a baby?

In my experience, it is about frequency and regularity. I have adult friends whom I have not seen for a while, and do not expect to see soon, but the relationship continues. With a baby this does not happen: you have to be there to have a relationship. New-born babies barely communicate, and once they have passed that early promiscuous stage, they tend to be selective, and choose to relate only to those they see often enough.

They also change and grow fast, and that growing is part of their personality. Yet being with them is not about "quality time"; it is about endless, often tedious, repetition. (How many times can you build a pile of bricks for someone else to knock down?) It is boring, it is constant, and it is out of your control.

Babies choose when they will do their relating; you are at their mercy. If a baby wants to sleep now, it will sleep. It does not believe in "reciprocal". If you wake it up and demand a smile now, because you'd like a smile now, you won't get one. And yet there is no smile in the world like the smile of a six-month-old child welcoming you. Of course, for a baby, this glorious grin is a crafty evolutionary device. It is also an accurate image of our relationship with Christ in prayer.

A relationship with a baby is physical. You have to be there: no answering machines or e-mails. Now is when you relate to a baby — whether now is 2.30 a.m., when a voice that does not sound like the "still small voice of calm" summons you to pay attention; or 5.30 p.m., when the baby is collapsed in sleep just when you are ready to play. That is the relationship. And, still more physical than that, a baby must be tended: lifted, moved, washed, fed. It is dependent, heart-breakingly vulnerable: you have to be a grown up to take care of a baby.

What is it in us that prefers, in prayer, to sit and watch a young man being tortured than to change a baby's nappy? Is it a pride that finds such service degrading; or infantility that does not want such responsibility? Do we crave being the child?

I am now old enough to be not merely Jesus's mother, but his grandmother. The central characters of the Gospels — Jesus, the disciples — are the age of my children. (This helps me with them: "John came to you fasting, and you said he needed counselling; I come to you eating and drinking, and you say I'm a layabout.")

But when I pray I see myself usually as a sad little eight-year-old girl. I want Jesus to be the grown up. But to become spiritually grown up, I must cherish his vulnerability in the mewling baby.

LUCKILY, we have a role model. Joseph has tended to get a shabby deal. Appalled at the thought that a healthy young male should be deprived of sex for the whole of his life (while glorifying Mary for the same "loss", in the doctrine of her perpetual virginity), the medieval Church made Joseph so ancient and doddery that it is unclear how he survived the trek into Egypt.

But, about the time when the young couple's decision might begin to be understood, "demythologising" becomes fashionable, and Joseph gets written out on rather different grounds. At the same time, though for quite other reasons, the stepfather suddenly takes over from the wicked stepmother as the cultural villain. (I have read Christian literature that urges women to stay in unhappy and violent marriages rather than expose their children to the "risk" of stepfathers. How irresponsible of God to allow his own son to have one.) I can think of only one truly human image of Joseph, and although it is touching, it is not kind. In "The Cherry Tree Carol", Joseph comes in

A shabby deal: Joseph is mostly sidelined — as in Robert Campin's triptych of The Annunciation *(centre and right-hand panels shown)*

from work. He hates Egypt. It is hot, they don't like Jews, and they measure differently. Both the baby's grandmothers are miles away; so he and Mary can never get out for a little walk beside the river of an evening. He doesn't like the beer, and he misses his mates. She is sitting there, lovely, serene, focused on the child. He can see the beautiful dark blue veins on her honey-coloured breast, to which the child has infinite access and he has none, ever.

She looks up, smiles and says, "Darling, get me some cherries." And he loses it: "Let the father of your baby gather cherries for you."

But we have strong evidence that it was not like that — or at least, not too often. The biblical account shows something very different. A man who can change his mind, trust his dreams, and risk social scorn. A man of resource, who can find a dry and warm place despite the shoving crowds and the scary onset of labour; who can organise overexcited shepherds, discuss politics with foreign princes, and make a quick getaway when he perceives danger. A man who will give up his home and career for the sake of a woman's baby.

But more, even, than that. A man who brings up a stepson to respect women, honour children, touch lepers, search out the heart rather than the letter of patriarchal law, and never grovel to the Romans. A stepson who lives joyfully and dies bravely, and is not obsessed by his mother.

We have spent a good deal of time in the past 30 years recognising that we cannot name God outside our own experience. When Jesus seeks to name God he says Father, Abba, Dad.

Surely Jesus wants my relationship with him to be that of a free, adult human being. Here, as a vulnerable baby, he gives me a chance to develop that maturity. This does not deny my more childlike moments, any more than his human weakness denies his divine power.

This does not mean I have to organise flights to Egypt, any more than I have to be a virgin mother. It just offers me yet another model of infinite love.

(2002)

125

Worship Kevin, born in Brighton

What we know about children helps us to understand Jesus,
John Pridmore argues

IT is an absurdly audacious and conceited claim, but I shall make it. We are better equipped than before to make sense of Christmas. We have new tools to help us unfold the mystery of the incarnation. Whether we use them or not is quite another matter.

How can we be so presumptuous, so arrogant, so foolhardy as to suppose that we can understand Christmas any better than those who, in heart and mind, went to Bethlehem before us? The reason is that it is only in our own time that we have begun to think about what children mean. We have the possibility of a clearer theology of Christmas because, at last, we have the rudiments of a theology of childhood.

For most of the first two millennia of Christian history, children were hidden from view. On the whole, the theologians who did notice them did not like what they saw. Augustine saw the tantrums of toddlers as proof of their fallen state. Aquinas consigned unbaptised babies who died in infancy to an eternity in limbo, a melancholy realm that is neither heaven nor hell. (Picture the transit lounge of a bleak and soulless airport — Schiphol perhaps — with no departure gate.) Luther believed that sin stirs swiftly in little children, and that the catechism must be drilled into them if they are to escape the power of "the flesh, the world, the Turk and the devil". John Wesley, taught by his terrifying mother, insisted on the necessity of "breaking a child's will betimes". Evangelical leaders, until not so long ago, clung to the biblical precept, "Iniquity is bound up in the heart of a child, but the cane will thrash it out of him."

Quite how these worthies celebrated Christmas — a feast that sets a child, tiresome creature that it is, centre-stage — must be the subject of someone's next book.

TO be sure, across the centuries there have been a just a few Christian thinkers who have loved children, and who have believed that we must become like them. It is significant that perhaps the two greatest of these shape their thoughts about children in the context of Christmas. Before turning to those who, in our own day, are thinking Christianly about children, we must honour these prophets.

I am minded to replace the fairy on the top of our Christmas tree with a figure of the German theologian Friedrich Schleiermacher (1768–1834). Schleiermacher saw in his own day what we are losing sight of in our own, that we can never be liberated by an illiberal gospel.

In 1806, Schleiermacher published an enchanting little book, which is difficult to categorise. The slim volume is entitled *A Celebration of Christmas: A conversation*. A Prussian family gathers on Christmas Eve. They exchange presents. They eat, drink, and make music. And they talk. They talk about what Christmas means and what it means to be a child. The little daughter of the family, named Sophie, joins the conversation. She turns to her mother. "Mother," she exclaims, "you could just as easily have been the mother of God's little child — and aren't you sad you're not?" The mother's response to her daughter's remark — and here I paraphrase Schleiermacher's German — is simply, "Perhaps I am."

The Christmas Eve conversation resumes. Someone observes how sad it is that so many people are "alienated from their childhood". The response to this reflection, voiced at the fireside, is Schleiermacher's own. "Christmas — the celebration of the childhood of Jesus — is nothing other than the recognition of the union of the divine and the childlike. No further conversion is necessary." We may have to put away childish things, but childhood itself is never to be jettisoned.

Schleiermacher's daring line of thought — no wonder alarm bells rang in orthodox ears whenever he spoke — was this: it is my newborn child who, at Bethlehem, rests in Mary's arms, and it is the Christ-child who, weighing seven pounds and seven ounces, was safely delivered last night in Brighton General hospital.

George MacDonald (1824–1905), another persecuted by the thought-police, would have welcomed Schleiermacher's understanding of how childhood and "the feast of childhood" interpret each other. It was MacDonald who wrote the lines:

> *They all were looking for a king*
> *To slay their foes and lift them high:*
> *Thou cam'st a little baby thing*
> *That made a woman cry.*

In the rarest of his novels, *Adela Cathcart* (my kingdom for anyone who can find me a first edition), George MacDonald writes of two travellers, an old bachelor and a much younger man, who fall into conversation in a railway carriage on Christmas Eve. The older man remarks: "Every year, as Christmas approaches, I begin to grow young again. I enjoy Christmas like a child." The carriage is cold, and the night is dark. Again, the older man shares his thoughts: "I believe that he always comes in winter. And then let winter reign without. Love is king within. Love is lord of winter."

The travellers get out at the same station and go their separate ways. But they meet again next day, Christmas Day. The family, with whom the young man is staying, go to church — where the older man appears in the pulpit as the visiting preacher. This surprising turn of events allows MacDonald to do what he loves doing, to hang one of his own sermons on the lips of one of his compliant characters. The interwoven themes of the sermon are the childhood of Christ and the child each of us must become.

"It is as if God spoke to each of us according to our need: 'My son, my daughter, you are growing old and petty; you must become a child. You are becoming old and careful; you must become a child. You are becoming old and distrustful; you must become a child. You must become a child — my child, like the baby there, that strong sunrise of faith and hope and love, lying in his mother's arms in the stable.'"

The rest of *Adela Cathcart* is a rag-bag. The family with whom the young man is staying spend their Christmas telling stories, and the book is little more than a compendium of the tales they tell. But the mutually interpreting Christmas themes of Christ's childhood and ours lend it some semblance of structure.

In one of the stories, for example, a schoolmaster dreams that a half-frozen, abandoned child comes to his door. The schoolmaster takes the child into his own home. In his dream, the child speaks to him. "I am the child Jesus." "The child Jesus!" says the dreamer astonished. "Thou art like any other child." "No, do not say so," returns the boy, "but say, 'Any other child is like me.'"

Schleiermacher and George MacDonald understood that what we believe about Christmas must be determined by what we believe about the child Christ. Thus far, we are with them. But they also insisted — and here we are only just beginning to catch up with them — that our belief about the child Christ and the significance of the incarnation must be shaped by our belief about children.

SO we turn to those in our own day who have been thinking theologically about what it is to be a child. Their primary intention in doing so has not been to make Christmas more meaningful — their subject has been childhood, not its feast — but the possibility of a fresh understanding of Christmas has been an immeasurably beneficial consequence of their work.

This work began with searching studies from some of the most powerful theological minds in Europe. Karl Rahner, Hans Urs von Balthasar, and Jürgen Moltmann — giants all — have all written about childhood. There is no space here to take account of what they say. But, for all their different

perspectives, they are unanimous in insisting that a Christian understanding of childhood is far from what passed for it throughout most of
Christian history.

Childhood is not a parlous state from which we must escape as soon as
possible. Childhood is ours for good as Christ's childhood is his forever. By
which token, there are not 12 but 365 days of Christmas, on the first of
which my true love gave me a partridge in a pear tree.

WE leave Europe and cross the Atlantic for new light on childhood and,
hence, on its feast. We turn to three theologians — though there are several
more — who are teaching us to look at children afresh and who thus bathe
Christmas, too, in a new light.

David Jensen is a professor of theology in a Texan university. He and his
wife, Molly, have two young children of their own. In wishing them all a
very happy Christmas, we must thank him, too, for a book with a clever
title: *Graced Vulnerability: A theology of childhood* (The Pilgrim Press, 2005).
"Graced vulnerability" — the term is as accurately and precisely calibrated
as my much-prized Leica camera. It is exactly right, both to describe the
child Jesus, born in Bethlehem, and the child Kevin, born in Brighton.

The achievement and importance of Jensen's book is that it recovers the
truth, lost in so much pious reflection on the Christmas story, that the
Christ-child is one with all our children. To be a child, for Jensen, is to be
chosen by God. It is to be open and vulnerable to the grace that makes life
possible. It is to be a pilgrim, to be on a journey to God, but, at the same
time, to be acutely attentive to the present moment. That is how Jensen
invites us to see our own children.

But by the same light we look at the child whose birth we celebrate this
Christmas. We recognise that his, too, is this condition of graced vulnerability. "The baby Jesus," Jensen writes, "comes into the world not to ignore
the stigma of vulnerability, but to enflesh it." If we build on that thought, we
may begin at last to bridge the gulf between the plaster doll in the crib and
the bemused kiddie looking at it.

Jensen has more to say about what properly characterises childhood,
the childhood of our own boys and girls and — because he has made our
kids' flesh his — the childhood of Jesus. But Jensen would have us remember
that many children miss out on what we take as definitive of childhood, all
the fun and games, simply because they are too tired, too sick, or too hungry.
It is a consideration that should temper speculation about the happy
childhood of Jesus, given that, from all accounts, he was born the wrong
side of the tracks.

IT is on the wrong side of the tracks that the American theologian Kristin
Herzog anchors her Christian understanding of childhood. She has spent

much of her life with poor children in Peru. For Herzog, childhood is both "goal and gift of life, not a stage to be overcome". She quotes the Hasidic saying: "When a child walks down the road, a company of angels goes before proclaiming, 'Make way for the image of the Holy One.'" With the approach of a child, the angels announce the coming of God.

The resonances with the Gospel accounts of Christ's birth, in which angels work overtime, are powerful. Once again, the radical re-envisioning of childhood enables us to see more sharply what took place when the Word became a child's flesh. Herzog's seminal study drives us to reconsider who it was that God in Christ became; for, when she writes, Herzog does not have in mind cute and cosseted American kids, but the diseased and hungry children she serves (*Children and our Global Future*, Pilgrim Press, 2005).

SUCH children do not always have the energy to play. That consideration brings us to our third thinker who requires us to reassess children and Christmas. Jerome Berryman is the creator of Godly Play, a Montessori-based approach to nurturing children in the Christian faith, which has been widely adopted in recent years. But Jerome Berryman, as well as being an educator, is also a theologian. His publication, *Children and the Theologians: Clearing the way for grace* (Morehouse Publishing, 2009), is the culmination of a lifetime's reflection on what it means to be a child.

Jerome's bold conclusion is that we should see children in sacramental terms. They are, for us all, a means of grace. Berryman writes movingly from his own experience of how children can be ministers of grace to us at times of deep sadness. Many would endorse that testimony. They would wish to add that the presence of children has constituted the grace — and often the saving grace — of Christmas.

Berryman argues that the notion of the child as sacrament provides at least the framework for formulating a formal doctrinal understanding of the status and role in the Church of those whom Christ placed in our midst as emblematic of his Kingdom.

ALAS, other matters have muscled their way to the top of the Church's agenda. Any formal recognition of the place of the child at the heart of the Church is probably beyond the vanishing point of the ecclesiastical imagination. But a final suggestion is perhaps within possibility's realm. My argument has been that, by engaging with the mystery of childhood, a task that the Church was long disinclined to undertake, we may enter more deeply into the mystery of the incarnation.

Whether or not one day the Church recognises the sacramental character of the children in our midst, we can at least begin to think of the Christian seasons — starting with this Christmas — in sacramental terms.

(2009)

Honouring more than our fathers and mothers

The Christmas story subverts ordinary understanding of the family, suggests **Jane Williams**

THE Christmas story remakes all kinds of concepts, and does so over and over again, each year, however fast we try to stuff them back into their "proper" shape as soon as Christmas is over.

To begin with, Christmas gently and insistently remakes the "ideal" family. Christmas cards may try to make this look like a father, a mother, and a child, but Joseph is not the father of the baby, and Mary gives birth far from home, with no mention of her own parents' support, and there are all kinds of oddities around the edge of the idealised threesome: animals, shepherds, and astrologers, to say nothing of angels.

When Mary agrees to become the mother of the Lord, she sings out her knowledge that this will not be a private matter: in this act, God is reversing the world order, to realign it with God's order. "He has brought down the powerful from their thrones, and lifted up the lowly; he has filled the hungry with good things, and sent the rich away empty," Mary sings, out of the prophetic insight given to her by God's choice of her — God's "lowliest servant".

She, the handmaiden, is to become the Queen of Heaven. God does not undo power by using power, or violence by using violence, or keep the promise to Abraham by dishonouring the Creator's promise to the rest of humankind. Instead, God calls all people to be fathers and mothers, brothers and sisters, of this baby, and thus remakes the whole human race into a family.

WHEN this particular baby, Jesus, grows up, he invites all kinds of people to travel with him, work with him, live with him; and he refuses attempts by Mary and his siblings to make him give due honour to the ordinary family unit, as though reminding Mary of the lesson she taught him, that the love of God is bigger than conventional human family love.

In agony on the cross, Jesus invites a thief to share his eternal home, and asks his mother and his beloved disciple to become a new family, an adoptive mother and son. When we find Mary in the Upper Room at Pentecost (Acts 1.14), we realise that Mary has understood: she is now the mother of all the disciples, women and men, but she is also their sister, their daughter, a disciple, just as they are. That early Christian community develops along household lines, sharing food and resources, as you do with your family.

Our Christmas pictures of Mary, Joseph, shepherds, animals, Magi, all gathered around the baby, prove to be prescient, as Christmas begins to challenge us to dig deeper, discover more and more connections with each other, more and more ways in which we belong together, as we take care of Jesus. For Christians, the basic unit of human community is the Church, all human families and all those without human families, and everything in between, equally adopted into God's family.

The story of creation suggests that we all have the same origin, and so its fulfilment is that our destination is also one.

IN remaking the family, the Christmas story inevitably starts to remake the parts played by women and men within it. St Matthew's Gospel signals that God has been subtly doing that for a very long time: Mary has "forerunners", in Tamar, Ruth, and Bathsheba, among others — women who do not fit the mould, but who are vital to the coming of the Messiah (see Matthew 1). They prepare the way for us to encounter Mary, who responds to God's invitation entirely on her own initiative, without consulting anyone else. She steps out into a place of mockery and exposure, not knowing whether or not Joseph will support her, simply trusting that God is true, and that this despised place will become a place of blessing.

Again, a pattern begins to emerge. Jesus accepts a degrading death, and makes it a place where death is destroyed, where hope and life spring into being, as though Jesus's response of trust — even when the way ahead is so unclear — is learned in his mother's womb. The Son of God is both the giver and the receiver of this gift.

In Luke's Gospel, Elizabeth is the first human person to give Mary the assurance she must long for. "Blessed is she who believed that there would be a fulfilment of what was spoken to her by the Lord," Elizabeth says, obliquely comparing Mary's trust with her own husband's lack of it. Zechariah certainly did not believe God, and could not speak again until he could speak an acknowledgement of his mistake. But Elizabeth's praise of Mary is more than just a marital dig: it is also a celebration of a human obedience that begins to unravel the old disobedience of Eden, which will be undone completely when the tree of death becomes the tree of life, with Mary's son as its strange fruit.

MARY's trust in God, God's trust in Mary, are seen again in Jesus's trust of women, particularly the ones who are not occupying the usual female positions and places. Jesus accepts ministry from them, and entrusts it to them. There is the woman who anoints Jesus, accepting — as his disciples can not — that the Messiah must die (Mark 14.3-9). What a welcome change it must have been for Jesus to be supported and not undermined in his hard decision to accept the cross.

There are the women who do not run away from the cross, but creep back at dawn to minister to Jesus's memory, and whose courage and devotion make them the first — astonished and terrified — witnesses to the resurrection (Mark 16). The pattern goes on into the earliest Church, as Lydia throws open her home (Acts 16.11-40); as Phoebe travels with the good news (Romans 16.1-2); as Philip's unmarried daughters prophesy (Acts 21.9).

It is not that women become more important, more faithful, than men, but that the unravelling of knotted relationships continues, until we can begin to glimpse again a human race who are bone of each other's bone, flesh of each other's flesh, not separated as though into different species.

THE list of ways in which Christmas makes us reimagine our world goes on. But the underlying coherence of it all is in the nature of God. John 1.12 says that that is the reason the Son comes into the world: to give "power to become children of God". That is the kind of power that Jesus exercises throughout his ministry — the power of the Son of God, to call people home to the Father.

What we see at Christmas is a glimpse of the reality of all that is, which is based in the unity-in-trinity of God: Father, Son, and Holy Spirit. We can only imagine, first, the Threeness, then the Unity — not both at once — because we are fragmented beings, still seeking the power to become children of God. So, God, the Son, comes to live with us, to make himself at home with us, so that we may be at home with God.

Christmas challenges us to accept and then to live out the radical love of God, who made all things, loves all things, and has room at the table for all who will come. The Christmas crib scene is a peephole into the new world.

As we kneel beside the shepherds and all the other strange and wonderful creatures whom God invites, our hearts and our imaginations begin to be enlarged. We begin to imagine that we might be at home with God, and with each other, around this simple cradle, in company with this strange family group.

(2017)

Dear tokens of my passion

In 2014, **Cally Hammond** was diagnosed with breast cancer.
It was Christmas.

HARD cases make bad law. We gather our best principles for living from what is typical — in other words, not from what is extreme or extraordinary. Apply this to theology, though, and the opposite turns out to be the case. Then, difficult or extreme ideas turn out to be essential for making sense of what is typical or ordinary. In particular, we need the extraordinary (sinless, virgin-born) humanity of Jesus to make sense of our ordinary humanness.

Now apply this to Christmas, and the same fact is underlined even more emphatically. It is the extraordinary nature of the season that makes sense of what we call "Ordinary Time". Most of the year, we trundle along in the familiar grooves and habits of life, doing the same things, following the same pattern. Then, at the darkest season of the year, there is a collective sense of pressure to be different, to do differently. We buy food we would not normally buy — why all the nuts, dates, and shortbread we are perfectly happy to do without the rest of the year? We invite people we don't normally spend time with. We might even break the habit of a whole year's idle reluctance, and actually go to church.

Something about Christmas calls forth extraordinary behaviour in us; but it is that shift out of our habitual comfort zone which is telling us the true message of Christmas.

IN the course of any human lifetime, the Christmas season is overlaid with a varnish of memories — inevitably, not all of them are good ones. Alongside the crisp, cold mornings of early half-remembered childhood, there are failures, bereavements, and broken relationships, which make the Christmas mixture more than one of neat joy.

Four years ago this month, I was diagnosed with a disease I didn't even know existed: inflammatory breast cancer. One day I was taking the college carol services, the next I was having a scan in hospital. The day after that was clinic, and the next day was my first cycle of chemotherapy. My life was handed over to medical professionals, and I had to trust in them, because, as the Prayer Book collect puts it, I "had no power of myself to help myself".

The paradox of treatment for cancer is that it is the treatment itself rather than the disease which causes most of the initial suffering. But curative suffering is something that Christians really do understand, thanks to the cross. The willing acceptance of suffering, not as an end in itself but as a means to new hope, has only begun to make full sense to me several years after my treatment ended. It took that intensity of experience to open up to me new insight into the meaning of the incarnation.

Everyone has the same potential to use their most challenging life-experiences as a way into divine truth. Hard cases make bad law; but hard experiences make good theology.

The two ends of the human life of Christ are knit together into a single message: that the Son of God accepted weakness and mortality, turning his back on the power and dominion that were his due — all so that we could share the life of his divinity, and learn to accept, and even love, our broken-ness, as the part of us which unites us most closely to him. This way, our suffering becomes a way to enter into the mind of Christ.

CANCER treatment is lonely and frightening, but that is not the whole story. There are good things, too, and perhaps addressing them here, in the context of the incarnation, will help to deflate the balloon of fear that a diagnosis tends to inflate in people's chests. The whole experience of suffering — whether illness, bereavement, or other kinds of sorrow, such as lost hope — really can draw us deeper into the truth of God and the meaning of that incarnation.

Many people cope with having cancer by becoming experts in their own condition. I tried not to go down this route; not because I thought it an inappropriate way to manage my fears — after all, people are different, and have different needs and ways of coping. Rather, it was because I felt that I was never going to be in a position to acquire enough understanding to approach the matter objectively, and with intellectual rigour.

I chose, instead, to take a different path, and the only one I saw that suited me was the path of trust. I tried to keep in mind the Passion of Christ: how he handed himself over into the power of others, through whose actions and choices salvation was effected, in him, for the whole world. His willingness to let go of power and control over his own destiny seemed to me like a better model for what I was enduring in my treatment.

It is only looking back, four years later, that I can see that it was just as much about the incarnation as the Passion: a lesson in human vulnerability which is common to us all. Whereas the extreme suffering of the cross is something that few of us endure, the experience of the incarnation is universal. Every one of us is born vulnerable (literally "can be wounded") and mortal ("subject to death"). The vulnerability of being born unites us all to Christ in his incarnation.

That pattern is clearest to us Christians in the story of the Passion, in that the life of the man Jesus was given to us precisely because we could not otherwise accept the divine "truth sent from above". But it actually begins before the foundation of the world. This is what the Welsh poet and priest R. S. Thomas had in mind in his short poem "The Coming": Father and Son look down on the needs of humankind, its hunger and yearning, and the Son's response is what we have come to know by its theological name: the incarnation.

> . . . *The son watched*
> *Them. Let me go there, he said.*

The theological message of Christmas is rooted in this divine choice to side with human vulnerability. It has become so familiar to us that we often fail to see how radical it is. Gods are not supposed to be vulnerable. They are supposed to be powerful. Above all, they are supposed to be our powerful allies, and we can win them over to our side by prayers, offerings, praise, and flattery. According to this model, if we serve them obediently enough, and promise them offerings enough, then our god or gods ought to exercise their power in our favour, by making us well again. We are their servants — their slaves, even. Obedience and submission are our duty.

It is a very understandable take on divine–human relations. But it is not the Christian way. The incarnation cuts across all that. It is the ultimate expression of what St Paul said: "When I am weak, then I am strong."

NO one feels weaker or more helpless than a cancer patient. Whether you try to be an expert in your own illness, or whether you opt for a doctor-knows-best approach, the experience of helplessness is unavoidable. There are the infuriating clinic waits. There are the crowded waiting-rooms, full of sick and miserable people, with helpless friends and relatives. There are the systems of where to go and what to do and whom to talk to, which no one explains; about getting weighed and having blood taken and making your next appointments.

There is the bubbling anger of the powerless always just below the surface.

The ultimate example of helpless vulnerability in such circumstances is surely chemotherapy. It is much feared, and understandably so. A complex system of poisoning, in fact. Cancer cells are abnormal and — oh, the irony! — themselves more vulnerable than normal cells. Because they are fast-growing, they can be killed without killing slower-growing normal cells. But other fast-growing cells get knocked out, too — white blood cells (hence the cancer patient's compromised immunity), and hair and nails.

For me, there were two kinds of chemo. One involved sitting in a chair, knee to knee with a nurse: over the course of hours she pushed three syringes of poison the size of kitchen-roll cardboard tubes into me through a vein in the back of my hand. Somehow, the obligations of human politeness drove me to engage in the most witless of small talk, as though such proximity to a stranger, and such willing co-operation with my own harm, was as normal as the cup of tea and biscuit that came round afterwards.

The second set of stuff was easier, administered through a drip; but I couldn't help thinking that putting it in a black bag (presumably to protect it from light) was unhelpfully gloom-inducing. The room was full of people co-operating in their own immediate suffering, accepting vulnerability for the sake of a longer-term good. Looking back, the parallel with the incarnation is striking.

It may seem strange to say it, but it was a life-enhancing experience, as are all human experiences lived at a deeper level than the surface trundling of the day-to-day. It mattered. The patients mattered, the staff mattered, the friends and family mattered; and the stakes were as high as they could possibly be. Whatever else it might be, chemo is not boring.

IT was Christmas and New Year when I went through chemo. But, at the time, my mind was not on the incarnation, and I took no comfort from the annunciation or nativity, except in the most general way: "Holy is the true Light."

I prayed the Advent Sunday collect daily, and that was it — content to think no further than casting off darkness, being clothed in light, and rising to the life immortal. Mary did not figure in my thoughts much, either. It was all Jesus. "What is not assumed is not saved" goes the old teaching on salvation. It was the God-Man who mattered to me then, and him alone.

I sometimes wonder if it is only our ability to live in the moment that allows us to endure life at all. We cannot safely be consumed with thoughts about the past (that way lies PTSD) or fears for the unknown future (that way lie phobias and anxieties of every kind).

During the time of my treatment, I did almost no academic work. Nothing had the power to interest me, with one exception. Worship. My son would drive me to Caius on the Sundays when I felt well enough, so that I could go to evensong in the college chapel. It had no discernible purpose — at least, not by worldly standards; it yielded no tangible harvest. And yet this alone brought me peace. I could not kneel or stand; so I just sat, and let it all wash over me. And I felt at one with God and the world, and not abnormal or broken, but just me.

During worship, I wasn't a sick person, or a dying person, or a burden, or an embarrassment. I was just God's beloved, fragile child, happy to be in my Father's company. It took cancer for me to understand this. But it could have been bereavement; or breakdown; or any kind of trauma. The insight is there for everyone to grasp, not just the sick.

I think this was why I wasn't thinking sad thoughts about its being my last Christmas. Our earthly celebrations, like all the worship I delighted in, must be pale shadows of the joys of heaven. There was nothing to regret in leaving behind the shadows, and clinging to the more reverent conception of heaven itself.

I was not afraid of dying, or angry about the likelihood of it. That is not a reflection on others who are. I wasn't being brave. It's just how things took me. The process of illness and treatment was physically gruelling, but, somehow, also mentally stimulating. After years going on an even path, I was being forced to think new thoughts, and make sense of new complexities — and I enjoyed that, although it took me a while to realise it.

CHRISTMAS draws us out of self-centredness, into a wider world. Mary and Joseph braved small hardships (a winter journey) as well as big ones (birth in a stable; Herod's persecution), to do their best for the child who was coming. The universal tidings of joy for the whole world were, first of all, personal tidings of joy for them.

All our human relationships cost us something, as they call us away from self-centred living; but they also set us free — from the oppression of the self and its demands. The kingly gift of myrrh is a powerful reminder that the suffering we associate with the end of Jesus's life is rooted in his incarnation.

The simplest way for human beings to share in the self-emptying love that is characteristic of Christ himself is parenthood. We must set self aside to focus on the needs of one who is helplessly dependent on our care. Through parenthood, the Christmas story takes on a new significance: the vulnerability of an infant embodies before us the fragility of goodness.

Our own experience of the protective fear that comes with love for something totally vulnerable acts like a lens, bringing the Christmas story into sharp focus. It is as sharp as the two-edged sword that is the incarnate Word of God (Hebrews 4.12). Love for others is also the best insulation against the loneliness that suffering can otherwise impose on us.

The simple truth of Christmas is that love hurts, but that not all pain is an evil. Cancer has taught me this afresh, from a new angle, just as new parenthood once did.

The interaction between Christians and their manifold pains and sufferings is a complicated one. Christian faith gives dignity to suffering; but we do not believe in fate, or punishment, or submission. Our faith legitimises questioning — even reproach of God.

But, somehow, in the midst of our darkness of body or soul, there is a spark of blessing which cannot be put into words — as if that darkness makes us newly aware of the preciousness of life, and those we love. We could not endure, day by day, the intensity that awaits us once time and history are done, but we never feel more alive, and blessed, than when a shard of that light, that love, pierces our soul and transforms it.

MARY was given a warning (Luke 2.35) by Simeon that a sword would pierce her soul. This, too, helps to make sense of the universal experience of suffering. The hardest pain of the whole cancer process, for me, was not what I endured physically: it was what my husband and children endured emotionally.

Their fears, their helplessness, their inability to find words, made sense for me, in a new and living way, of that ultimate Christian icon from the other end of Jesus's human existence: the cross. He hung on the cross, watching the grief of his mother and his friend, unable to do anything to comfort them, either by word or action; both parties were suffering, and neither had the power to change that suffering.

Hans Memling:
The Virgin Mary
nursing the
Christ-child
(c.1490)

The only word for this, surely, is agony. But even that, painful as it was, I experienced as a blessing. And I have come, over the past four years, to understand the cancer itself as a blessing, too. It showed me things that nothing else could: how much I am loved and valued; how my faith has been vindicated; how Jesus the baby in the manger, and Jesus the man on the cross, are the heart of my existence as a child of God.

And it is this paradox of blessing which I am trying to put into words here, in the hope that others may find it helpful, whether they are themselves going through such a grim experience this Christmastide, or whether they stand in the place of Mary, helpless observers of another's pain, or whether, for now, they are free from such burdens.

NOT everything about having cancer is horrible. Lying on a sofa feeling bored and sick and so unfit for anything challenging or complex that you find yourself binge-watching Jeremy Kyle, day in, day out, is not nice. But there is no human experience so dreadful that it cannot be turned to some sort of reflection or good.

I was dozing one day in between episodes, when the doorbell rang. Without my glasses, scruffy and unkempt — and bald, too, of course — I stumbled to the door and opened it. Outside were two people trying to sign up donors to the RSPCA. They took one look at me, and said apologetically: "We'll go next door." That's a perfect example of what I still think of as the "cancer dividend".

I didn't mind being bald, incidentally. Admittedly, it was a bit draughty in the winter; but if I had had an invisible illness, as so many people have, I could not have expected to be shown the same forbearance with my weakness, tiredness, and lack of focus.

I was a very impatient patient. I didn't want to have to go to hospital all the time. I wanted to be left alone. The word "patient" is rooted in a Latin verb meaning "to suffer", the same word from which the term "passion" derives. I might have striven for resignation and acceptance; but I still spent a lot of time immersed in anger, fear, and fatigue.

Although I went to church, and was glad to worship, I did very little praying. I was content to be the one prayed for, for a change, and was constantly grateful for the prayers of so many Christian friends that sustained me. At one moment, I recall seeing the prayers as a blanket, wrapping me with warmth and security, and finding comfort from that vision.

Christmas for us as a family, four years ago, was the first we had ever had to ourselves: just me, my husband, and our two children. It was overlaid with sensitivities — what if it's the last one? I managed to take midnight mass at our local parish church in Harlton; and a Christmas Day service, too. It was an effort, but it was also a labour of love — another cancer dividend, to be reminded that this work of a priest is never only work. It is also immense privilege. It mattered that I managed to celebrate the eucharist then, and, if I was a bit wobbly and lacking in concentration, people didn't seem to mind too much.

Afterwards, I spent the day on the sofa, and, on Boxing Day, I was back in hospital having chemotherapy. A strange kind of Christmas. But still a good one.

THERE are very few poems about Christmas which do any kind of justice to the mingled themes of vulnerability, suffering, love, and compassion which have always been part of the festival, and which make theological sense of the universal experience of being human.

One that does is by Rowland Watkyns (c.1614–64), and I offer it here as the best theological reflection in English which I know on the subject of the incarnation, and its meaning for the whole of humankind. The "four beds" of Christ stand for the life-journeys each one of us must travel, following the star whose light promises us the true Light:

> *Now in a manger lies the eternal Word:*
> *The Word He is, yet can no speech afford;*
> *He is the Bread of Life, yet hungry lies;*
> *The Living Fountain, yet for drink He cries;*
> *He cannot help or clothe Himself at need*
> *Who did the lilies clothe and ravens feed;*
> *He is the Light of Lights, yet now doth shroud*
> *His glory with our nature as a cloud.*
> *He came to us a Little One, that we*
> *Like little children might in malice be;*
> *Little He is, and wrapped in clouts, lest He*
> *Might strike us dead if clothed with majesty.*
>
> *Christ had four beds and those not soft nor brave:*
> *The Virgin's womb, the manger, cross, and grave.*
> *The angels sing this day, and so will I*
> *That have more reason to be glad than they.*

St Paul had to learn the truth the hard way: that when he was weak he was strong. He learned it because God told him directly what, through Scripture, he tells us, too, and not just at Christmas, but for every day of our lives: "My power is made perfect in weakness."

(2018)

The worst and best of times

Susan Dowell reflects on remembering the departed
at Christmas

*In the darkness of this age that is passing away, may the glory of your
kingdom which the Saints enjoy surround our steps as we journey on.*

"Preparation for morning prayer, Saturday, and daily in the
Kingdom season", *Celebrating Common Prayer*

"A HARD time for you," friends call to say, remembering that the darkening
days of autumn saw the anniversary of my husband's death and the feast of
All Saints fall on a birthday not quite reached three years ago. Now, hardest
of all, perhaps, there is Christmas itself — traditionally a time when families
gather together, and one in which we are made keenly aware of absent
members. For those whose loved one died at this time, it must indeed be
the hardest of times.

But the days leading up to and through Advent belong to the bereaved
in good ways, too. For these have been set aside as a time of remembrance,
a time when I feel the Church holding me and those like me close to its
heart. Blessed are we who mourn, it is promised for we shall be comforted.

Am I comforted, my friends ask. Yes, I answer; let us keep the feast: the
promise holds true. But, like all heavenly promises — including those of
the angels that I've been echoing in carols in my parish church and round
the town this past week — they aren't kept in the ways we expect, and
certainly not in the sweet, soothing terms in which comfort is offered today.

"All is well," we hear, because "I am I and you are you" — just as we
always were. This is not to condemn these words, their author Canon Henry
Scott Holland or those who choose them. But their widespread use at
funerals (almost overtaking the 23rd Psalm) seems to have coincided with
an understanding that these occasions are "really for the living".

They aren't. My husband Graham's wasn't, and I hope mine won't be.
The dead need our prayers, too, because they have more important things
to do than wait about in some next-door room (into which they have
"slipped") for us to visit them to chat over our memories. If we wish to draw
"nearer to our loved ones who are with Thee", we need to get to grips with
the nature of their business. That means getting to grips with those difficult

matters: last things, judgement, all that Advent has just drawn us to — and without which Christmas would not be Christmas.

I CLING to the reality of judgement, because, without it, what is there for mercy to do; what would it be tempering? I have found the concept of purgatory to be the most helpful way into the mystery. Purgatory has had a very bad press over the past half-millennium, even among Catholic Christians. But, like all good theology, it makes sense.

New medical techniques have changed the process of dying — that is, what the dying themselves experience, or appear to experience. Some of these techniques, effective pain relief, for example, are an unqualified blessing. My husband's illness was confusingly complex, and there was, until close to the end every reason to hope he might break through into restored health. What I and others read in his face those last days was a certain perplexity, a "Hang on, this isn't supposed to happen just yet."

I cannot regret the hope, nor the vigorous way it was pursued by Graham and his carers. Nor can I say that he lost the battle that he, his carers and I were "bravely" (in the language of so many newspaper death notices) fighting. If it was a battle, it was not — if the faith we shared is true — lost.

Yet I was distressed by his unreadiness, his being taken on the hop. I wanted his death to be a letting go, a joyful free-fall into the arms of God. Its seeming not to be is what I mean by the "business" of the dead, which the traditional funeral acknowledges as real.

Purgatory, as I understand it, addresses this wanting. It is a process in which all kinds of unfinished business are put before the beloved who alone can take away all the clutter, unreadiness, or whatever might prevent the free-fall into his everlasting aims.

If my perceived need for this became manifest at the gentle end of a long (72 years) and well-lived life of a faithful Christian priest, how much more so for other lives: lives unlived beyond infancy; the unnumbered, unrecorded lives cut short by deprivation or senseless slaughter? How else but through a belief in a process of preparation for the promised glory, unbounded by our earthly timescale, are we to make any sense of the unfinished business all people carry into their dying?

I seem to have left out lives disfigured by sin: an omission to which a small grandson drew my attention recently. "Do people go to hell if they are very bad?" he asked.

"No, but they have to learn to be good; and if they haven't learnt it when they're alive, God is there to teach them when they die," I replied. There's nothing like being made to do theology on the hop.

IF I am to be worthy of the special place I have been accorded as one who mourns, I must, as the prayer I began with makes clear, try to match my steps more closely to those of the cloud of witnesses that surrounds me. They are not easy companions, as countless others have discovered. One such was W. R. Inge (the "gloomy Dean" of St Paul's), whose book *Personal Religion and the Life of Devotion* was written after the death of a beloved nine-year-old daughter. He prefaced it with a poem: "Weep not for her who has been snatched away; but learn to follow her."

In his book, Inge suggests that our learning to follow can stand as a living sign of the promise of salvation — an example to our neighbours and fellow Christians: "Love remembered and consecrated by grief belongs more *clearly* than the happy intercourse of friends to the eternal world" he says (my italics).

I want to reflect this clarity, and thanks to the ministry of Christian friends, am reasonably certain about what is not required of me as one who mourns. I do not have to become a more solemn person, nor to require solemnity from others — and thanks are due to Canon Scott Holland for releasing countless people from this burden. Nor, more importantly, do 1 have to be stoical. To indulge in either posture would be to reduce mourning to a melodrama with me cast in the star part — a lonely role for me, and unedifying for the audience.

The trouble is that it is more difficult to work out what is required of me. Following the dead is hard mainly, of course, because the path is blocked by the pantechnicon of rubbish I travel with: my own sinfulness. So I need to act on what I told my grandson, and start shedding as much as I can now.

This is not something I can do alone. It has to be done alongside the community of which I am a part. This means the people who are there for me in a way that goes beyond keeping a benevolent eye out for me.

What I mean by "there" was movingly spelled out by Dr Rowan Williams in an interview broadcast on Advent Sunday 2002, *An Archbishop Like This:* "Who is it who can tell me who I am?" he asked quoting *King Lear.* The telling, Dr Williams suggested is what our faith and our Church offers: it is that upon which our common life depends.

The answer to Lear's agonised question can be only a partial one this side of heaven. But life, and dying, is like that. Our telling must reflect our uncertainties, if it is to be truthful. It has to be a disciplined telling, the kind that does not descend into pathos and personal drama.

In his reflections on the theme of telling *(Lost Icons: Reflections on cultural bereavement),* Dr Williams has shown this propensity for dramatisation to be symptomatic of the kind of self-awareness our culture promotes. He writes that this is a culture in which we have lost a knowledge of "how to belong with each other" (and in that loss, we are all bereaved as his sub-title suggests). If we cannot belong to each other now, how on earth can we belong to those who have travelled ahead of us? How can we ever learn to follow them?

The only cure for this cultural ignorance, Dr Williams proposes, is the recovery of what he calls habits of "self-understanding that are fast becoming unavailable". Habits are part of the basic stuff of life, and are things that, with enough discipline, we can change for the better.

In this effort to change, I have allies. My husband's life, as well as his death, was marked by the good habits — trustfulness, solidarity, irony — for which Williams pleads (especially irony: Graham's version of the seven "deadlies" added an eighth — not taking oneself too seriously).

A theologically informed friend pointed out that what *Lost Icons* also shows is that "the possibility of the discovery of the soul is linked to those moments of heightened self-consciousness, which typically are brought to bear on us through the frustration of our desires, through conflict and loss."

Can it really be that my soul and my present self, the self that needs attention from others, are not two separate and irreconcilable entities? Yes, Dr Williams affirms, but he warns that to say so is to enter "dangerous territory".

I may not have been accustomed to handling conflict and loss before, but I have become accustomed to it now, and my disinclination for the task is neither here nor there. What exemplary clarity can this attention-seeking soul/self hope to offer others? Perhaps not much, but one thing might be just enough.

In our must-have culture, I — like other bereaved people — am one who knows that what she most desires won't happen. Whatever else they might get up to, our loved ones will never return to us in the old familiar, next-door, slipped-off-for-a-moment way. They are no longer bound to our earthly seasons. I pray for those for whom seasonal coincidence has, seemingly for ever, associated Christmas with suffering.

Meanwhile, I need for my own earthbound soul's sake, to start desiring something that I can have. At Christmas, that something is revealed to us all, and it turns out to be a gift beyond our wildest longing. Let us, then, keep the feast with one another and with all the saints who, we are promised rejoice with us "on another shore and in a greater light".

(2002)

Salute the happy morn?

The world and his or her partner come to midnight mass,
but it is the congregation on Christmas morning that gives
Richard Coles pause for thought

IN Finedon, where I am parish priest, midnight mass is still one of the busiest services of the year. Three hundred or so dutifully turn up from gable-ended houses in the gingerbread-stone posh end; from the Banjo, as our streets of social housing are called; from shift work in the anonymous warehouses along the A45; and from the Conservative Club, the Old Band Club, the Gladstone Working Men's Club, and the Bell Inn (estd 1042).

Many of them are still fairly familiar with what we are doing, unfazed by the business with the crib or thurible. They are at home with candlelight, and with the trickier carols, some even remembering — with tremendous gusto — the descants they learned at school. Afterwards, they disappear into the night, feeling, as I felt, that faint conspiratorial pleasure at participating in clandestine acts of worship.

But the real conspiracy, the real clandestine act of worship, is not midnight mass, but Christmas morning. People might think that Christmas morning would be one of the busiest of the year, but, here, it is not. Perhaps, because of the relentless anticipation generated from bonfire night onwards, we peak early, on Christmas Eve, with our "living nativity" in the afternoon for the children, and midnight mass for the grown-ups. Perhaps it is the logistical necessities of the day, quite apart from growing indifference to Christianity, which have edged church out of the itinerary.

My Christmas Day timetable begins with Morning Prayer at seven — solo and perfunctory, I'm afraid, after four hours of sleep. The eight-o'clock follows, unusually well attended here with a congregation of between 30 and 40. But, this Christmas morn, Christians seem slow to awake and salute.

But Neil, the churchwarden, who does the early turn, is up and about. The altar is dressed, the candles are trimmed, and, once again, I thank God for calling him to this ministry. He is not only unfailingly reliable and diligent; he is also a builder, and will ascend ladders to do impossible things with light fixtures, and descend ladders to do impossible things with boilers, without demur, unlike his priest, who functions only at sea level.

BOB the server is also here, again unfailingly reliable and diligent, and we wordlessly fall into our routine, except the pews are much emptier than usual, and our routine is interrupted for some communion-wafer mathematics. As I do the headcount, I have a moment's sober realisation that our hard core is getting smaller, death having undone two of my most faithful eight-o'clockers in the past year. I try not to lapse into actuarial speculation about the next.

Those who are here, present and correct, prefer the quiet of the eight-o'clock — hymnless, and childless — and are usually of an age where it is preferred to get the business of the day done before nine. Their expectation, and the custom of the house, sometimes strikes me as being at odds with the character of the festival. Unto us a child is born, king of all creation; but it is business as usual at St Mary's, Finedon, as far as our eight-o'clockers are concerned. The pulling of crackers and wearing of hats is for later.

The old faithful, I think, look to the church to give a pattern to their lives, a sense of the passing year, and, indeed, the passing of their own years. They do not need or desire fireworks to help them do this, rather the formulae of words and actions that, in subtly altered forms, have been with them since childhood, learned in the parish's boys' school and girls' school, from curates whose names are forgotten, but not the catechism they taught.

IT is also a service where we try to keep a measure of stillness and silence, helped by the wonderful play of light in the clerestory, which seems to happen quite this way only around the winter solstice. It is silver gilt, unlike summer light, which is more golden, and falls across the 18th-century organ case in a gallery at the west end of the church, picking out the arms of Queen Anne, from whose private chapel at Windsor it came. I think of all the incumbents who have preceded me since 1350, and have watched the same play of light as Christmas morning dawned, weather and the world's unresting change permitting.

At the end of the service, I go to stand just beyond the porch and parvise, and have a minute alone, while people gather their hats and gloves. It is one of my favourite moments of the day, to stand under the gargoyles, looking down across the churchyard, past lichen-covered gravestones, and 1000-year-old yews, into the hall's park, laid out by Repton in the 1740s. There is a huge dead oak just beyond the haha, which always makes me think of Caspar David Friedrich, and, lest we surrender entirely to nostalgia, the smell of Weetabix, a 24-hour, 365-day operation, blows in from Burton Latimer, two miles down the road.

The first departing faithful pass by, to whom I wish Merry Christmas, and note how quickly it has come round again. I think of my grandmother, who lived to be 101, and told me that when you are over 90, you go to bed on Christmas night and wake up to find it's Christmas morning. That same year, she thanked me for the pashmina I gave her, but said that she hadn't opened it, because she was not likely to get much wear out of it, and I could have it back when she died and give it to someone else. And so it came to pass.

AFTER the eight-o'clock, I have a cup of coffee on the children's table with Jane, the churchwarden on the late shift. Jane, for whom I also give thanks daily, has readings for readers, and intercessions for intercessors. She also has a strategy for child management, which can be taxing, because we have no sound-proofed space for our children, which can lead to unchristian feelings when the twins decide to have a lusty shout out while the rest of us are trying to attend to the silent promptings of the Spirit.

Fun Bags are available, full of Christmas-themed materials, and wildly inflationary quantitative easing with chocolate coins is promised at the end. But we know that most of the children we see for Christmas we saw yesterday at the living nativity, a learning experience much enriched by the appearance among the three kings of Darth Vader wielding a light saber.

To add richness to the learning experience for grown-ups, Jonathan, our brilliant director of music, joins us, and we work out whether the choir will be strong enough in number to manage the "Hallelujah Chorus", which we love, not least because our organ was once played by Handel, or so the legend goes. And what better piece could we therefore perform with it on this most holy morning?

And it is here that we run into an inconvenient truth. While we are all geared up to mark this second most important day in the Church's calendar, with bells and whistles and a general pushing out of boats, our congregation is not. Those who are around may well have attended at midnight, but many have gone away to spend Christmas with children, and grandchildren — the first generations of Finedonians who left to go to university and never came back. Or some of the better-heeled members of the congregation are in second homes in sunnier places.

I CHECK the figures, and see that last year, on Christmas Eve, we had about 70 at the living nativity, and 220 at midnight mass. At the eight-o'clock we had 24 — not bad; but at the main eucharist on Christmas morning we had 54. On a normal Sunday, we could double that.

Who were these attenders? There are some solid 9.30 regulars who never miss; there are some parents with children too small to stay up for midnight mass; but, judging by the haggard expressions of their mummies and daddies, they woke up not long after. There are some posh townies, back from Islington and Putney, taking the grandchildren to see the grandparents in the country, the girls in dark coats with gold buttons, the boys in miniature jackets and ties. There are the local farmers and their families, in Sunday

Early to rise: St Mary the Virgin, Finedon

best, keepers of the tradition of Christmas-morning church, leaving their flocks in the fields, or — more likely — their winter barley.

And there are the non-classifieds, the Christmas walk-ins, the unrecognised: the Romanian who works in a packhouse, far from home, who tells me how he would kill his grandfather's pig on St Ignatz's Day, and gets choked with homesickness; the new divorcee, on her own this Christmas for the first time in 25 years; the man in his 70s, last in, and first out, whom I have never seen before, but guess to be a priest; and then there is the person I don't see.

Every Christmas, I cannot help thinking that I am watching Christianity become one degree more marginal to people's lives. This year, when we have had more explaining to do than usual, as the Archbishop of Canterbury put it, I feel it more acutely. Can we recover with confidence our place at the centre of our communities, by reaching out more readily, more intelligibly, to those who are retreating further into the margins and beyond?

Or do we need to recover, with confidence, the irreducible weirdness of what we do, to restore to the gospel its mystery and power, by rediscovering it ourselves? These are not easy questions to answer, but I do not think that we choose between them. I think that our choices lie somewhere in the configuration of these non-classifieds, in their different distances and proximities to the crib, still steady with light and silence in the bewildering *son et lumière* that cannot quite displace or replace it.

A happy and holy Christmas to all.

(2012)

Happy Christmas, folks

This is a time when churches can expect an influx of visitors
who 'just want to feel Christmassy'.
Malcolm Doney says that's fine by him

AS a priest with a regular Sunday congregation of about a dozen, I find it
heartening to welcome a packed crowd of 80-plus on Christmas Eve. And
then another, almost completely different, bunch of the same size, filling
the pews on Christmas Day. I don't know who most of them are, and I
know that I am unlikely to see them again until (possibly) next year. And I
am not about to try to persuade them otherwise.

I can tell them that "God is for life, not just for Christmas," but it won't
wash. A few years back, a cleric in Devon took to the pages of his parish
magazine to rail at those who turned up only at Christmas or maybe Easter,
saying that they were treating God "like an elderly relative of whom they
were not very fond". These occasional visitors, he said, "go and visit him for
an hour or two at Christmas, and perhaps at Easter, but they feel at liberty
to ignore him for the rest of the year (unless they want something from
him, of course)".

His frustration — with what have become known as "Chreasters" — is
understandable, but misplaced. In my experience, people do not come to
Christmas services because they feel they have some kind of obligation to
God for having sent his Son to save us from our sins — mostly, they just
want to feel Christmassy. And that's fine by me.

CHRISTMAS attendance is one of the few areas in the Church where the
numbers have remained stable over recent years. In *Statistics for Mission
2019*, the Church of England reported that the number of churchgoers on
Christmas Eve and Christmas Day was just under 2.5 million, a figure it has
hovered around for the last 10 years. During Advent, 2.6 million people
attended special services for the congregation and local community, and
2.9 million people attended special services for civic organisations
and schools.

The viewing figures do not exactly compete with the final of *Strictly Come
Dancing*, but they are respectable. People in our village love midnight mass
in particular, and expressed their dismay vigorously when — a couple of
years ago — it was cancelled because there was no priest available to preside.

Wanting to feel Christmassy is not to be sniffed at: in fact, it is to be positively encouraged. Dr David Walker, when he was Bishop of Dudley, wrote an essay, "How Far is it to Bethlehem? Exploring the ordinary theology of occasional churchgoers". He undertook a survey of people who attended carol services at Worcester and Lichfield Cathedrals. His findings support my own parish experience.

Christmas congregants do not believe that they are involved in a church activity so much as an event. The distinction, Dr Walker said, was that "the former carries some explicit or implicit expectation … that attendance on one occasion creates a commitment or obligation for future occasions. By contrast, an event stands alone; while the individual may attend a similar event, no wider contract is imputed or implied."

THE congregants, however, are not simply spectators or audience. Although many will rarely, or never, read the Bible, or take part in private devotions, they nevertheless buy into the Christmas service — they immerse themselves in it. A large part of the attraction is the retelling of the nativity story; they

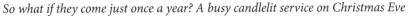

So what if they come just once a year? A busy candlelit service on Christmas Eve

relish the journey to Bethlehem, the birth in the manger, the angels, and the shepherds.

Christmas services, for most of these people, need to fulfil a fairly specific brief: there should be plenty of music — in particular, traditional Christmas carols; there must be a rehearsal of the Christmas narrative (a nativity play would be best); there should be candles; and the service should be uplifting.

There will be a spectrum of attitudes to the historicity of the narrative and its theological or moral interpretations. But the Virgin birth, the presence of angels and shepherds, and the divinity of the Christ-child are not deal-breakers. Instead, as Dr Walker pointed out, they want to "enter the story rather than to assent to any particular theological import". Of those surveyed, almost two-thirds agreed that "the Christmas mystery is more important than the historical facts".

Neil MacGregor, interviewed by Sam Wells about his Radio 4 series *Living with the Gods*, talked about religion as a "ritualised narrative". This is what we are enacting in our Christmas services. We might describe it as folk religion — Dr Walker calls it "ordinary theology" — but, however we dub it, it does suggest a felt need for people to connect with our tribal stories, to plumb into a deeper, older tradition that involves ritual, history, spirituality, and morality.

In a series of theological reflections on the birth of Jesus, Professor Elaine Graham, from the University of Chester, who is Canon Theologian at Chester Cathedral, wrote: "Christmas is not purely a religious festival, but rather a hybrid: of Christian festival — focused on birth narratives — folk religion, consumerism, pre-Christian winter festivals, post-Dickensian sentimentality, and so on."

What Christmas services do is to blend these elements into the kind of ritual event at which religion still has the capacity, in the words of Martyn Percy, Dean of Christ Church, Oxford, "to provide enchantment within the modern world". In his book *The Salt of the Earth*, which explores religious resilience in a secular age, he writes: "People know that there is more to life than the explicable and the visible." It is, he says, "part of a chain of social memory that enables society to cohere".

Professor Graham thinks that, at Christmas services, there may be "a kind of complicit negotiation under way with the original story that trans-forms it from the sacred sanctioned text into something that lodges more in the realm of popular affection and popular religiosity".

The warmth, the uplift, that these services generate have even inspired atheists to recognise the human benefit of this form of religion. It is what inspired the comedian Sanderson Jones to co-found the determinedly secular Sunday Assembly. In a blog introducing a Winter Solstice celebration he wrote: "I really love Christmas and first thought of starting a non-religious congregation of some type when I was at a Christmas carol concert." Having noticed the joy that it engendered, he had wondered "if it was possible to harness all those good bits to celebrate the awesome fact that we are alive".

Another comedian, Robin Ince, the co-presenter with Professor Brian Cox of *The Infinite Monkey Cage* on Radio 4, similarly thought it unfair that, at Christmas, God should have all the best tunes, and developed an alternative. "I decided that something must be done to prove that the godless enjoyed celebration as much as anyone who dwelt in pews and porches singing carols," he wrote (*Church Times* Features, 21 December 2012). "I came up with 'Nine Lessons and Carols for Godless People' — a night that celebrates the universe and its contents with scientists, musicians, comedians, and, occasionally, hula-hoopers and tap dancers."

Christmas has universal resonance. In his interview in the *Church Times*, Neil MacGregor observed: "I think that [it] is clearly very difficult for truly secular societies — which ours is in many ways becoming — to know what its shared festivals are. Christmas is very interesting in the way that it has, I think, uniquely, remained the one moment where the community thinks of itself as a community; where everybody would acknowledge that part of that is thinking about the poor, the weak, the destitute; and that is articulated through some kind of celebration — because it's almost the only moment, as a nation, where the whole nation pauses to think about all parts of the community and the obligations that should bind it."

Narrative, vernacular, folk, ordinary. Our nativity plays, our carol services, midnight masses, and family worship are important cultural and spiritual resources that play an important part in helping occasional churchgoers to build their world. As the American Rabbi Michael Lerner recognised: "There is a beautiful spiritual message underlying Christmas that has universal appeal: the hope that gets reborn in moments of despair, the light that gets lit in the darkest moments of the year, is beautifully symbolised by the story."

It's the story, stupid. Dr Walker calls it "a gateway into the mystery of God". When people turn up at Christmas, they come in hope that they will be transported, that their spirits will be lifted. They are hungry beggars wanting to be fed. Not for ever. Just now.

We have a banquet for the taking, and — like the convener of the great feast in the Gospels — we should demonstrate largesse. It does not mean expecting people to have this plenty rationed out over the course of a year. If they get a taste for this, and want more, then fine. In the meantime, let's just give the folk religion.

(2017)

The Christmas sermon: what to say and how to say it

Kate Bruce advises preachers how they can engage people and not bore them

CHRISTMAS is coming. The goose is getting fat. Time for the preacher to pull something out the hat ... again. But what to say? How to say it? How to avoid the Scylla of schmaltz and the Charybdis of irrelevancy? How to speak with passion and authenticity, blending lightness with profundity, hitting the right notes and avoiding the trivial?

Time for the preacher to think deeply about the hearers, ponder Scripture, read the context carefully, pray sincerely, and get creative.

Who are the hearers? Probably a mixture of people. Rich; poor; those locked into internecine family warfare; happy families; lonely people; those with firm faith; those hanging on by their fingertips; enquirers; cynics; those who have chosen to be in church; and others press-ganged into seasonal attendance. The sermon must welcome and make space at the table for all comers.

Hospitality is vital. No matter how infrequently these people might come, here they are. Give them something to smile about. Give them the truth that they are deeply and profoundly loved. Give them hope.

Whichever text you are working with, stick close to it so that the particular voice of the writer is heard, and you avoid conflation that flattens out the distinctiveness of the particular. Sticking with the biblical text keeps us anchored, and the themes that spring from the readings are rich and resonant.

Take Luke. Just before the infancy narrative, from the mouth of a young woman, pregnant, unmarried, vulnerable, we hear explosive, powerful words, laden with political and spiritual ramifications. All right — strictly speaking, these verses belong to Advent, but there's always room for a swift flashback.

Mary — what a role-model in an age when many women feel silenced. On to Luke's birth story — he paints a picture of people displaced by political decisions: Joseph and a heavily pregnant Mary are part of a human caravan wending their way towards Bethlehem. Will the travellers meet a wall, or a welcome? (Note how language can be used to describe the action in the text while simultaneously evoking a more contemporary story.)

Walk inside the story with an attitude of curiosity, and the applications fall out: if I had a place in Bethlehem, would I have opened my doors and offered hospitality? In what way do I offer hospitality now? What can we do to support those who are in situations of vulnerability? What does it mean to welcome the stranger today?

Now Luke's camera zooms in: some scruffy shepherds on the receiving end of an angelic greeting are being drawn into the heart of the story. The ordinary and the extraordinary elide and the little people are, by divine invitation, first on the scene. At the epicentre of this story of human vulnerability is Divine presence: God thrust through the birth canal, a new-born, feeling the precariousness of the human experience.

Simply staying with Luke offers resonant themes. Here is a story that we need to tell. Here is a story that many people don't know any more; a story that speaks to our times with surprising relevancy, and profound hope. After all, if God is to be found in the midst of this messy story, perhaps he might be found in the midst of ours?

MATTHEW's birth narrative is also full of rich preaching possibilities. Jesus's identity as the Messiah is declared at the outset. What does this mean to us? What kind of Messiah?

The text explains that "he will save his people from their sins," that this is "Emmanuel, God with us". Bear with me: a sermon based on Matthew could reclaim the concept of sin.

Perhaps we are a bit squeamish about bringing such a heavily freighted word into the season of festive celebration — but, unless we can name the problem, how can we speak of hope? This is not about peddling guilt, it's about framing reality honestly. We are wrecking the environment, and the earth is suffering; we allow petty squabbles to wreak havoc in relationships; our consumerism drives up debt and traps people; we easily lose sight of the reality of God's presence in our desire for presents. Often, we realise that we are stuck in old patterns of relating and behaving. The truth is that we need help.

Without being a killjoy, we can suggest that there is more going on in this season than turkey and Twiglets, much as I like both. I love Christmas — but the stuff of the season doesn't see me much beyond the Boxing Day bloat. The sermon could offer the invitation not to miss the presence of God by focusing on the wrappings of Christmas. Why not invite people to promise themselves a few quiet moments of reflection over the washing-up, an openness to the possibility of God meeting them in the ordinary, in an afternoon walk with the dog? The invitation, in whatever form, must be to give attention to God, to be open to encounter, to risk trusting that there is something more.

THE early verses of John 1 offer a smörgåsbord of preaching possibilities, stretching our vision out of time and space, before zooming back down to earth with: "The Word became flesh and lived among us," more colloquially translated as "Christ shares your postcode".

At a university carol service, preaching on this text with the expectation of a more evangelistic style, I asked people to suspend their disbelief and ask a "What if … ?" question. Here, the Grinch who stole Christmas came into conversation with John Betjeman: a pleasing and unlikely pairing. Both were asking questions of meaning and truth. The Grinch: "What if Christmas, perhaps, means a little bit more?" Betjeman, in his poem "Christmas": "And is it true, This most tremendous tale of all?"

My sermon strategy was deliberately invitational rather than declamatory: "Come and consider this. Just imagine for a moment …". In an age that is suspicious about claims to truth, invitation and suggestion help the preacher to inhabit an attitude of homiletic humility: "This has been the experience of many ordinary people, but what do you think?"

If people decide it isn't true, well, OK, they can shrink-wrap Christmas and call it Winterville. But if they conclude that it is more than a nice story told in stained glass, then this might change absolutely everything. At the very least, the question of the truth of the incarnation, and how that connects to the wider gospel story deserves some exploration, a willingness to engage with the idea of God; perhaps by attending a course looking at faith, by learning to pray, even joining the church community.

The question for the preacher and the church is, again, one of hospitality. How might a person who wants to experience more be helped to engage, in an accessible and down-to-earth way? In other words, how does the Christmas sermon connect with the wider life of the Church?

GIVEN that the heart of the Christmas narratives is the incarnation, it would be a tad ironic to preach an abstract sermon full of ideas but not earthed in the soil of the now. Whatever the final sermon looks like, it needs to be grounded through the use of resonant images and examples. Abstract ideas will not stick, and what will last is the impression that the sermon was dull, boring, and hard to follow, possibly leading the hearer to make an internal note to self: "Glad that's over. Let's never do church again."

The preacher's words need to be accessible, and delivered in an engaging way. While the sermon should not become a mere trivial pursuit, there is room for laughter, for joy, and for gentle mockery of the seasonal traditions: the horror of sprouts, the fear of the Christmas jumper, or the opening notes of the *Casualty* theme tune as Uncle Nigel insists that he can skateboard. The Christmas sermon, following the pattern of the incarnation, is a place where the ordinary must elide with the extraordinary, and must offer, above all, hope.

A FINAL suggestion: do spare a thought for the harried parent wrestling with a squirming infant. Keep the Christmas-morning sermon punchy and short — and, if the earsplitting wails of an infant cut across your finely crafted words, then, brilliant! It's Christmas, when a child has always been centre-stage.

(2018)

Tidings of comfort … if no joy

Lucy Winkett hopes that more churches will observe
a 'Blue Christmas'

LATE last Advent, I spent time with a man who had come to see me to "talk about God". The impending festival had caused him to seek out a priest, because he felt somehow out of kilter with the tinsel-decked streets. The playlists of the shops were driving his spirits down, not up.

In the course of our conversation, he told me that he had spent the previous Christmas Day alone in his flat. It's not that he did not have family or friends to go to, if he had really wanted to. He just told everyone that he was with someone else. And he found himself alone in what, on Christmas Day, was an unusually quiet flat in the city.

Before he knew where he was, he was Googling "How to make a noose". It wasn't long before he had thought about where to buy a rope, and had worked out where in his flat to hang it.

He was in despair. Freefall. At what the Christmas songs say is "the most wonderful time of the year".

THIS is not another article complaining about how the "meaning of Christmas" has been lost. This is a suggestion that, as part of our offering of Christmas carol services, churches hold a "Blue Christmas" service — as many now do. In our case, this is an hour on a Sunday afternoon before Christmas, billed as a carol service "for those who find this time of year difficult".

Blue Christmas services are not bah-humbug events. The atmosphere at our Blue Christmas service this year was less grumpy than tender; less protest than a nod to the truth expressed in the lyric from a hit song of the 1980s: "Every day's like Christmas Day without you. It's cold and there's nothing to do" (from "Come On Home", on the 1986 album *Baby, the Stars Shine Bright* by Everything But the Girl).

But, at the Christian festival of joy at the birth of the Saviour, is the Church right to be so downbeat? Surely, it's the moment to take us out of ourselves and rejoice — whatever our circumstances — that God is with us. To count our blessings. Be thankful.

Well, yes. But also, no. If we take the theology of liturgy seriously, then there is a clear rationale for holding something like a Blue Christmas service.

Because all we are doing, when we pray or take part in liturgy, is joining in the praise of creation that is already happening — seen and unseen — in time, and for all eternity.

This is praise, yes; but good liturgy will also be able to lament. It will be able to hold these things together, even in the exuberance of the carolling and wassailing that goes on in churches, pubs, shopping centres, and high streets.

FOR the Church, the shadow of the cross will always fall across the cradle. Good liturgy puts into sacred words what is already true about God and humanity; and, for some, that will include the desperation of the season as well as the joy. But, apart from its being liturgy, the primary lens through which a Blue Christmas service is understood and received is pastoral.

A Blue Christmas service, held alongside the joyful services, is a pastoral acknowledgement of the ambiguity of enforced jolliness. It is an open and gently held sacred space for the sheer misery of missing some one; a space for acknowledging the feeling that the whole of society is having an expensive party to which you are not invited.

As one of the prayers we used this year puts it: "God, you have promised to go before us into hospital rooms, empty houses, into refugee camps, into war zones, into graveyards ..." It is acknowledging the fact that Christmas is celebrated in a time of war and poverty. But even in less politically dramatic circumstances, Christmas, for many people, often has a tinge of personal sorrow about it.

What is it that makes Christmas — the festival of light, peace, goodwill, and joy — so poignantly sad? I think it's because it touches very deep themes that throw into relief the day-to-day reality of what it's like to be alive in the world.

Christmas marks the passage of time. We think to ourselves: "Last Christmas, he was still here." "This is the last Christmas we'll be in this house." "This is the first Christmas I haven't been able to afford a proper present for my mum." It is a moment of reckoning: a moment of comparison with the past, and tentative hope that, next year, things will be better than they are now.

ANOTHER, more contemporary reason that Christmas can feel so hard is that we are still peddling the Victorian expectation that everyone has a safe family environment to withdraw to, and that that is the ideal.

For some, of course, this is really true — and good for them. For many, though, family is complicated and fragmented. Many families have had to come to terms with a "new normal", after divorce or estrangement, for example. And the pressure to treat everyone equally — or even to continue to try to create that Victorian ideal — means overanxious catering, causing huge stress (mostly to the women of the family, aiming for Nigella-like perfection); or exhausting car journeys, travelling hundreds of miles in a 48-hour period so that everyone sees everyone else, and no one feels left out.

And then there's the commercialism of a contemporary Christmas, and the expectation of present-buying — hard for many families to bear after years of austerity.

AT our church, it is my colleague, the Revd Lindsay Meader, who has pioneered the Blue Christmas services. There is Scripture, silence, and poetry, and always some beautiful music to listen to, as well as carols. There are candles, but no trumpets. There is evergreen, but there are no baubles.

One person who came to a Blue Christmas service a few years ago wrote this to Lindsay afterwards: "This year, whilst longing for Jesus, I approach Christmas with dread. Yet in that service, the darkness was so beautifully held in the warmth of God's love and promises. It was visually extraordinary. One little candle. By the end, a sea of light. I think that tells the gospel story in and of itself.

"I held that in my mind as the very next day circumstances in my life took yet a more upsetting twist, out of my control, yet deeply impacting me. To be allowed to light candles whenever we felt the moment was right meant so much. For me the service said, 'Come as you are. God loves you and will hold you.'"

A visitor who stumbled across the service on a Sunday afternoon, wrote: "You don't know me. I was at the Blue service. I wanted to say, from the depth of my heart, thank you. Thank you for creating this space, somewhere in the busy, tinsel-filled city, to sit with grief, loss, pain, bewilderment, fear, darkness, whilst at the same time holding up the hope we have, and doing it so exquisitely, gently, lovingly."

IF there is a line in a carol that encapsulates this kind of service, it might be "O hush the noise, ye men of strife, and hear the angels sing!" For us, it has been important to offer a space afterwards — with tea and nice cakes, and someone to talk to, if people want it. But no pressure.

And, for those of us who are able to receive the joy of the season this year, taking part in a Blue Christmas service reminds us that, some years, we aren't — and that we are just human beings, in whose messy lives Christ is born once again, not to neaten us out, or cheer us up, but to love us. And be with us. Always.

(2018)

Back to the old joy and innocence

Carols reconnect people with mixed emotions and depths,
says **Paul Vallely**

AT my son's school Christmas concert, a close-harmony group of the older boys performed a version of the Angelus which was new to me. The teacher introduced Franz Biebl's *Ave Maria* with a striking story. It had been written by a fireman, he said, for a firemen's choir. The piece is a haunting setting of the Angelus prayer, with sonorous *Aves*. Throughout the rendition, I could not escape the thought of a group of fire-fighters who met to sing at night to subsume the tensions of the day into the luxuriant harmonies of this gem of 20th-century church music.

We live in a time when skills are increasingly developed and exercised through a profession. The impulse of the amateur has become the realm of the dilettante. Friends who are professional actors offer only mild disdain when amateur dramatics are mentioned. Yet the season of Christmas provides something of a reminder of the fact that participation in a community — and in the forms of art and ritual which celebrate that — is something central to our humanity. The division of professional labour in an indirect way diminishes that.

Canon Alan Billings touched on this in a *Thought for the Day* on Radio 4, when he spoke about school nativity plays, carol services, and concerts to celebrate Christmas. Most particularly, he offered the example of the Sheffield Carols, for which people gather in country pubs on the edge of the Peak District to sing a singular set of carols that are peculiar to the area.

Locals say that folk carols were driven out of the area's churches in the 19th century, when the Tractarian Movement brought robed choirs, high-church medievalism, and music played on organs into the churches. But it was not just the old folk carols that were driven out, but also many of the people who sang them. They had been turned into a kind of audience at worship. Feeling driven out of the church, the people took to the pub for their carolling.

Yet the mystique of the carol lingers. Partly this is because, as one vicar pointed out at another carol service, the nuggets of theology buried in the carol — "veiled in flesh the Godhead see" — reconnect us with the depths beneath the shallow busyness of our contemporary Christmas. Partly, however, it is because it also reconnects us with the unspoiled potential of childhood. We go to the school nativity play to see our children or grand-children, and they make us reimagine the story through their uncompromised eyes. Christmas celebrations, as Canon Billings pointed out, lead to mixed emotions because we get caught up in the joy and excitement of the children, but something also triggers memories of our own long-forgotten childhood, whose innocence was lost in the slow attritions of life.

It is not all our own culpability. When I got home, I looked up Biebl on the internet. He was not a fireman, it turned out, but an assistant professor of choral music at the Mozarteum, the celebrated academy of music in Salzburg. But he had had in his parish choir a fireman, who in 1964 asked him to compose something for his workplace choir at the fire station. The *Ave Maria* was the result. So the teacher's story was half true. The piece was an intermingling of the educated talents of a professional and the enthusiasm of a group of amateurs. Perhaps there is a lesson in that, too.

(2013)

It all began in Truro

Howard Tomlinson looks at the origins of the
Festival of Nine Lessons and Carols

ALMOST 140 years ago, on 24 December 1880, the first Nine Lessons with Carols service took place, not in the magnificent surroundings of King's College Chapel, but in a temporary wooden "pro-cathedral", situated in the north-east of the precinct adjacent to a masons' yard in Truro. It was set there because St Mary's, Truro, the parish church that had been designated the cathedral in the 1876 Bishopric of Truro Act, which established the independent Cornish diocese, was being dismantled — its early-16th-century south aisle apart. This was to make way for the building of John Loughborough Pearson's design for a new cathedral for the new see. A wooden shed, like the wooden manger, was the humble setting for a service that has now become a mainstay of Christmas observance in the Anglican Church.

It is evident from local newspaper reports that St Mary's had been the scene of successive carol services on Christmas Eve in 1878 and 1879. These took the place of the choir's former practice of perambulating around the parishioners' houses, singing carols on their doorsteps — and, no doubt, receiving hospitality (and collections) at many of them. The new services were popular. In 1879, it was reported that "the cathedral was crowded, many non-conformists as well as church-goers being present."

There is good reason to believe that their originator was Somerset Walpole — one of a group of able young men who served in the new diocese — who had both conducted the carols and intoned the prayers in the two services. What is certain is that Walpole did not devise the famous Nine Lessons service of 1880. This was put together in a burst of creative energy by Edward White Benson, the formidable first bishop of the new diocese.

When Benson undertook this labour of love amid his frenetic endeavours to build up the Cornish Church is again conjectural. It is likely, however, that it was compiled in the days after the last service in St Mary's on the evening of Monday 11 October 1880, when the Rector celebrated in the old cathedral for the final time.

We know more definitely that Benson's service was not an entirely original composition: the nine-lesson sequence, after all, had been the custom at the greatest feasts of the Church in the Middle Ages. Moreover, Arthur Benson, the eldest surviving son, remembered that his father's festal service had been arranged from ancient sources, and Walpole later suggested that it had been largely compiled from medieval service books. One such source was Grandisson's *Legenda*. Although the evidence relating to Benson's composition of his Nine Lessons is slight, its nature can be reconstructed with greater certainty.

We are fortunate in being able to examine both the content and structure of the service through the survival of Benson's draft and two printed orders of service in the Cornish archives at Kresen Kernow. From these sources, the differences between the 1880 service and ours today are immediately apparent.

The first five lessons are all from the Old Testament, only two of which are now included: the first from Genesis 3 (Adam and Eve), and the fourth from Isaiah 9 (Unto us a Child is born). Of the four New Testament readings, there is only one Gospel narrative: from Luke 2, about the shepherds. The Magi are ignored in the Word, although not, with the inclusion of "The First Nowell", in the music. The great Johannine Prologue ("the Word became flesh") forms the seventh lesson rather than the ninth, and the final two readings are from Galatians and 1 John. The latter epistle — preceded by Benson's benediction: "Unto the fellowship of the citizens above may the King of Angels bring us all" — forms a fitting climax to the service.

It could well be that the draft of lessons and readers, which was marked "private", was intended as a template for Walpole to insert the music. Benson, however, would have had the final word, no doubt insisting on a different translation — perhaps his own — of the original fourth-century Latin text of a hymn from the one printed in *Hymns Ancient and Modern*. So "Earth has many a noble city" became "Bethlehem! Of noblest cities" to fit in with the preceding Lesson from Micah. The rest of the music — four carols, three "anthems" from *Messiah*, two "hymns", and the concluding Magnificat — was probably planned by Somerset Walpole.

We have a good idea of the sources for most of this music, although no choir scores survive. All four carols, with some editing for "Once again, O blessed time", were taken from the 42 published in *Christmas Carols New and Old*, edited by Bramley and Stainer. The three anthems were all chosen from Handel's *Messiah*. The two hymns, "O come, all ye faithful" (the only piece with extensive dynamic markings) and the different translation of "Bethlehem! Of noblest cities" were from *Hymns Ancient and Modern*.

As for the actual service, in the *West Briton* of 23 December 1880, mention is made of "the usual festal service" that was to be held the next day, and for which "a small pamphlet" would be issued. The following week, there was a fuller and more accurate report of proceedings, suggesting that "the service was very hearty and impressive throughout, the singing being particularly good."

We can also be sure of the state of the wooden "pro-cathedral" in December 1880. The same journalist reported that "the church was tastefully decorated with flowers and evergreens and presented a very neat appearance, the chancel having had special attention paid to it." But it was likely to have been cold (a stove heater was not installed until 1886), poorly lit, and badly ventilated.

To our eyes, used as we are to the splendour of the celebration, it seems an incongruous setting for the first Nine Lessons service, but the church had a distinctive spirituality. As Bishop Wilkinson remarked some years later: "The services in the wooden cathedral seemed ... like a scene out of Primitive times — like the Acts of the Apostles; the surroundings so plain, the ceremonial so simple, the religious feeling so spontaneous."

We can only guess the size and nature of the congregation. Perhaps the wooden church was as crowded and the worshippers were as mixed as for the 1879 carol service in old St Mary's, and the numbers as large as the 380 people who crammed into the church in 1883 for Bishop Wilkinson's enthronement. As for its timing, Bishop Benson marked on his own copy of the printed Order that the service took 70 minutes: "from 10.5 to 11.15pm", and a *West Briton* journalist reported that "the service [was] terminated at 11.20 by the bishop pronouncing the blessing."

While some uncertainties abide, of Bishop Benson's purpose we can be absolutely sure. As he had earlier observed, his professed mission was "to preach Christianity without contention, and to advance ... [the] Church without party or faction, without animosity, without disputation". And here, in his Nine Lessons service, he was intent on teaching the true Christmas narrative to a mixed gathering of Anglicans and Nonconformists.

Just as Benson himself had used ancient sources for his festal service for Christmas Eve, I am sure that he would have approved of Milner-White's reworking some of his benedictions, the short blessings that preceded each of the original Nine Lessons. As he confided to his diary after his attendance at an Easter Eve service at the Duomo in 1894: "Must not the English Church try some way to seize on the possibilities of edification which these holy services of the Holy Week present? ... Why should we not add the Prophetiae to our services, like my Nine Lessons?"

Benson well understood the importance of appropriate liturgical adaptation for a declining Anglican Church.

(2020)

Word from Wormingford

Ronald Blythe plans the carols
and appoints the lesson-readers

PERCY Dearmer wanted carols to be sung at church services throughout the year. Instead of the anthem, for instance, and as an extra delight after the blessing, now that the choir and congregation were in good voice. He described them as "songs with a religious impulse that are simple, hilarious, popular, and modern".

"Please, sir, may we sing a carol?" begged a member of Parson Woodforde's congregation on Christmas morning. "You may, but not until I am out of the church."

Some remote intelligence presumably told him that a carol was a dance. Or maybe, his *Diary* revealing his appetite, he flinched from having to listen to the eating- and drinking-carols of his day such as "Wassail, wassail, all over the town!"

Our carol services — Henry takes one; I take the other — have to be the same every year, though different, his at Little Horkesley, mine at Wormingford. They must begin with Mrs Alexander and end with Charles Wesley. I religiously destroy each year's copy so as to hold on to a mite of freshness in the latest selection; and I am always startled, as is everyone else, by the heart-wrenching power of the familiar.

Into its English Gothic setting comes a Bethlehem so at variance with the grim concrete town we see on the screen that it is hard to find a connection. Out goes all debate. The wonder, the wonder! And all of it just saved in time; for, if Cecil Sharp and Ralph Vaughan Williams, two young men, had not suddenly realised just before the First World War that a rare kind of song was slipping into silence, the carol book would have been a flimsy affair.

I love the secular borrowings, such as singing Bishop Brooks's "O little town of Bethlehem" to Vaughan Williams's tune of "The Ploughboy's Dream". As for Gustav Holst's setting of Christina Rossetti's "In the bleak midwinter", the chancel arch shivers as we do our best to re-enter poverty.

"Where do Christmas songs begin?" asks Timothy Dudley-Smith. "By the stable of an inn Where the songs of hosts on high Mingled with a baby's cry." Where do Christmas songs hit the roof? In King's College Chapel.

Borrowed from Truro Cathedral, the Festival of Nine Lessons and Carols was first heard at Cambridge in December 1918 in a world of mourning, in a tall church of empty stalls. In a sacred cage where, to adapt Shakespeare, once the sweet birds sang. Now all shot and buried in mud. Come, thou Redeemer of the earth.

I strew nine lesson-readers through the lectern Bible. No names. By their deeds shall ye know them. A churchwarden, a hospice director, a farmer, a bell-ringer, a commuter, a schoolboy, a schoolgirl, a parish councillor, a lay canon. Then I hand the whole thing over to Christopher the organist and wait for the village to swarm in. Which it usually does.

Waiting, I remember learning Frances Chesterton's "How far is it to Bethlehem?" from mother, I suppose, and definitely from the curate's wife, a large Welshwoman with a surprisingly small, true voice. "Lullay my liking, my dear son, my sweeting; Lullay my dear heart, mine own dear darling!" and other carols which remain outside our nine. As is Geoffrey Shaw's robust "Unto us a boy is born!". Carols are filled with exclamation marks. Our handbell-ringers stand round a table and make a silvery noise. The Advent candles burn out.

There is the crib, invented, they say, by St Francis, ours with knitted creatures, human and farmyard. There is the gale outside, and the music within.

(2006)

How a carol was born

Did you know that 'While shepherds watched' was once sung to 'On Ilkley Moor baht 'at', asks **Adrian Leak**

NAHUM Tate, the author of "While shepherds watched their flocks by night", was an unlikely hymnwriter. Born in Ireland in 1652, the son of a clergyman called Faithful Teate, he settled in London after the Restoration, changed his name and made a precarious living by his pen. He wrote a number of largely unsuccessful plays, and translated or adapted the works of others.

Apart from his "Christmas Hymn", his most memorable achievements were the libretto for Purcell's *Dido and Aeneas,* and an adaptation of Shakespeare's *King Lear* which eliminated the Fool entirely, and had Edgar marry Cordelia so that they all lived happily ever after. This version was still popular much more than a century later, at the beginning of Queen Victoria's reign.

Like many of his trade, he led a rackety life. Chronically short of money and harassed by creditors, he produced work far beneath his abilities, and took to drink. He did, however, have his successes: King Charles was amused by one of his plays, and his ode "Panacea — a Poem on Tea" was generally well received.

To the surprise of many, he was appointed Poet Laureate by William IV. Southey called him the second-worst Laureate ever, and Pope made a waspish comment about him in the *Dunciad.* George I declined to reappoint him, and Tate closed his career by dying suddenly and unexpectedly in the Royal Mint, in 1715, while taking refuge from his creditors.

The work by which he is now best known, "While shepherds watched their flocks by night", was probably not one he would have considered highly. It first appeared in 1700 in a supplement to the new metrical version of the Psalms, which he and Nicholas Brady had published in 1696.

Since the suppression of carol-singing earlier in the 17th century, there had been no authorised Christmas hymn; indeed there had been no authorised hymns at all. Only biblical texts, such as metrical psalms, or paraphrases of passages from the Bible, were thought appropriate for singing in church. Tate's hymn is a metrical version of St Luke's narrative; comparison with Luke 2.8-14 shows how closely he followed the King James Bible.

"While shepherds watched" soon became popular. People could now sing a carol in church without censure. Its metre matched a large number of popular tunes; and one of the first that it was sung to was *St James* ("Thou art the way", AMNS 128). Later in the 18th century it was sung to some wonderfully roistering "chapel" tunes, such as *Northrop* (EH, Appendix No. 8), *Lyngham, Old Fosters* and *Cranbrook*. The last two are still sung as pub carols in Yorkshire, though *Cranbrook* is now better known as the tune for "On Ilkley Moor baht 'at".

It was not until the editors of *Hymns Ancient and Modern* (1861) linked Tate's Christmas hymn to *Winchester Old* that the world got used to singing it to its staid little "church" tune. But what a loss to our carol services has been the ousting of those wild "Old Methodist" tunes, with their repeats and flourishes and splendid bravura.

In Tate's day, singing in the parish church, when it was attempted, was mostly deplorably bad. This was owing not only to the wretched verse of Sternhold and Hopkins's Old Version (1562) of the metrical psalms, but also to the custom of singing the tunes at a funereal pace: the clerk first reading and the people then singing one line at a time.

This laboured progress through verse after verse of stumbling doggerel was rendered even more lugubrious by the introduction and conclusion of each line with a long "gathering" note. Just how long that note could be is evident from the instruction in a late-17th-century manual that the length of the breve should be equivalent to "eight pulses at the wrist of a person in good health and temper".

"'Tis sad to hear what whining, toting, yelling or screeking there is in many country congregations," wrote Thomas Mace, a lay clerk of Trinity College, Cambridge, in 1676; and many people agreed.

"Whining and screeking": Village Choir (1847), by Thomas Webster

IT had not always been thus. When the old metrical psalm tunes were first introduced in England by Protestant exiles returning from the Continent, Queen Elizabeth is alleged to have referred to them as "those Geneva jigs", a comment that casts an interesting light on how, for example, *The Old Hundredth* must have originally been sung.

Tate and Brady's New Version of the Psalms went some way to unlocking church singing from its 17th-century straitjacket. Tate claimed that the lack of singable tunes in the Old Version had been part of the problem. After its publication, the New Version acquired a series of supplements, each introducing new tunes. These included *Hanover* (originally set to Psalm 149, but now usually sung to Robert Grant's majestic version of Psalm 104, "O worship the King all glorious above"); and *St Anne* (set to Tate's Psalm 42, "As pants the hart", but now invariably sung to Isaac Watts's version of Psalm 90, "O God our help in ages past").

Another reason for the low standard of music was the dreadful verse the congregation had to sing. Neither Sternhold nor Hopkins was a competent versifier. In the New Version not every psalm is good verse, but comparing Tate's version of Psalm 34 ("Through all the changing scenes of life") with Thomas Sternhold's shows the difference. Take, for example, verse 5. Sternhold wrote:

> *Fear the Lord all ye his saints,*
> *Who is a mighty king:*
> *For they that fear the living Lord*
> *Are sure to lack nothing.*

Nahum Tate's familiar version is:

> *Fear him, ye saints, and you will then*
> *Have nothing else to fear;*
> *Make you his service your delight,*
> *Your wants shall be his care.*

The last two are elegant lines, graceful in sound and sense, whereas Sternhold's lame diction cannot be uttered or sung without a lowering of the spirits. However, it is for his "Christmas Hymn" that Tate is now best remembered. But, for all its being one of the first non-psalms authorised for use in church, "While shepherds watched" was not the start of something new. It was not a forerunner of the great tradition of 18th- and 19th-century hymnody. It was the last example, and perhaps the best, of a tradition that was falling out of use: the literal, biblical paraphrase.

Biblical paraphrase had its roots in the pre-Reformation Church, and provided the laity with a vernacular version of the Scriptures, usually in verse. What was new, though not applied to the "Christmas Hymn", was

Tate's insistence that, in verse written to be sung for worship, literary excellence and freshness of language should outweigh a slavish adherence to the Bible. In his version of Psalm 42, "As pants the hart for cooling streams, When heated in the chase", he introduced a wholly new element: the idea that the deer was hunted. The psalm simply has: "As the hart panteth after water brooks".

He and his co-author Nicholas Brady were criticised by some for being unfaithful to the text. But gradually the New Version gained popularity, though it never entirely replaced Sternhold and Hopkins. As late as the mid-19th century, Old and New Versions were still being bound together as supplements to the Bible and the Book of Common Prayer. They remained until the 20th century, the only authorised "hymn" books of the Church of England. Not even *Hymns Ancient and Modern* attained this official status.

That spirit of cautious conservatism preserved Tate and Brady's work for years after it had been superseded by popular, unauthorised hymnody. Even during Tate's lifetime, his attempts to loosen the grip of formal psalmody were being overtaken by unofficial publications. It is in these that the true beginnings of English hymnody can be found.

At that time England did not lack writers of fine religious verse. George Herbert, Richard Baxter, Henry Vaughan, Richard Crashaw, Samuel Grossman, John Austin, Thomas Ken, Joseph Addison and supremely, Isaac Watts all wrote poems that were either intended to be sung as hymns or, during Tate's lifetime, were adapted for that purpose. They contributed to Anglican and Nonconformist worship that balance of personal devotion and sound doctrine that became the basis of the best in English hymnody.

As for composers, Orlando Gibbons in the earlier years of the 17th century had contributed 15 tunes to Wither's *Hymns and Songs of the Church* (1623), a book suppressed by the intervention of the Company of Stationers, which had an interest in the sales of the Old Version. "Forth in thy name, O Lord I go" and "Jesu, grant me this, I pray" are two of the eight hymns still sung to Gibbons's tunes. And in the Restoration period Jeremiah Clarke wrote beautiful melodies, among them *Bishopthorpe*, now set to "Immortal love, for ever full". The Church of England, hidebound by its fear of any departure from biblical text, did not make official use of this treasury of words and music available to it from the 17th century. It was the Nonconformist Churches, and particularly Methodism, that kept English hymnody alive and well.

Tate and Brady's New Version stood between the death of the old tradition with its roots in Calvin's Geneva, and the birth of a more gracious and fluent style. But not until the publication of *Hymns Ancient and Modern* in 1861 did Anglicanism in this country discover what it had been missing.

(2002)

Time of rites in turmoil

Christmas has long been a focus for disputes,
says **William Whyte**

AH, Christmas: a time of celebration, good food, and epic family rows. As any fan of *EastEnders* knows, nothing makes the festive season more special than a really bitter argument. Over the years, 25 December has brought murder, suicide, assault and battery, and a whole host of other gifts to Albert Square.

The worst of it all is that, however exaggerated it may seem, the soap opera's bleak vision of mid-winter turns out not to be so far away from the truth. Divorce rates soar after Christmas, as couples rush to confirm a split that developed over the break.

What is true for families is also true for churches. Indeed, the quarrels that often occur at Christmas can make the petty disputes of the rest of the year seem inconsequential. Freighted as it is with all manner of emotional significance, the most minor changes to a special service or an ostensibly long-standing tradition threaten to spark the ecclesiastical equivalent of a civil war: rival factions each contend for control of the Christingle, or insist on their version of the nine lessons and carols.

If this is the case when it comes to apparently trivial issues, then it does not require too great a leap of imagination to see what trouble a more significant upheaval might cause. And, of course, we do not just have to imagine what this might be like. In the decade between 1549 and 1559, the Church suddenly, radically, and controversially changed its liturgy four times, and, in so doing, made the celebration of Christmas a particularly significant focus for discontent.

CHRISTMAS was not always important. In the Early Church, it was the Epiphany that mattered most in winter — and presumably caused the majority of fights. But, in the Middle Ages, Christ's mass came to assume an almost overwhelming importance, as it accreted innumerable customs of its own.

By about 1500, almost every parish in England would have experienced a similar December: fasting through Advent, followed by a celebration. On Christmas Eve, churches and houses alike were decorated with evergreen plants. On Christmas Day, the Sarum Use prescribed three masses, the first starting before dawn and lit by candles specially bought for the occasion.

The solemnity of the Latin service, the brightly lit and brightly coloured church, the songs, the processions, the invocations of the saints, and the reading of the genealogy of Christ from the rood loft: all these marked the birth of Jesus and the start of a huge party. Outside the church, people broke their fast with a banquet — the first of many, in a festival that might last for the Octave or for the 12 days of Christmas, and which could continue right up to Candlemas at the start of February.

Inevitably, not everyone felt that all was well with this combination of religion and high spirits. The pious were shocked at the drunken antics that invariably accompanied these celebrations. The civil authorities regularly had to deal with problems of public order. There were petty squabbles aplenty, as individuals and groups competed to take centre-stage. But it is hard not to feel that Christmas was one of the moments when sacred and secular time actually came together, and the community celebrated as much in church as out of it.

ALL of this changed with the Reformation, or, more precisely, with the imposition of the 1549 Prayer Book. This rupture did not emerge out of nothing. The break with Rome in the early 1530s and the creation of a vernacular liturgy in the mid-1540s each reflected a serious attack on traditional religion.

None the less, the accession of Edward VI in 1547 increased the pace and scale of reform exponentially. That year, a series of injunctions outlawed many of the commonplace practices of parish life. Images were to be removed from church and destroyed. The use of candles was reduced. Processions were prohibited, and bells were not to be rung. A new liturgy was to be created — one that was not open to the sorts of superstition that the reformers believed had characterised popular belief for so long.

That new liturgy was promulgated in 1549 as the Book of Common Prayer. It finally fully replaced the old rites with a new one. What is more, the old services were not simply to be discontinued: the old service books were actually to be burnt by Christmas Day. Royal proclamations, ecclesiastical visitations, Acts of Parliament, and the whole force of the Tudor state were deployed to ensure uniformity.

Not surprisingly, there was resistance. In June 1549, there was a rebellion in the West Country, led by people unable to accept these innovations. The new liturgy, they said, "was but lyke a Christmas game". In other words, the defenders of tradition believed that the reforms were actually secularising worship, inappropriately bringing the celebrations that should be kept outside the church into the service itself. In particular, they objected to the practice of having men and women approach the altar on separate sides of the church, seeing this as comically close to the sorts of country dances that marked the yuletide season.

Neither argument nor rebellion could halt the reforms, however. Even in Morebath, a little Devon village near the heart of the West Country revolt, the decision was taken to sell the altar cloths to buy a copy of the new Prayer Book. Christmas 1549 was consequently unlike any that had gone before it. In almost every parish, the evergreens were absent, the images were whitewashed or destroyed, candles were removed, and the processions were ended. The church was quieter than it had been before. Bells were silenced, and, as Eamon Duffy points out in *The Stripping of the Altars* (Yale, 1992), the switch from Latin to English rendered the musical repertoire of the Church obsolete. Choirs now had nothing to sing.

Outside, the festivities continued, but shorn of its Octave and much of its solemnity, Christmas inside the church must have seemed a pale shadow for many congregations.

AS a result, the traditional Christmas went underground. Some parishes, many families, and a number of Oxford and Cambridge colleges celebrated secret masses. Others reinterpreted the Prayer Book, treating it as though it were just the mass in English.

So the government hit back: not just by punishing offenders, but by producing a still more severe liturgy that was simply not open to any such interpretation. The revised Prayer Book was published at the end of October 1552, and for most parishes, Christmas would have been the first significant event marked with this new form of worship.

The priest now stood at the north end of a wooden table, instead of facing eastwards towards a stone altar. He no longer wore vestments, but was robed in a simple surplice. There was only one communion service — and any bread and wine left over was to be taken home by the officiant and consumed as though it had not been consecrated. This was about as far away from the old idea of Christ's mass as could possibly be imagined.

YET this new service did not last long. The death of Edward VI and the accession of the Catholic Mary I in 1553 ensured that there was only ever one Christmas celebrated according to the rites of the previous year's new Prayer Book. Mary was determined to roll back the Reformation — and so the festivities of 1553 were all meant to be in Latin, a revival of the old Sarum liturgy. The evidence suggests that this was a popular move. Indeed, many congregations went even further than the Queen intended, restoring things such as the Christmas tradition of decorating the church with evergreens, something even the Catholic hierarchy now looked on with suspicion.

It was not possible to eradicate reform completely. In many parishes, there was continuing battle between priest and congregation, Protestant and Catholic. Bishops even demanded to know whether any good singer, "since the setting forth and renewing of the old service in the Latin tongue, absent and withdraw himself from the choir". When the Catholic controversialist and Chancellor of Wells, Roger Edgeworth, came to preach in Bristol, in the midst of all this change, he showed that he was all too well aware of the problems. "Here among you in this city some will hear mass, some will hear none ... some will be shriven, some will not ... some will pray for the dead, some will not. I hear of much dissension among you."

ALTHOUGH most congregations probably welcomed the return to tradition, many individuals did not — and some did all they could to frustrate this Catholic revival. Mary was thus able to compel conformity, but never succeeded in enforcing uniformity.

Worse was to follow. Although Queen Elizabeth I initially retained the Latin rite on her accession in 1558, the new Book of Common Prayer of 1559 brought about another change in religious practice. Back came the vernacular, out went the altar. But this was a more conservative version of reform than the 1552 Prayer Book, not least in its insistence that the priest should be robed in appropriate vestments. The Christmas communion service of 1559 must thus have felt rather as though the congregation had been transported back a decade, and that the reforms of 1552 and 1553 had never happened.

The truth was, though, that time could not be turned back, and that this attempt at compromise did not satisfy anyone — not even the Queen who had insisted on it. She was a far more conservative figure: one who claimed that she "differed very little" from Roman Catholics, and who insisted on keeping a crucifix and silver candles on her private altar.

For her Protestant advisers, in contrast, the new Prayer Book did not go far enough, and another wave of iconoclasm swept across the country as a result. Other "godly" reformers went further still, increasingly doubtful of the veracity of any written liturgy, much less formal prayers.

Catholics could never accept anything less than the Latin mass. Ten years later, another rebellion — this time in the north — revealed just how strong these traditionalists still were, as the old ways and old church furnishings made a brief but telling comeback.

EVENTUALLY, as Judith Maltby has shown in her *Prayer Book and People* (Cambridge, 1998), the 1559 service was accepted by a majority as the right and proper way to worship God. Within a generation, indeed, it became the tradition — one that parishes sought to perpetuate entirely unchanged from one year to the next.

Yet the controversies of the 1540s and 1550s did not go away. In making one change, further changes became possible, with only unanimity an impossibility thereafter. Increasingly, this meant that Christmas itself became a matter of debate. For the Laudians of the early 17th century, it was vital to rediscover the older spirit of Christmas, the one that had been lost in the Reformation. Not for nothing did Laud's own college — St John's in Oxford — stage a celebration of Christmas in 1607 which lasted from All Souls' Day until the start of Lent. Complete with a play, ribald songs, and the election of a "Christmas Prince", it was a little glimpse of the olden times.

For the Puritans, by contrast, it was precisely this sort of behaviour which made the whole season itself seem dubious: the relic of a superstitious, papistical past. Little wonder that Christmas was banned by the Puritan Parliament in 1647, and covertly celebrated by High Anglicans until the Restoration of 1660 (see p. 186, "Christmas: why the ban didn't work").

IN 1662, yet another new Prayer Book produced what was meant to be yet another final settlement. It actually drove thousands out of the Church, as many Protestants refused to accept the set prayers and formal liturgies it imposed. Christmas, again, was a point of dissension. The Prayer Book set aside a special service for the day, but Puritans refused to accept such a dangerously Catholic practice. As late as the mid-18th century, indeed, Quakers condemned the Christmas pudding as "an invention of the scarlet Whore of Babylon, an hodge podge of superstition, Popery, the Devil and all his works". If this was true of a sweetmeat, then one can easily imagine what was thought of a Christmas Day communion service.

Two hundred years later, in 1928, a further attempt at resolution was made in a disputed revision: passed by the Church, but rejected by Parliament. In 1966, there were more reforms, and in 1980 the Alternative Service Book was published, only to be replaced by Common Worship in 2000.

More importantly still, individual churches have continued to do exactly what they did in the 16th century: pick and choose among the texts to find something that seems to suit. Then, as now, this irritates the authorities. Then, as now, it leads to rows — and never more than at Christmas.

But that, in a way, is what Christmas is for: to make us focus on what matters — and what does not. And for the Church of England, what does not matter is uniformity. We have never had it, and we never will. Or, leastways, we will not have it so long as we remain alive. It means crossness and difficulties, and it will doubtless result in people's not speaking to one another because of quarrels over the festive season. But that is a small price to pay for freedom. Happy Christmas.

(2011)

We are all made for sharing

It really is about the present. **Jane Williams** considers
the true gifts of Christmas

"'CHRISTMAS won't be Christmas without any presents,' said Jo." So begins one of my favourite books, *Little Women,* by Louisa May Alcott. The March family are poor this Christmas, even poorer than usual, and the prospect of a Christmas with no presents is a real one. Each of the four girls in the family has at least one thing that she was desperately hoping for at Christmas. Their wants seem very modest compared to the huge pile of presents that many children in Britain expect for Christmas; but Jo's despairing exclamation would be echoed by many — Christmas is really about presents.

What the March girls learn is that although presents are, indeed, a vital part of Christmas, giving them can be as much fun as getting them. On Christmas morning, they hear of a family even worse off than themselves, so poor that they don't even have food, let alone gifts, and the girls decide to take them their own breakfast, or at least part of it.

The awed gratitude with which they are met in the desperate household they visit feels like the greatest gift of Christmas. They know perfectly well that they will be only slightly hungry because of what they have done, but that the family they go to will remember their food and warmth and care as a Christmas miracle.

And, of course, when they get home, there *are* presents. Perhaps not as grand and expensive as they had hoped for, but suddenly wholly satisfactory. Although this may mark the formal end of the Christmas episode in the book, the consequences of that discovery about Christmas are far reaching. Beth, in particular, never forgets what she has seen in the Hummel household that morning, and she continues to visit regularly. She catches a terrible disease from the poor children, which leads, eventually, to her death.

But even this is not the end of that Christmas, because it is Beth's illness and death, at least in part, that lead Jo to abandon the stories of fantasy and violence that she has been writing, and write instead about reality; about the world that she actually knows.

CHRISTMAS *is* about presents, giving them and getting them, but it is also about death and about reality. Implicit in the birth of Jesus is his death — all the Gospels are clear that that is what he came for.

Implicit, too, in this birth is the creation of reality. John is, of course, the Gospel that makes this most explicit. What is given to us at Christmas is the source of all that is. Many will reject it and prefer their fantasies, but the fact remains that only in Christ does life come into being; only in Christ are we part of God's creation. We can choose to live constantly regretting the presents we haven't got, or fantasising about the presents we would like, while all the time ignoring the gift God holds out to us at Christmas.

Luke's Christmas story does not lay the options out so starkly, but they are still there: gift, life and death. In Luke, we see God the Son, laid in a manger. He is to be food for the world, the source of its nourishment and strength. But, while we thank God with joy, our imaginations should be asking: "Why a manger? Why an animal trough as the place from which the world will be fed? Why are shepherds the first ones to hear about what God has given us for Christmas?"

Luke's is a subversive Gospel of humility. The gift is magnificent and beyond price, but it may be that we will turn up our noses at it because we don't like the wrapping paper. Perhaps we will tell ourselves, as we turn to our groaning tables, that we do not need such plain and basic food. Most of us are already planning our post-Christmas diet, even as we overeat now. No more food from God, thank you very much. But Luke knows, as John does, that if we reject this food, then we reject God. He knows, too, how tempted we are to turn away from such a God, a God who really does not know how to behave as we know he should.

Matthew, too, weaves together glory and humility at the birth of the Son at Christmas. His conception is shrouded in mystery, but not numinous mystery, simply shameful and distressing mystery. His birth is marked by a star, and by a visit from three romantic strangers. But their presence leads to fear and death and disruption, and their gifts are troubling and significant.

Mark, of course, wastes no time at all on the birth of Jesus, but plunges immediately into the ministry of the suffering Messiah.

WITH the unerring instincts of born fantasists, most of us go straight for the trappings of the Christmas story, and studiously avoid looking directly at the life-giving, death-bearing gift of God at Christmas. We go for the sweet, woolly lambs; we go for the ox and donkey, with their adoring brown eyes. We go for kings, splendidly dressed, with gifts in gorgeous boxes. Above all, we go for a plump, smiling baby, safe and healthy and well cared for.

But surely the question that shouts through Christmas is: "Why? What on earth is God up to?" If this is indeed God's gift to us of life and food and salvation and restoration, is this really the best way to get it to us? A baby's life is always fragile. Conception and birth are dangerous moments, even now. Two thousand years ago, the chances of survival were even smaller. Why does God choose such a very vulnerable means to come among us?

And then there are all those years in which we hear nothing at all of Jesus: years and years of ordinary, unremarked life. Such a strange investment of something so valuable, and for what? For a couple of years, perhaps, of public ministry.

What's more, partly because God oddly chose not to be born to rich and influential people, nobody much hears the Son's message. Those who do, largely reject it, apart from a handful of baffled men and women, and even they give up when their leader is put to death. For, of course, that is the culmination of it all; that is what the Son is born for; that is the point of God's Christmas present to us — Jesus's death on the cross. You might as well put the present straight in the bin, if you are only prepared to look at the sweet little baby, and not at the man dying on the cross.

This is not how we would choose to save the world. Has God got it horribly wrong? Or is there some vital clue in this strange and terrible present? The fact of the matter is that most of the ways in which we choose to save the world simply compound the problem.

We fight violence with violence, and more violence is born. We improve our health and wealth in the rich world, but we need the poor world to stay poor if our standard of living is to be maintained. We are comfortable and entertained beyond the wildest dreams of our ancestors, but there are as many abused and neglected people as there ever were, and we need to turn to our computers and televisions for advice on how to live together and love one another.

Perhaps God's way is the only way that might actually change things. God comes just to be with us, living as vulnerably and hazardously as we do. When violence is done to him, he absorbs it, never returning it, even when it costs him his life.

He presents to us, simply, over and over again, the reality of God's love.

GOD made us; God lives our lives with us; God is our beginning and our end. Nothing we can do will change that. Nothing we can do will drive God away. When we think we pushed him out of our lives onto the cross, we find he has used our petty attempt at force to open his life up to even more, through the resurrection and the gift of the Spirit.

When the March girls discover that the joy of giving presents is as great as the pleasure of getting them, they are actually learning something about the baby in the manger. As they feed the hungry and care for the sick, they know something of God's pleasure in sharing his life with us. This sharing of what we have with others, so that we can be enriched by their life, is what we were made for.

Sharing involves risks, as Beth discovers. But not sharing in God's self-giving way in the world is far more risky, because it continues to build higher and higher the towering cities of our fantasy world, which is bound to topple into nothingness. Risk accepting God in exchange for nothing. Receive God's present of himself, and share it with others. It will last for life — and beyond.

(2003)

Bethlehem, Easter, 2002
by Pádraig Ó Tuama

Arrived, in a dark
pitching, two thousand and
two wintertimes ago.

Warmed by animal heat
and the nighttime sweat of
his exhausted mother

surrounded by angels,
singing peace and pleasure
to all who follow,

while timid shepherds bring
kind gifts — a lamb,
   a reassurance —
a gentle prophecy for
long years ahead.

And now, huddled in
the hidden corners
of nativity's cathedral

lie fighting men
and praying men,
warmed by each others' blood
and the nighttime sweat
of tired vigilance.

They are surrounded
by the keepers of Zion.
Those seen,
and those unseen.

And their harmony together
is found in rounds of fire
and occupation
seeing occupation
and resistance of each other.

Today, I saw a white clothed nun
scurry like a frightened animal
past a green cloaked tank.

Her prayers, I'm sure,
are ones for safety for two troubled
   peoples,
for quiet ambles round Monday
   morning markets,
for stars of promise to
shine again in Bethlehem.

(2013)

(from Sorry for Your Troubles,
Canterbury Press)

The gifts that we are asked to give away

Sister Wendy Beckett suggests where to look
to find joy at Christmas

CHRISTMAS is the only feast that comes to us clearly labelled: on the highest authority, we know that it is "tidings of great joy" (Luke 2.10). It is not, of course, the feast of the greatest joy. That will always be the resurrection, Easter; when Jesus, "our pioneer", as Hebrews calls him, takes us with him into heaven, and all the Father's desires have been fulfilled. But that greatest joy can happen only because of the first great joy of the birth. One joy is absolutely untarnished, complete: the joy that makes it possible is great indeed, but it is relative and strangely ambivalent.

Think of the shepherds, roused at night from their huddle over their watchfire, staggering to their feet in bewilderment at their angelic summons. What was their joy? At the stable, they were offered nothing that made any apparent change to their lives; no gift to take away; no life-transforming words. They saw what they were told they would see: an infant lying in a manger. What did they make of it? Did they realise that, from now on, God had become visible? That, from now on, human life, with its sorrows and frustrations, would be illuminated from within? That we were no more alone? Or did they come and look and go away again?

In after years, were they different — men of joy — or did it all seem like a collective dream, which led nowhere? Because God gives us grace, it does not follow of necessity that we are changed. Grace can lie inert in the soul. We who know what Christmas means can experience it, and yet see life no differently.

Was it joy for Mary and Joseph? Surely there was overwhelming joy for them both in the safe accomplishment of the holy birth. Mary, especially, must have longed to see the face of her divine child.

Yet they must also have felt a sense of crippling failure. For a man of Joseph's time to be unable to care for his family was a painful humiliation, yet here was the child entrusted to him in a vision, come at last into the world, and his father could not provide even the minimum of warmth and comfort. The stable sounds romantic, but it must have been wretchedly draughty and chilly: no water at hand, no heat, no access to food. . .

We know that Mary had come with swaddling bands, but what else had they to welcome Jesus? They had only their love and their grief at their poverty. It boded ill for the future, showing them that the world into which the Word of God had so generously come was not a receptive place. Soon Mary would be told that "thine own soul a sword shall pierce" (Luke 2.35), but the sharp cut of that sword had already wounded her. Her child was to die, rejected by his people, and the sorrowful foreknowledge of that is implicit in the conditions of the Lord's birth.

Did our Lord feel it? Or was it, for him at least, joy? We Christians have never wholly managed to understand that Jesus was total man, "like us in all things, sins alone excepted". So he was a total baby. There was no loving recognition of his mother; no blessings for the shepherds; only the natural actions of a newborn. The human mind cannot fathom the sacrificial love of a God that could condense his immensity into the extreme limitations of what it means to be a real baby. Jesus did not pretend, did not stay hidden and adult within the semblance of neonatal incapacity. No, he surrendered to the true helplessness of a stage we have all lived through and forgotten, and he did this because he loved us.

So, then, joy for us, great joy: theologically, we have no doubt; yet, emotionally, this feast is strongly nuanced. On one level, nobody could fail to delight in children at their nativity plays, at cribs, and (within reason) carols, at the beauty of church services. Yet this great day brings with it difficulties. Many people are exhausted by the sheer work involved: the cooking, the shopping, the socialising, often with relatives with whom they have little in common. The difficulties exist, and we cannot magic them away with spiritual thoughts.

Yet the essence of the incarnation is that everything has become a means to God. He is with us. He offers himself as Love. Accepting all that Christmas brings, good and bad — trusting to our Saviour to make the good something that we give to others, and the bad something that we are content to bear in peace — is a living affirmation of what Christmas means.

But, if we desire to understand this joy at a deeper level, then let us try, even for a few moments, to find a place apart. (No one will miss us for so short a time.) Be still; let the wonder become real to you; accept the child as Lord; and thank him for such inconceivable love. Let Jesus give himself. Then go back to the festivities and give him to others.

(2004)

Christ's annual sun day

The date of Christmas can be traced back 2600 years,
suggests **David Keys**

EVIDENCE from classical and other ancient sources strongly suggests that the date and some aspects of the festival of Christmas had their origins up to 300 years before the birth of Christ. It has long been known that the decision to make 25 December Jesus's birthday was made by the Church under the influence of the fourth-century Roman Emperor Constantine. The date was chosen because the Emperor seems to have believed that the Roman sun god and Christ were virtually the same — and the sun's birthday had been decreed as 25 December some 50 years earlier by one of Constantine's predecessors, the Emperor Aurelian.

Aurelian, in turn, seems to have chosen 25 December because, since Julius Caesar's calendar reforms of 46 BC, that date had been fixed as the official winter solstice, even though the real date for the solstice in Caesar's time was 23 December. Scholars have therefore always been puzzled as to why 25 December was chosen. The sun's birthday was almost certainly first allocated to the ancient equivalent of 25 December back in the first half of the third century BC, when 25 December really was the mid-winter solstice, and therefore marked the sun's annual rebirth — the day on which the sun began once again to climb higher in the sky.

It is likely that one particular event triggered the whole 25 December tradition. That event was the consecration of the Ancient World's largest sun-god statue — the 34-metre, 200-tonne Colossus of Rhodes. The probable consecration date was 283 BC — and, in that year in Rhodes, the solstice occurred around sunrise on 25 December.

Artist's impression of the Colossus of Rhodes

The Colossus was a giant statue of the Greek sun god, Helios, a deity who became associated in the Greek pagan philosophical tradition with ethical values. Plato, in his *Republic*, portrayed Helios as the symbolic child of the concept of goodness.

The date of the consecration of the Colossus of Rhodes was probably preserved by academics in Rhodes or Alexandria, and is likely to have been passed to Julius Caesar by the Hellenistic Egyptian scientists who advised him on his calendrical reforms.

After Caesar's time, the sheer size of the Roman imperial system meant that its unity could never be taken for granted. By the third century AD, emperors were increasingly using the cult of the sun god as a unifying force within the Empire. By the later third century, the sun — by now referred to as Sol Invictus (the unconquered sun) — was beginning to be seen in quasi-monotheistic terms. Other gods were regarded by some as either subservient to the solar deity, or even as different facets of him.

THE quantum leap forward, as far as "proto-Christmas" was concerned, came in AD 274, when the Emperor Aurelian declared that Sol Invictus was "Lord of the Roman Empire". The promotion of the sun god to this supreme position occurred because Aurelian believed that Sol Invictus had helped him defeat Middle Eastern rebels who were threatening the unity of the empire. In gratitude, the Emperor built a massive temple in Rome in the sun's honour. In it, Aurelian installed two large cult statues seized from the rebel capital, Palmyra — now a ruined city in the Syrian desert.

One was an Eastern sun god, Shamash-Helios, while the other was either the rebels' chief god, Bel, or more likely his associate, the partly solar deity Yarhibol, who was depicted with solar rays emanating from his head. The new temple in Rome was consecrated on 25 December — the day that Aurelian thought was the sun god's birthday.

About half a century after the consecration of the temple, the first pro-Christian Roman emperor, Constantine, merged the sun cult with Christianity, implying that Christ was the earthly manifestation of Sol Invictus. The twenty-fifth of December became Christmas. The day of the sun god had already become Christ's holy day, Sunday. The Christian "man-god" was referred to as the Sun of Justice, and, in a mosaic in the crypt of St Peter's Cathedral in the Vatican, Jesus was — and still is — portrayed adorned with sun rays and riding in a chariot — just like Sol Invictus.

The emperor Constantine appears to have seen his divine patron — initially Sol Invictus, but later Christ — in much the same way as Aurelian had viewed the sun. The imagery of Christ, like that of the ruler cults of the Hellenistic and Roman worlds, owed much to solar iconography.

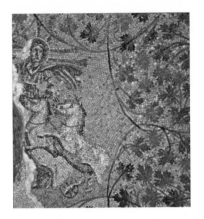 

Above left: Christ the sun – Christ depicted using the imagery associated with Sol Invictus, the sun god, with rays emanating from his head and riding in a chariot, from a mid-third-century mosaic in the crypt of St Peter's in the Vatican

Above right: Roman Imperial silver disc of Sol Invictus (third century)

JESUS'S real date of birth is not known — although various pre-fourth-century traditions and computations put it either in the January–March period, or in November. One thing is sure, however: he was not born on 25 December; but the ancient sun god's association with goodness and ethical values, as well as the sun's gift of light, warmth, and life, eased the transition from pagan to Christian "Christmas Day".

It was the people of Rhodes who opted to build their Colossus, and so inaugurate the 25-December tradition. The bronze giant had been built in the early third century BC as a gesture of gratitude to the patron deity of the island of Rhodes, Helios. The rich but tiny island state had just defeated a takeover bid by one of Alexander the Great's immediate successors, backed by a 40,000-strong army. Siege equipment worth the modern equivalent of £75 million was sold, and the money raised was used to construct the Colossus.

It survived until 226 BC, when an earthquake caused it to collapse. The Rhodians wanted to rebuild it — but the Oracle of Delphi appears to have warned them not to, and so its massive remains lay there until AD 654, when an Arab scrap merchant bought it and sold the bronze to clients across the Middle East. Not a fragment has survived. But its legacy — 25 December — has fared better.

(2007)

185

Christmas: why the ban didn't work

The Puritans should have known that they could not hold back the people's celebrations, says **William Whyte**

THE diarist John Evelyn found himself a prisoner on 25 December 1657, detained for attending church. He was in the chapel of Exeter House, on the north side of the Strand, when he was arrested. The sermon had ended, and the priest was distributing communion, when soldiers burst in. "These wretched miscreants", he later wrote, "held their muskets against us as we came up to receive the Sacred Elements, as if they would have shot us at the Altar."

Evelyn's offence was celebrating Christmas. This had been made illegal in 1647, and would not be permitted again until 1660, when the restoration of the monarchy also brought about the restitution of the Church of England and its traditional rites and ceremonies.

As the soldiers who arrested Evelyn made clear, Christmas was proscribed for three reasons. In the first place, it was maintained, the festival was "super-stitious". After all, the Bible gave no sanction to it, nor any date for it. Second, such celebrations involved using the Book of Common Prayer, which had also been outlawed, and was nothing "but the *Masse* in *English*". Finally, Christmas could act as a rallying point for Royalists: it was politically, as well as theologically, unthinkable.

This Puritan attack came as something of a surprise. When the Civil War began, few could have imagined that its victims would include Christmas. Christmas was a big deal in Early Modern England, marked by religious worship and secular celebration. Hospitality at Christmas was one of the key duties of any gentleman — the obscure Roman Catholic layman Nicholas Wadham was one of many celebrated for keeping their home "an inn at all times, but a court at Christmas".

Even English Puritans of the early 17th century tended to observe this practice. In the 1630s, as Ronald Hutton has shown, a Bristol shopkeeper who ignored the law and opened up on Christmas Day escaped prosecution precisely because she was so unusual. Her religious protest was written off as simple eccentricity.

But the victory of the puritanical parliamentary forces in the Civil War changed all that. The public celebration of Christmas was outlawed: churches were ordered to be closed, and worship was forbidden. Initially, there appears to have been some resistance to this. Christmas Day 1647 was marked by rioting at Ipswich, Norwich, and Canterbury — where a full-scale Royalist uprising began.

None the less, the power of the state — and, more particularly, of the army — soon proved too great. Evelyn's diary, for example, shows that he was simply unable to find a service to go to until 1656 — and he was, of course, detained for unlawful worship just a year later. In that sense, at least, the Puritan attack on Christmas seems to have worked.

OUTSIDE the churches, however, the spirit of Christmas was harder to crack. All the evidence suggests that the season continued to be marked by more secular celebrations. In 1650, the hard-line Puritan MP Sir Henry Mildmay complained that he had witnessed "very wilful and strict observation of the day commonly called Christmas Day". Shops were shut, he lamented, and there were "contemptuous speeches" in defence of the festival.

Likewise, six years later, in 1656, Ezekiel Woodward admitted that "the people go on holding fast to their heathenish customs and abominable idolatries, and think they do well". Even in puritanical Cambridge, Francis Throckmorton gave presents to his servants, and paid musicians to sing carols. Throughout the country, Puritans repeatedly protested that they were kept awake by Christmas revellers. Court records reveal that alehouses

Frontispiece to John Taylor's pamphlet "The Vindication of Christmas" (1652)

and inns were still being used by those seeking to mark the day.

Ironically, what the Puritans had done was not only unpopular; it was entirely counterproductive. They knew what they were against, without being entirely clear what they wanted to offer in its place. Their religious reform did little or nothing to prevent secular excess, while actually condemning many faithful Christians. The result was a situation in which pious people were actually prevented from attending church, and arrested if they took communion.

THE first legal Christmas, in 1660, was greeted with great enthusiasm. Although much evidence is lacking, it would seem that the secular celebrations were now given full rein. Not only could shops and markets shut; they were required to do so. Not only could people eat and drink to excess; they were positively encouraged to.

Christmas traditions that the Puritans had condemned as idolatrous or wasteful were now, no doubt, seen as signs of loyalty to the restored monarchy and the re-established Church of England. The "good ribs of beef roasted and mince pies ... and plenty of good wine" with which Samuel Pepys typically marked the festival were symbols not only of Christmas, but also of the return to right order of the nation as a whole.

These secular celebrations, however, were not nearly as important as the revived religious aspects of Christmas.

Image from "The examination and tryal of old Father Christmas", a pamphlet by Josiah King, first issued in 1653

It was the Church's worship that the Puritans had really objected to and punished. Eating, drinking, and making merry had continued throughout the ban. The link between Christmas and churchgoing was what the Puritans had most wanted to destroy: the "idolatrous" celebration of "Christ's Mass" was what they had hoped to end.

The fact that Christmas Day 1660 witnessed wide-open, well-decorated, and well-attended churches and cathedrals was sufficient proof of their failure. As for John Evelyn, he went to Westminster Abbey, where he was thrilled to find that "The Service was also in the old Cathedrall Musique."

To be sure, not everyone was pleased — nor was everyone as excited. Samuel Pepys, for one, slept through the afternoon service on Christmas Day 1660. Nor was the enthusiasm that greeted this first Christmas always sustained. John Evelyn, indeed, recorded on 25 December 1661 that "ill weather kept me from Church". A year later, he noted that the curate had preached on "how to behave ourselves in festival rejoicing".

Clearly, the Church still had some doubts about Christmas merrymaking. None the less, no one seriously suggested a return to prohibition. Indeed, with time, even some Puritans seem to have reconsidered their views. The devout Dissenting minister Ralph Josselin recorded on 25 December 1667 that he had "Preached and feasted my tenants and all my children with joy."

The whole experience should have taught the Church a valuable lesson. Excluding people in the hope that they will go away and become better does not work. It is only by including them that any progress can be made.

(2007)

The rumour of angels

Simon Jenkins goes in search of celestial beings in Scripture and popular culture

An angel of the Lord appeared to them, and the glory of the Lord shone around them, and they were terrified.

Luke 2.9

THE golden icons of the Eastern Church are famously still; Christ and the saints gaze out at us from images that contain no flicker of movement. But one great exception is the icon of the Annunciation, which is frequently given pride of place on the royal doors of the icon screen. The Angel Gabriel enters from the left in strong forward motion, his wings flexed, his legs stretching his robes, his knees bent, his feet practically running. He is an angel in a hurry.

Meanwhile, Mary turns where she sits, her hand flies up in surprise, and she almost drops her spindle of scarlet thread. Gabriel has just swooped down from heaven with the most joyous news ever told, and the bright colours and quick movements of the icon buzz with it.

THE Angel Gabriel has always known how to make an entrance. I first noticed this when I was about four, watching the nativity play at my Presbyterian church. The angel arrived for his big scene by being thrust through a doorway and onto the stage by an unseen Sunday-school teacher. Over the door was a naked lightbulb which pinged on, suddenly lighting up little Gabriel's tinfoil wings, the tinsel halo, the voluminous white nightie.

The juxtaposition of the lightbulb and an angel brings to mind the theologian Rudolf Bultmann's assertion that "it is impossible to use electric light and the wireless and at the same time believe in the New Testament world of spirits and miracles". Bultmann, like the Sadducees of Jesus's day, did not have a lot of time for angels.

Indeed, Matthew and Luke's nativity accounts have come in for a fair bit of this kind of "demythologisation" in recent years. And these stories positively crackle with angels. In addition to Mary's encounter with Gabriel, there is an angel to announce John the Baptist's conception; an angel to urge Joseph to marry Mary; an angel to address a band of stunned shepherds; a whole multitude to sing a burst of praise; and an angel to tell Joseph to return from Egypt.

THIS clustering of angels (the English word is derived from the Greek for "messenger") at the opening of the Gospels tells us that the event to come

189

falls outside of normal human experience. The angelic company turns an ordinary Bethlehem hillside into a temporary outpost of heaven, saturated with glory, worship, and divine presence.

This event creates ripples in time which expand across the whole surface of Scripture. They reach back to the fugitive Jacob on his lonely hillside at Bethel, trying to get some sleep with only a stone for a pillow, and his dream of a ladder up to heaven on which angels ascend and descend.

The ripples extend to the lowly parents of Samson, to whom an angel appears in a field and tells them they will at last have a child. When they ask the angel's name, his reply is utterly disarming: "Why do you ask my name, seeing it is wonderful?" The ripples of Bethlehem find Isaiah, who sees the Lord surrounded by the seraphim (angels with six wings) crying "Holy, holy holy!" as the temple fills with smoke.

Angels answering to a wide variety of description and modus operandi fill the Scriptures from beginning to end. We see angels riding horses, ascending on flames, hurling millstones, opening locked doors, delivering cakes, carrying pots of ink, and striking down armies.

There are terrifying angels, with faces like lightning, feet like polished brass, and voices like the sound of a multitude. Rather than "wings of drifted snow", the angels on Jacob's ladder ascend like builders, by climbing. But the angels of Revelation fly in abundance, announcing ruin and redemption.

IN the 2000 years since the canon of Scripture closed, the theological and artistic response to the breadth and depth of the angelic world has been hugely varied. In Jewish tradition, from the time that the book of Daniel was written, there was a huge expansion in speculation about angels. Exegetes became preoccupied with calculating their size — one tradition claimed that an angel, Sandalfon, was so much taller than other angels that it would take 500 years to walk the difference.

According to other rabbis, the angels defer to humans, waiting in silence for the people of Israel to recite the *shema* ("Hear, O Israel ...") before singing their own songs of praise.

Meanwhile, in the Byzantine world of the sixth century, the mystical writer Pseudo-Dionysius the Areopagite wrote a small book, *The Celestial Hierarchy*, which offers a detailed breakdown of the executive branch of heaven. Dionysius divides the angelic population into three hierarchies, each of which is subdivided into three ranks of angels.

The first hierarchy, which abides in the immediate presence of God for ever, includes seraphim, cherubim, and thrones. The second group, which is ruled by the first, includes dominions, powers, and authorities. And the third group, which rules over all human hierarchies, is made up of principalities, archangels, and angels.

It is obvious to a modern eye that *The Celestial Hierarchy* is a rather over-zealous attempt to get the divine bureaucracy into the kind of shape that a Byzantine potentate would appreciate. And, of course, it has been criticised for compromising the place of Christ as the mediator between God and humankind. Nevertheless, the idea took wing, and Christian thinkers throughout the Middle Ages began reshuffling heaven into different angelic departments.

Thomas Aquinas (among others, including Dante) followed Dionysius's ninefold scheme, but, in the end, all the speculation about the lives and habits of angels caused a backlash. The scholastics, it was said, had reduced themselves to arguing over angels dancing on the head of a pin, the criticism most wittily put by the English writer William Sclater in 1619, when he said that the philosophers spent their time arguing over "how many angels might sit on a needles point; and six hundred such like needlesse points".

PERHAPS the dead end of speculation about angels came in the 1960s and '70s, when the Swiss flying-saucer enthusiast Erich von Däniken produced a book, *Chariots of the Gods?*. He claimed that the vision of the cherubim in the opening chapters of Ezekiel — which includes shining creatures with four faces, wings, wheels full of eyes, and flashes of fire — were the prophet's attempt to describe a visiting spaceship, piloted by alien astronauts.

The story was splashed across the tabloids at the time, and generated further headlines when a NASA engineer, Josef F. Blumrich, set out to disprove von Däniken's theory, but ended up a convert. Blumrich decided that Ezekiel's creatures looked like a lunar lander he had designed a decade previously, and went on to produce detailed plans of the cherubim "mother ship" in his book, *The Spaceships of Ezekiel*.

ALTHOUGH the angel narratives of the Jewish and Christian Scriptures have been twisted into strange shapes in some corners of modern culture, they remain powerfully and positively symbolic. From Robbie Williams's hit single "Angels" to Antony Gormley's *Angel of the North*, the idea of angels offers a folkloric kind of hope that there is a beautiful world beyond ours: a perfect life beyond this one. "The rumour of angels", to borrow the sociologist Peter Berger's memorable book title, offers a point of contact between genuine faith and today's culture.

Certainly, at Christmas, the angels over that Bethlehem field, in their great and numinous flood of light and love, in their overwhelming heraldry of God, offer a meditation to balance against the horrors and uncertainties of modern life. All Christians are evangelical, in the wide and generous sense of inhabiting, celebrating, and sharing the evangel of Jesus. The song of the angels is a reminder to keep the *angelical* in the *evangelical*.

(2016)

191

The naming of names

Robin Gill explores the implications of parental identity
on birth certificates

*Joseph went to be registered with Mary, to whom he was engaged and
who was expecting a child. While they were there, the time came for her
to deliver her child.*

Luke 2.5-6

REGISTRATION for non-Romans in the Roman Empire was concerned
primarily with taxation rather than birth and identity. But, apart from that,
some of the mysteries surrounding the birth of Jesus do have odd symmetries
with complexities that surround birth registration today.

Various experts contributed to a recent symposium on birth registration
in the context of IVF and surrogacy. All were aware that, although the
formal questions asked on birth registration forms differ little today from
those that were first issued two centuries ago, actual practice is different.

Most significantly, two parents of the same sex can now be entered on a
birth certificate. For example, two men whose sperm have been mixed
together to enable an unnamed woman to conceive and give birth can now
be recorded on the resulting child's birth certificate. And two women, only
one of whom is genetically related to the child, can both be recorded, with
no mention of the male who provided the necessary sperm.

Elsewhere in the world there are so-called three-parent children (with
the third parent providing mitochondria): how have they been recorded?

FOR one of the lawyers who spoke at the symposium, there was no problem:
"Birth records are simply administrative evidence of a child's current legal
parentage. They are not, in and of themselves, legal determination of
parentage." From this perspective, there is nothing new about putative
fathers appearing on birth certificates when (with or without their
knowledge) some other male provided the sperm. The Archbishop of
Canterbury has just such a birth certificate. And adoptive parents have long
been able to add their names to birth certificates.

Another lawyer, who was also a family expert, was more ambivalent: "Is
it the registration of an event, a person, legal relationship, or a mixture of
all three?" A social worker also took a wider view of birth registration
beyond the narrowly legal: "Birth registration is an official record of our
parentage. Or is it? Which 'parents' shall it include: those who contributed

their genes to us, those who carried us in their wombs, or only those who are our legal parents?"

Significantly a donor-conceived person also contributed, and she asked: "What is a birth certificate for? Is it a record of a birth? An identity document? A legal statement of biological parentage?" Asking the question in this way points beyond intention to practicalities that many of us face at times, and their implications for family rights and entitlements, and for citizenship rights. Because my father and paternal grandfather were born in Gibraltar, I, my wife, and my children and their spouses can all claim citizenship there.

We now have full Gibraltar citizenship identity cards, which allow us to visit the monkeys at the top of the Rock without being charged (at least by the humans). Theoretically, the cards also allow us to travel around Europe without a passport (although I do not recommend this, even before Brexit, as few officials have ever heard of Gibraltar identity cards).

SOME New Testament scholars argue that there are hints in the Gospels about Jesus's birth identity, especially in Mark 6.3: "'Is not this the carpenter, the son of Mary and brother of James and Joses and Judas and Simon, and are not his sisters here with us?' And they took offence at him." What is the "offence" here? That a local man is teaching in the synagogue at Nazareth? But the previous verse says only that they were "astounded" by his teaching, rather than offended.

Or is that he has demonstrated "deeds of power", or that he claims to be a "prophet"? Possibly. But why did the offended people mention only his mother (and brothers and sisters), and not Joseph? Might it not be a question about his birth legitimacy that was causing such offence here? Local communities have long memories.

In addition, there is the well-known oddity of Matthew 1.16. Matthew goes to great lengths to trace the Davidic genealogy of Jesus through Joseph, rather than via Mary's family tree, concluding: "… Jacob the father of Joseph the husband of Mary, of whom Jesus was born, who is called the Messiah".

Matthew, of course, did believe that Mary was "with child from the Holy Spirit" (1.18), just as we affirm today in our Creeds. But his use of the word *parthenos*, or "virgin" — found in the later Greek version of Isaiah 7.14 rather than the Hebrew version's "young woman" — has been debated by scholars since Irenaeus and Origen.

A GENERATION ago, some theologians speculated about the possibility of parthenogenesis as a naturally occurring phenomenon. Since asexual reproduction is possible in plants and single-cell creatures, could more advanced forms of animal life also reproduce asexually? Worms chopped in half were often mentioned at this point.

Eventually, it dawned on most of us that any examples of naturally occurring parthenogenesis were entirely irrelevant to the birth of Jesus, born spontaneously of Mary. He would have had to be female, since Mary had no Y chromosomes.

Fortunately, the Creeds make no mention of chromosomes. I have always considered it anachronistic and impertinent to speculate about the origins of Jesus's Y chromosomes. Theologians need to tread carefully here, in order to avoid an account of Jesus that presents him as not fully human. Today, it also seems anachronistic and impertinent to enquire about the origin of a donor-conceived person's chromosomes or DNA, if he or she chooses not to enquire beyond the information given in the birth certificate.

Those people of Nazareth who were offended by Jesus obviously knew nothing about chromosomes or DNA, but their suspicions about his birth legitimacy (if that is what they were) seem equally impertinent.

BEYOND such impertinence, we might show compassion for those embarrassed about having non-standard birth certificates. And we might show understanding for those who love and care for children who are not genetically related to them, but whom they do wish publicly to affirm.

I have no idea how, or whether, this should involve a change in legislation, or what by-products such legislation might entail — although at least some consequences are already obvious. For example, the new practice of not naming sperm or gamete donors on birth certificates carries a risk, however small, of consanguinity. (That danger, of course, was there from the introduction of birth certificates, since some putative fathers named on them were not in fact the biological fathers.)

In addition, the 20th-century practice of anonymous sperm donation carried a similar danger of consanguinity (today, at least, regulated sperm or gamete donation in the UK can no longer be anonymous, although even now parents are not legally obliged to tell their children that their conception depended on such a donation). Lawyers will doubtless be alert to other off-target consequences, relating perhaps to inheritance or political rights; so I will trespass no further in this area.

But we can, in my view, avoid theological impertinence by going no further than Matthew in affirming that Mary was indeed "with child from the Holy Spirit". The doctrine of the Virgin Birth is surely an affirmation about God's unique initiative in Jesus Christ, rather than a statement about the origin of Jesus's Y chromosomes.

(2016)

A genealogy meets its end

Advent and Christmas services invariably leave out the long list of ancestors from the Gospel accounts.
Neil Patterson asks why this is

EACH year, we retell the Christmas story, most memorably in school nativity plays. Like most clergy, I suspect, as I hear the tinselled angels sing, I often reflect on how this coherent "story" is in fact a conflation of the infancy narratives of Matthew 12, and of Luke 13, given deeper meaning by the theological umbrella of John's preface. He was humbly born as one of us; God come down from heaven to save us. Bring on the turkey.

Yet even in those short chapters we seldom, if ever, read Matthew 1.1-17, or Luke 3.23-38, the purported genealogies of Jesus through Joseph. But the evangelists included them, and we ought at least to consider what they might mean to us today.

There are several possible reasons for this. We do not like reading long lists of Old Testament names. The lists are inconsistent. And I say "purported" above, because neither is actually the genealogy of Jesus himself, only Joseph, his foster-father. Perhaps we are afraid to emphasise earthly descent, in case we should be thought theologically unsound on his divine parentage. Or maybe they are just boring.

BUT it was not always so: witness the innumerable medieval illustrations and windows of the Tree of Jesse, a visual celebration of Jesus's descent from the father of King David. Therein lies, I suggest, the issue. For Matthew and Luke, the list of ancestors, like Jesus's birth in Bethlehem, was intended to emphasise his status as the rightful heir of the kings of old. This is not as implausible as it may seem; until the tenth century AD, the Jewish community in Babylon was led by an exilarch, believed to be directly descended from Zerubbabel.

Deep roots: the Tree of Jesse, from a 12th-century illuminated manuscript

And to some, it may still matter: a friend whose congregation included a member of our royal family recalls preaching a conventional sermon on Jesus, humbly born among us, and being told afterwards, "humbly born, but of royal descent". But to most of us today there is a certain awkwardness about the idea that Jesus may have been born "with a silver spoon in his mouth". It is deeply important that God became one of us, and, to an extent, that the genealogies back to David set him apart, born of a special and ancient family.

Even in the mid-20th century, C. S. Lewis and J. R. R. Tolkien can be found wrestling with this problem. A thwarted rightful king regaining his throne is an appealing traditional myth, but the audience was Everyman. Thus Prince Caspian (in Lewis) and Aragorn (in Tolkien) are such heirs, who claim kingship by adventure. But in the foreground are the Pevensie children and the hobbits respectively, in both cases characters with whom any reader can identify.

A MORE contemporary (and obviously less serious) manifestation of the theme is Disney's *Lion King*, where the trope yields childish excitement and (at least on stage) high camp. We have come a long way from the King of the Jews.

The irony is that in a more democratic age, genealogy itself is extremely popular — or, as it is now called, family-history research. In summer, especially, I receive a call or email perhaps once a week from someone researching their family's background in one of my parishes. The better organised are planning a visit, and can be told that the older registers are all archived in Hereford, and can be given details of who holds the churchyard plan. There are still a surprising number of people, though, who will ring on a mobile from a churchyard, in the touching belief that the priest can tell them immediately where their ancestor, who died in 1847, is buried.

Hereford diocese received, at one stage, so many enquiries that there is now a dedicated link on the website to channel them. In the search for identity and roots, many believe that they can find an answer in their ancestry, and, once you reach your 32 great-great-great-grandparents, the odds are good that you will find somebody interesting.

THE problem for us as Christians is that the Bible has a clear message about genealogy. The Old Testament is full of it. It did (and does) matter enormously to the Jewish people to know from whom they were descended, and the genealogies in the Gospels are part of this.

But the Epistles offer a very different view. In Philippians 3, Paul dismisses as rubbish his honourable Jewish descent. And, in 1 Timothy 1.4, and Titus 3.9, Christians are warned of wasting time on genealogy. In the context of the Gentile mission, the sense is clear; it does not matter if you are of respectable Jewish descent (or, indeed, a highborn Gentile) — what matters now is willingness to follow Jesus Christ, and to be reborn as his son or daughter. This is a challenge to all those who are keen to find confidence in their ancestry, but a ringing hope that all can alike be fellow-heirs of God.

The challenge for us as we prepare to acclaim the one "born of David's line" at Christmas is to understand how it is important that Jesus came of a particular, privileged line (within his particular, privileged Jewish race), but leaves no such particular physical inheritance himself.

His genealogy was, to use the expression of Wittgenstein from another context, a ladder that, once climbed up, can be thrown away. The hopes of Israel, both for leadership and, more cryptically in later Isaiah, for redemption, focused on one who would inherit the kingship of David. Jesus was born to fulfil those, and thus demonstrated that God's ancient promises were not in vain.

IN two profound ways, however, Jesus subverted the inheritance of kingship into which he was born, and revealed God's greater purposes. In the first way, he came as a king who did not rule, but suffered.

There are elements of conventional leadership in his actions: he taught; he appointed followers to their duties, and delegated them to spread his message; and he demonstrated the coming Kingdom by powerful spiritual works, chiefly of healing. But he resisted the desire to take political power, or associate with rulers, or call his Father's angels down to save him.

His only crown was that of thorns, his royal robe that of mockery, and his throne the cross. To every ruler and governor of every age, the lesson is laid down: kingship is a duty of service and suffering that none should willingly seek.

The second way is less often spoken of, but equally important. Jesus did not marry, and did not beget any children. He made a literal end to his own genealogy. This stands in striking contrast to the concerns of Old Testament patriarchs and kings to carry on their line, and the basic Jewish assumption of a duty to marry and propagate the race.

There is an interesting contrast with Muhammad, whose descendants are still honoured among Muslims, and include many of the ancient royal houses. But Jesus, through whom came the original message "be fruitful and multiply", came to change the message, and sow the seed of a different fruit: of eternal life in him, and the multiplication of his spiritual children.

The truth revealed at Christmas is that neither kingship nor inheritance would ever be the same again.

(2013)

Feathered friend or predator?

Robins are traditionally associated with Christmas,
but, **Ian Tattum** writes, they are not what they seem

ALTHOUGH the penguin now competes with the robin for the honour of
being the emblematic Christmas-card bird, the robin has been dominant
since the Victorians first acquired the habit of sending cards at this time
of year.

The ornithologist David Lack, in his pioneer bird biography *The Life of
the Robin* (1943), suggested that the association between robins and
Christmas originated when the red uniform of postmen earned them the
nickname "robins"; many of the earliest Christmas cards actually featured a
robin bearing a card in its beak.

*You've got mail: a Christmas card
showing a robin as postie, c.1870*

Now, however, it is recognised
that, although the Victorian postal
service cemented the connection,
the appropriation of the robin as a
Christmas symbol antedates it by
many years. Robins can be found in
18th-century Christmas pictures by
urban artists, and had a reputation
for tameness and friendliness from
much earlier. The fact that the robin
is one of the few birds that sings in
the winter, and has plumage which
makes it conspicuous in snow, are
likely to have had some influence,
too. But we owe a debt of gratitude
to Lack for revealing to the world
for the first time the robin's true
nature — and the picture that he
paints is not a cute or cosy one.

LACK was born in 1910, and died in 1973. He conducted groundbreaking
studies, not only of the robin but also the swift; and undertook seminal
work on Darwin's finches and island ecology. He was a key figure in that
reconciliation of the ideas of Darwin and genetics which became known as
neo-Darwinism. Agnostic after a traditional Anglican upbringing, in 1948

he became a committed Christian, and he wrote thoughtfully about the relationship between evolution and Christianity. (I cannot help thinking that A. N. Wilson would have written a better book about Darwin had he drawn on Lack's wisdom.)

In his study of robins, Lack revealed that most of what was popularly believed about the birds was misleading. He was drily witty about the tradition that they and all other birds sang for joy: "Why do birds sing? The most popular answer is because they are happy. From which it could be concluded that, whereas cock robins are happy most of the year, the hens are happy only in the autumn; that cock robins are happier before than after obtaining mates, and they are happiest of all when fighting."

Lack went on to show, through numerous examples, that singing was a sign of territoriality and belligerence rather than friendliness or joy. As for the belief that robins befriend gardeners and actively seek out their company, he revealed that robins are opportunistic feeders who are there to gobble up any insects that are exposed by the gardener's work, and that they live for barely a year. The bird often fondly thought of as "my" robin turns out to be a series of strangers, taking advantage of our love of horticulture.

None of this need diminish our sense of delight at encountering the robin during the winter months, since it deepens our knowledge and appreciation of a familiar creature now known wondrously to be — like all avian kind — a surviving tiny, feathered dinosaur.

THIS time of the year brings out the inner puritan in the hearts of many people, believing or not, who lament the commercial subversion of "the true meaning of Christmas", whether they believe that to be the innocent joy of children, the celebration of family or community, or the glory of the incarnation and the blessedness of the lowly and the outcast. The robin can serve as a sign of both the comfort of the hearth and the wild summons of the manger.

The poet R. S. Thomas, who was devoted to the lonely pursuit of bird-watching, and was a knowledgeable amateur ornithologist, may well have known Lack's *Life of the Robin*, which was published in a popular paperback edition in 1971. Certainly he embraced the robin's symbolic ambiguity in his poem "Song", in which he observes that, like Christ, the robin comes to us "in his weakness, but with a sharp song".

(2017)

Word from Wormingford

Before cards and Christmas trees,
there was the piety and misrule of
the Court, says **Ronald Blythe**

AFTER the country funeral, drinking sherry, seeing the worried widower, I murmured the usual comforting things. "And now I will have to write the Christmas cards," he said. I wrote mine all day, the white cat rumbling on my lap.

The cards had beautiful Renaissance paintings on one side, and Alzheimer's or Stroke on the other. Where appropriate, I added love to the official kind wishes. The frosty garden grew green and returned to white before I had finished. The recipients spread through time, ran from school friends to recent acquaintances, but were mostly people who comprised my world, other writers, priests, rural society, and, of course, far-scattered relations.

Certain cards have to contain little letters or extra devotion. Some must praise the beauty of those I have already received. I used to excoriate this ritual, but now I am glad to have it; for thinking of old John in Natal, still teaching organists, I see him walking into the pub in his RAF officer's uniform. And remembering the elderly plantswoman and her brother, I see them arrive at the fancy-dress party in costumes far too old for them, and laughing away. And so I add "love" with conviction.

Tomorrow, I shall walk to the village post office and buy 100 second-class stamps, pick up *The Times* where Peter leaves it outside Harold's, and then start on the presents, a far weightier matter.

Advent Two and evensong for three. The ancient building wavers in candlelight. Pam reads Zephaniah, and I read Luke. We sing a hymn, but say the rest, our voices rising and falling, I and the brother and sister. I talk about the cousins Jesus and John — the boys on the Christmas card — for a few minutes.

By now, whatever faint irritation we may have felt at being so deserted has disappeared. Prayer has overtaken us. A trapped silence feeds us. It is with some regret that I place a full stop to it all with the blessing. In the black churchyard, we urge each other not to fall over the tombstones, most of them to John Constable's uncles and aunts. No Christmas cards for him. Maybe a pencil-sketch of a tree.

I have cleared the back of the farmhouse of its summer detritus, the sticks and soggy leaves, the elder, the nettles. Malcolm the window cleaner arrives, and the panes shine like a coal seam. In a couple of hours, between us, we have done marvels.

In the meadow known as Lower Bottom the horses wear their winter blankets. There is early moonlight and ice in the air. I fetch the washing in from where it has been stiffening on the orchard clothes-line. Night creatures are about, rats, rabbits, badgers.

On the radio, someone is reading Cavafy's amazing poem "Ithaca", only, of course, it isn't quite the same destination. But the name resounds, like Yeats's "Byzantium", in the ear like a longing. Like the only worthwhile journey. Like Bethlehem.

High above, the grey-black sky, silver planes head for Calcutta with 400 passengers reading novels and drinking Cinzano and gin, or Coca-Cola, looking down at starry Norwich. They don't make a sound.

I spend a good hour looking for my Collected Cavafy poems, having tidied them away. And there is "Ithaca" at last. We are all on the move in Advent — God, too.

A MEDIEVAL king would "keep his Christmas" at Woodstock or Westminster, or wherever he happened to be. And God keeps us wherever we happen to be. "Keep me as the apple of the eye."

James I liked to keep his Christmas at Whitehall, a vast palace of which only Inigo Jones's Banqueting Hall remains. Fresh from Scotland, no longer scalded by its Kirk, James was alternately entertained, if this is the description, by Lancelot Andrewes and William Shakespeare. The mighty Bishop at the beginning of the feast, the peerless writer at its end. The sermon kept to the solemn rules with a vengeance — the often disgraceful Court pulled itself together — the play, *Twelfth Night*, kept it entranced. Rarely were there such festivities as these. They were talked about for months afterwards.

In his Christmas sermon, Andrewes's learnedness would sometimes forsake him, rather as the intellectuality of the Wise Men would forsake them as they entered the stable. Like every good preacher, he knew when to abandon the script. Or, rather, he knew that there would be moments in the Gospel story when he would go to pieces. Thus there began these emotional unscripted asides in the retelling of it.

Nobody was more understanding than James, for whom the word "Baby" was so wonderful that he went on calling his son and lover this when they were in their twenties, signing his letters to them "Your Dad and Gossip".

Seated below the pulpit, he heard Bishop Andrewes approaching the stable on Christmas morning with his theology pat, his severe face all set for the great occasion, his notes crackling in his hand. And then — a newborn boy! The Saviour of mankind. The preaching went out of his voice;

King and Court went silent. Not a sound in the freezing chapel. But Andrewes was not in it, he was in Bethlehem.

"An infant — the infant Word — the Word without a word — the eternal Word not able to speak a word — a wonder sure ..."

Then, almost a fortnight later, it would all end with Twelfth Night, the holiness, the feeding, the exhaustion — and the order. For the latter was strictly enforced, whatever else occurred. Twelfth Night was misrule, when the sacred pattern was reversed, and rich and poor and male and female exchanged roles. It was wild. But so would the climate be until springtime, dark and cold and deathly.

For a few hours, dukes would become servants, boys become girls. Being divine, Kings couldn't become anything else, of course. James watched his Players perform *Twelfth Night*, a final Christmas entertainment which Mr Shakespeare had written especially for him, and maybe Bishop Andrewes watched it, too. Christmas had been a box of gifts, Twelfth Night was a box of tricks. In between were the parties and the worship. Now had come the reckoning.

It is not quite Christmas Eve, however, and neither the Boy born to be King nor the bills are with us. In the Suffolk market town, an immense conifer sways and glitters. Teenagers who haven't as yet shown any of the wear and tear of Christmas look beautiful under the swaying lights. The clergy are looking to their laurels as they hurry from Nine Lessons to Nine Lessons, and from Midnight to Midnight.

The bells, some of them as old as Shakespeare, rock in the towers. One should long since have been surfeited with all this. How does it stay so fresh? How do babies cause one to be at a loss for words? How strange it all is.

(2008)

Milton's "On the Morning of Christ's Nativity"

This Christmas, read Milton's great poem on the nativity, in which old gods yield to the holy infant, says **David Scott**.

MILTON is quite impossible in one way. He writes from within a view of the world which seems completely archaic, and will mean nothing to most people. It is even difficult for scholars and for the most well read.

T. S. Eliot gave the difficulty a name. He called it "the dissociation of sensibility". Put simply, we do not feel about things the way other people used to — we think rather than feel our thoughts with the immediacy that people used to. Also, we have got separated from great chunks of our ancient culture. So there are two immediate hurdles: the words that are no longer in common parlance, and a world-view that has dipped below the horizon.

I am in no position to right any of that. I am reminded that the Church spends a great deal of its time working in the old cosmology, where "up" means good, and "down" means bad, and nature gets personified. But being aware of that brings us halfway to managing it.

As with the old cosmology, so with "the old gods". In the course of Milton's poem, Pan, Cynthia, Peor, Baalim, Moloch, Isis, and Osiris all disappear, leaving Christ, although in a stable, firmly at the centre of the universe. Being aware that the panoply of the gods is, in comparison with Christ, largely stage-paste, it ceases to threaten. Their work is done, and the mystery that they represented (as in "mystery religions") is replaced with a new purged form of mystery, or wonder, which now lies in the babe which "the virgin blest … hath laid to rest".

Christ's birth does not reduce the world's mystery. The mystery of the world and the knowledge of the universe are not incompatible. The alchemy of poetry allows them to live side by side, both contributing to the task of telling the difficult truths of faith.

Milton's poem on Christ's birth works within those two givens of mystery and of knowledge. In the sensitive and large-hearted response to that paradox lies the key to coming alongside "On the Morning of Christ's Nativity".

Milton was born in December 1608. In December 1629, when he was 21, he took the opportunity to write about Christ residing at the centre of the universe. After the prelude, the ode proceeds in three movements, which describe the setting, the angelic song, and the flight of the pagan gods at the birth of a new and more divine deity.

But, first, note the title of the poem: "On the Morning of Christ's Nativity", the very day itself. Milton has "On the Morning": the wakening hour of resurrection, or perhaps the time he would have gone to church. There is something good and clear-cut about "the Morning of Christ's Nativity". It narrows the event down, and saves us from weeks of stretched-out Christmas, starting before December and going on as far as Christmas Eve, and then dropping us into a dreary sense of emptiness. Christ is born on Christmas Day, and that is the day on which we celebrate:

This is the month, and this the happy morn
Wherein the Son of heaven's eternal King,
Of wedded maid, and virgin mother born,
Our great redemption from above did bring ...

THE strangeness and the ordinariness of the birth of Jesus fused in Mary's womb to give us the child who is Christ. The birth was as ordinary as you could get it, and yet as extraordinary as it ever has been.

Being born below from a God above, Christ holds out the possibility, through faith, of redeeming the fault lines of the past. Milton took with utmost seriousness the biblical realities of a paradise lost. No one in English literature has gone to greater lengths to put the biblical story into such dramatic form, and to remind us that the paradise we lost, and continue to let slip away from us through sin, was regained through God's love manifest in Christ Jesus:

That glorious form, that light unsufferable ...
He laid aside; and here with us to be,
Forsook the courts of everlasting day,
And chose with us a darksome house of mortal clay.

God became man, took on an earthly form, and taught us the truths of love and service, penitence and worship. He died for us and rose again. So, with Milton this Christmas, we could ask ourselves what gift shall we afford the infant God who has done so much for us.

Hast thou no verse, no hymn, or solemn strain,
To welcome him to this his new abode ...?

THE poem is divided between an introductory poem of four verses, and "The Hymn". Most people think that the introductory poem of four verses is it, but, no, the extra 27 verses of "The Hymn" take us into the most amazing cosmic realms.

It needs a fair amount of patience in decoding, and yet what looks indigestible turns out to be as basic as you could want:

It was the winter wild,
While the heaven-born-child
    All meanly wrapped in the rude manger lies;
Nature in awe to him ...

Milton's Christmas gift to the Lord is the hymn that follows, and it takes up a new rhythm, nine lines with differing lengths for each verse, breaking up the sedentary rhythm of the prologue. It was a scheme that Hopkins used for "The Wreck of the Deutschland".

Things are beginning to happen. Nature, once in competition with grace from the fall, now lays a carpet of pure white snow over the hills of Bethlehem, and likewise over the sins of the past.

God sends down "meek-eyed Peace":

The hooked chariot stood
Unstained with hostile blood,
    The trumpet spake not to the armed throng,
And kings sat still with awful eye,
As if they knew their sovran Lord was by.

The reign of peace has begun; "the mild ocean" has "quite forgot to rave". Milton draws the whole universe into the ambit of the holy birth. The sun bows to the Son. "The stars with deep amaze Stand fixed in steadfast gaze." Cynthia, the moon goddess, acknowledges a new reign: "She knew such harmony alone Could hold all heaven and earth in happier union." The seraphim and cherubim cry:

Ring out, ye crystal spheres,
Once bless our human ears ...
And let your silver chime
Move in melodious time ...

And then at last our bliss
Full and perfect is,
    But now begins ...

Milton is not allowing us to get to the crib without a final battle. Nothing is that easy, since the old gods had to be overcome by "the dreaded infant's hand" and "the rays of Bethlehem":

Our babe to show his Godhead true,
Can in his swaddling bands control the damned crew.

"THE HYMN" is all about change — change from an old contract to a new. A new vision of the world opens up, as the old gods, in the light of the infant Christ, lay down their arms. The old culture of the gods, the world-view that personified nature into a cross between a Baroque carnival and a badly acted school play, turns into something approaching the modern stripped-down universe. Its centre is the stable:

> *But see, the virgin blest*
> *Hath laid her babe to rest …*
> > *Her sleeping Lord with handmaid lamp attending:*
> *And all about the courtly stable,*
> *Bright-harnessed angels sit in order serviceable.*

Yet one senses also that Milton still needed the old regime. This is partly because it was so rich and poetic, and partly because he understood quite a bit about what went into the schemes that excited Satan in the Garden of Eden.

Of the 27 verses of this hymn, the majority are about the dismantling of the old order, and precious few about the construction of the new.

> *And sullen Moloch fled,*
> *Hath left in shadows dread,*
> > *His burning idol all of blackest hue;*
> *In vain with cymbals' ring,*
> *They call the grisly king,*
> > *In dismal dance about the furnace blue;*

All the time, one is hoping for a deeper sense of the spiritual capacity released in the incarnation, and not simply a reliance on the power of its opposite to make the point.

It was T. S. Eliot who wrote about "the alien people clutching their gods", and Milton is expert on the old dispensation. Yet, like Eliot, we may no longer be at ease in the old dispensation, and be glad of another death.

What I hope is that Milton's poem will encourage us to come out from the drowsy hours of post-Christmas feasting, and confront the realities of the faith that sustains us. Christmas is soon over, but the victory of Christ over the cosmos will see us through the years, and through the toughest times that the world can bring to us. Milton writes from that serious perspective, and we may be glad that while we were on this earth we read this poem.

(2008)

"Eating Turkies" and being snowed in

Pamela Tudor-Craig looks at Jane Austen's Christmas

"... that festival which requires a more than ordinary share of private balls and large dinners to proclaim its importance"

THUS Jane Austen marked the space between Marianne Dashwood's doomed flirtation with the rogue Willoughby in Devonshire and its prolonged and agonising dénouement in London. Are we to note a touch of asperity in the writer's description of the mismatch between the first humble Christmas and the worldly extravagance with which it was commemorated in her time? Probably: the context in which she refers to it again is the spiteful letter where the horrid Miss Bingley exults that she has contrived to drag away her charming but pliable brother, who had been showing symptoms of falling in love with Jane Bennett:

"I sincerely hope", writes Miss Bingley, in one of the most insincere letters immortalised in print, "your Christmas in Hertfordshire may abound in the gaieties which that season generally brings, and that your beaux will be so numerous as to prevent your feeling the loss of the three of whom we shall deprive you."

If there were any doubt as to the distasteful impression that letter was intended to convey to the reader — and the heroine Elizabeth saw through it at once — that doubt would be allayed by the use of the word "beaux". On the lips of Miss Steele and Sir John Middleton in *Sense and Sensibility*, or those of the dreadful Thorpes in *Northanger Abbey*, it is the epitome of vulgarity. We are reminded that, while the blood of the aloof Mr Darcy is dark blue, the large fortune of the Bingleys has been gained in trade.

With the single exception of *Northanger Abbey*, which opens after the Christmas season, when the Allens take Catherine Morland to Bath, and closes within 12 months, the action in each of Jane Austen's immortal novels spans a little over a single year. It follows that they move through Christmas, and each Christmas tells us something, but amazingly little, about what she is prepared to reveal about her understanding of it, and what part it played in polite society at the time.

The emphasis is on "polite", because it is undoubtedly the case that a strong thread of the customary celebrations of the Middle Ages survived among the less "polite", ready to be picked up and enhanced and enjoyed again by the antiquaries and enthusiasts for folk lore of the Oxford

Movement. There was much about ancient customs of merriment and worship — there still remained much into the 20th century — to glean in the pub and on the village green. It would be fun to imagine that, though Emma's Hartfield was a modern house, there survived at the back an ancient hall and outbuildings, accommodation for surreptitious apple-bobbing, Yule logs, and bunches of mistletoe. Such junkets at Northanger Abbey would have been kept with great caution from the eagle eye of General Tilney.

IT might be wise to enquire what Jane Austen said about Christmas in her own voice. Here there is a theoretical problem, in that her letters to Cassandra, which, when they were parted, formed an almost continuous diary, cannot be expected to cover Christmas, when surely they were not separated.

As the novels testify, a family gathering was the one staple of her fictional Christmases. Jane and her sister were, however, sundered over the Christmas of 1798, and Jane wrote to Cassandra, starting on 24 December and finishing on the 26th. Jane was at home at Steventon, Cassandra with the Knights in their grand Kent house of Godmersham.

In the midst of balls (she was but 23 years old) and hopes of promotion for the Austen men in the Navy, Jane says, in an aside: "I wish you a merry Christmas, but no compliments of the Season." She adds, however, probably on Boxing Day: "Of my Charities to the poor since I came home [on 24 October] I have given a pair of Worsted Stock(in)gs to Mary Hutchins, Dame Kew, Mary Steevens and Dame Staples; a shift to Hannah Staples & a shawl to Betty Dawkins, amounting in all to about half a guinea …" (It is a relief to hear that the fashion for muslin dresses was underpinned in the winter months in this way. Had you realised that Catherine Morland was driven about in an open curricle by the lamentable John Thorpe in February and early March?)

We hear again of gifts to the poor as a feature of the Christmas season as early as 30 November 1812, when Jane writes to her great friend Martha Lloyd from Chawton: "We are just beginning to be engaged in another Christmas Duty, and next to eating Turkies [sic] a very pleasant one, laying out Edward's money for the Poor; & the Sum that passes through our hands this year is considerable, as Mrs Knight left £20 to the Parish …"

The adoption of her brother Edward by the wealthy Knight family was the source of the modest prosperity of Jane, Cassandra, and their mother in her widowhood.

THE giving of gifts, not only to the poor, but within the family, was clearly a Christmas activity, though gifts were not necessarily exchanged specifically on 25 December. When the delightful and eminently sensible Mr and Mrs

Gardiner, brother and sister-in-law of the silly Mrs Bennett, arrive with their four children as usual to spend a Christmas week with the Bennetts at Longbourn, "The first part of Mrs Gardiner's business on her arrival was to distribute her presents ..."

The importance of a Christmas reunion, especially where families were seriously divided and journeys were hazardous, lends a special focus to the painful parting of Fanny Price from her cherished brother William, the only person whom she could love without constraint. The Ball at Mansfield Park, which she had been reluctantly obliged to open with the dangerous Henry Crawford, took place on 22 December. William left to rejoin his ship early the following morning. After a hasty breakfast, Fanny was left to cry in peace among "the cold pork bones and mustard in William's plate" and the broken eggshells in Mr Crawford's.

Her uncle Sir Thomas Bertram hoped that her tears would be divided between them, but in fact all her sorrow was over the pork bones. That image of dismembered remnants, in all its crushing ordinariness, epitomises the lot of women whose relentless role it is to be left behind. William embarked on Christmas Eve. Yet critics complain that the Napoleonic Wars play no part in her writing.

THE most disappointing handling of the event of Christmas occurs in *Emma*, granted that the grand climax of the first of the three triangles constructing that novel — that of Emma–Mr Elton–Harriet Smith — occurs in a snowfall in the coach returning from a seasonable party at the Westons: the débâcle of Mr Elton's profoundly unwelcome proposal to Emma herself. The rest follows with a rapidity that leaves unsaid the whole unfolding of Christmas Day.

The impediment of snow was a reality in Jane Austen's life. In the postcript to that letter of 24–26 December 1798, she wrote: "The Snow came to nothing yesterday, so I did go to Deane, and returned home at 9 o'clock in the little carriage — and without being very cold." Perhaps the only true reflection of Christmas in her time is the persistence in our shops of Christmas cards showing stage coaches galloping through the snow — not that the Austens knew of the custom of Christmas cards any more than they knew of Christmas trees, Christmas stockings, carol services, or, above all, Christmas cribs, still in her day confined to Roman Catholic countries. (In Naples and Bavaria, craftsmen were contriving some of the most beautiful ever made.)

Considering that she had just refused an offer of marriage from her clergyman, it was as well for the baffled Emma to discover in the morning "a great deal of snow on the ground ... though Christmas Day, she could not go to church". But that is all. The writer has brought together the entire family, with five children, and their entourage, plus their parents and an uncle, under the elegant roof of Mr Woodhouse, on 25 December; yet all we hear is that the weather continued to provide an excuse to stay indoors for several convenient days.

Emma could not have gone to church with such a father to fuss over wet shoes; but surely the two redoubtable Mr Knightleys went, and took the boys with them? Was not the village orchestra at work in the gallery? And did not that shepherd boy of Robert Martin's with a lovely voice have a chance to sing a carol? Surely the unquenchable Mr Weston came over in the afternoon, his wife on his arm ... Were there not charades to chase down the turkey? That is the passage, between chapters 16 and 17, in all the exquisite contrivance of these novels, that I long to see expanded.

MANSFIELD Park is the most overtly religious of the five completed master-pieces, and declaredly so, a very moral book, with young characters clearly labelled "good" (Fanny and Edmund) and "bad" (Mary and Henry), and others ill-trained to distinguish and therefore seriously hurt (Henrietta and Louisa) — not to mention the failures in guidance of the older generation. Indeed, it might have been a trifle predictable without the almost irresistible charm of the immoral people.

The novel that really deals with religion in the inward sense, the religion of the author herself, is *Persuasion*, however. Here at last she has found a way to refer to the inner springs of her heroine's life in a way that does not embarrass the casual reader. Anne Elliott is cruelly placed at the beginning. The love of her life returns eight years after she had been persuaded to reject him — and returns minded to look for a younger partner. At the painful twists of the plot, Anne keeps her serenity by escaping to her room. After the first occasion when Captain Wentworth showed her the slightest kindness, "it required a long application of solitude and reflection to recover her".

At the centre of this occasionally heartrending plot, there is a Christmastide scene that we should examine with some care. The reader has already had more than enough of the empty-headed, socially ambitious Sir Walter Elliot and his eldest daughter before they meet the open-handed, generous naval circle to which the hero belongs.

At a watershed in the plot, about to transfer the suffering Anne from the neighbourhood of the family home of Kellynch Hall to Bath itself, there is a vignette of Christmas in the great house at Uppercross, home of the Musgroves, into whose family the heroine's other sister, Mary, has married. After the serious accident where Louisa Musgrave fell on the Cobb at Lyme, she has been nursed there in their tiny house by Captain Wentworth's friends the Harvilles. The elder Musgroves return from visiting her there, bringing with them the Harville children, to relieve the congestion.

Anne Elliot visits them with Lady Russell. "Immmediately surrounding Mrs Musgrove were the little Harvilles whom she was sedulously guarding from the tyranny of the two children from the Cottage, expressly arrived to amuse them. On one side was a table, occupied by some chattering girls, cutting up silk and gold paper; and on the other were tressels and trays, bending under the weight of brawn and cold pies, where riotous boys were holding high revel; the whole completed by a roaring Christmas fire, which seemed determined to be heard, in spite of all the noise of the others …

"Mr Musgrove made a point of paying his respects to Lady Russell, and sat down close to her for ten minutes, talking with a very raised voice, but, from the clamour of children on his knees, generally in vain. It was a fine family-piece."

So much Anne's view of the scene. Mrs Musgrove observes to her that "after all she had gone through, nothing was so likely to do her good as a little quiet cheerfulness at home".

Anne's sister Mary, the essential snob, cannot understand what her in-laws see in the Harvilles. Lady Russell says to Anne: "I hope I shall remember, in future, not to call at Uppercross in the Christmas holidays." But we are left to warm our hands at the generous simplicity of the Musgroves.

IT is difficult, I understand, to get into the spirit of Christmas pudding on a picnic on a New Zealand beach: easier to long to "put on the armour of light" (Romans 13.12) when the sun is at its lowest, and to watch around us the return of spring flowers as we visit again the empty tomb. Jane Austen would have found every encouragement among her favourite poets to set her actions in the appropriate seasons of the year.

To go for a walk with William Cowper at the opening of his "The Task" is to go hand in hand with Marianne Dashwood on the hills around Barton. Marianne declares: "To hear those beautiful lines, which have frequently almost driven me wild, pronounced with such impenetrable calmness, such dreadful indifference!"

"He [Edward Ferrars] would certainly have done more justice to simple and elegant prose. I thought so at the time; but you would give him Cowper!"

Marianne and her family leave beloved Norland and its trees in the fall of leaf. Anne Elliot shares a walk, melancholy for her, to Winthrop, "fraught with the apt analogy of the declining year, with declining happiness". The sultry climax of the intrigue between Frank Churchill and Jane Fairfax is played out in a heatwave in the grounds of Donwell Abbey and upon Box Hill. The eventual coming together of Emma and George Knightley takes place at the first return of summer after the nearest Jane Austen gets to suggesting a storm.

But the matching of the seasons of the year and the seasons of the Church, which are for us so enriching a feature of the annual cycle, would in 1800 have smacked of Rome. In Cowper's poetry, Jane Austen would have found an aversion to all things Roman Catholic reinforcing her avoidance of the smallest mention of the visual pageantry of Christianity. Another poet and artist of her time, however, thought otherwise. In July 1809, the little family of Austen women moved back to Hampshire, this time to a simple house in Chawton, after apparently uncreative years in Bath and Southampton. She took up again the even, probably monotonous, routine that, as every creative person, every contemplative, knows, is the best background for the adventures of the mind and spirit. Thus opened the most productive years of her writing life.

In the same year, 1809, William Blake produced several illustrations for one of the first poems of John Milton's "Ode on the Morning of Christ's Nativity". It is doubtful whether Blake could have found a congenial text among the poems of his contemporaries, but in 1629 the 21-year-old Milton had been untouched by Puritanism. He had not yet learned to fear Christian imagery, and had more in common with the other Caroline poets George Herbert and Richard Crashaw. He opened his hymn with just such an association of the cold season and the crib as comes naturally to us northerners:

> It was the winter wild,
> While the heaven-born child
> All meanly wrapped in the rude manger lies;
> Nature in awe to him
> Had doffed her gaudy trim,
> With her great Master so to sympathize …
>
> Only with speeches fair
> She woos the gentle air
> To hide her guilty front with innocent snow …

So Blake represented Nature as a nubile lady, covering herself with virginal snow as she lies on the ground outside the shed. The poem turns upon the Virgilian belief that the nativity was marked by a moment of peace on earth:

> But he her fears to cease,
> Sent down the meek-eyed Peace;
> She crowned with olive green came softly sliding
> Down through the turning sphere …

The last stanza opens:

> But see, the virgin blest,
> Hath laid her babe to rest …

Stable: William Blake's
*The Night of Peace: Milton's
Hymn — "On the Morning of
Christ's Nativity"*, 1809

*Heaven's youngest teemèd star,
Hath fixed her polished car,
Her sleeping Lord with handmaid lamp attending:
And all about the courtly stable,
Bright-harnessed angels sit in order serviceable.*

In his 11th stanza, Milton had told us that the cherubim were helmed and
the seraphim bore swords. So, somewhat confusedly, the guards around the
"courtly stable" are identified. The steeds bearing the heavenly chariot and
its new star through the night are resting while the Child sleeps; so time
stands still. It is all, admittedly, rather clumsy and stilted, a first attempt to
reclaim a thread lost to northern artists for nearly 300 years. There is more
natural warmth in one rejoicing sentence of Jane Austen's where, at the end
of *Pride and Prejudice*, Elizabeth Bennett tells her beloved aunt and uncle
that all is well: "Mr Darcy sends you all the love in the world he can spare
from me. You are all to come to Pemberley for Christmas ..."

So the love of family, and the love between Darcy and Elizabeth, have
broken down social barriers that were as strong, if more nebulous, than
those between the crib and the three kings. If Jane Austen had lived to a
reasonable age, she would have known a different visual Christmas world.
When the Gardiners left Gracechurch Street and their warehouses to spend
Christmas in the fictional equivalent of Chatsworth, a younger Ebenezer
Scrooge was already bending over his desk.

(2009)

213

Diving into the deep end

John Donne's poem "Nativity", provides theology, emotion, and spritual insight, says **David Bryant**

Nativity

Immensity cloistered in thy dear womb,
Now leaves His well-belov'd imprisonment,
There He hath made Himself to His intent
Weak enough, now into the world to come;
But O, for thee, for Him, hath the inn no room?
Yet lay Him in this stall, and from the Orient,
Stars and wise men will travel to prevent
The effect of Herod's jealous general doom.
Seest thou, my soul, with thy faith's eyes, how He
Which fills all place, yet none holds Him, doth lie?
Was not His pity towards thee wondrous high,
That would have need to be pitied by thee?
Kiss Him, and with Him into Egypt go,
With His kind mother, who partakes thy woe.

John Donne

FOR a Dean of St Paul's, John Donne had an impressively racy background. Born into a recusant family, he saw close friends and family suffer torture, exile, and death. His brother died of bubonic plague while in prison for sheltering a priest. Donne's youthful womanising, reckless expenditure, and lust for travel have echoes of St Augustine's *Confessions*.

He served a spell in the Fleet Prison, thanks to the furious Sir Thomas Egerton, whose daughter he had seduced. Three of his 12 children died before they were ten, and his anguish was so great that he contemplated suicide.

The disillusioned Donne wrote a fiery polemic against the Roman Catholic Church, as a result of which King James I became his champion. The King took him in hand, appointed him a Royal Chaplain, and swiftly advanced him through the higher echelons of the Church of England, and he became Dean of St Paul's.

Out of this seething cauldron emerged a poet whose love lyrics and erotic verse raised more than a few lay and clerical eyebrows. In his latter years, he mellowed, and turned to religious poetry, whose hallmarks are powerful imagery, sensuality, provocative God-talk, and pithy epigrams. His poem "Nativity" is a marvel of punchy theology, emotion, and spiritual insight. The opening lines are an unforgettable paradox.

Immensity cloistered in thy dear womb,
Now leaves His well-belov'd imprisonment.

Addressed to the Blessed Virgin Mary, this throws us straight into the spiritual deep end. God in his vastness lies beyond human comprehension, hidden in a cloud of unknowing. He is the "Light inaccessible, hid from our eyes", in the hymn-writer's words. At the same time, God is immanent, entwined like a thread through every atom of the universe.

This omnipresence of God opens a wide field for different approaches to prayer. It speaks to those who respond to a holy, elusive, transcendent God through silence and contemplation, and paves the way for a more earth-based spirituality, centred on the humanity of Jesus exemplified in the Christ-child.

FORGET the frivolities of Christmas, mistletoe, mince pies, and silver glitter. What follows is heavyweight theology. God has intentionally chosen to enter the world homeless and vulnerable.

This is *kenosis* — God emptying himself, so aptly described by St Paul in Philippians: "Christ … though he was in the form of God did not count equality with God a thing to be grasped, but emptied himself." This concept had its genesis 2500 years earlier, when Isaiah proclaimed a God who was revealed as a suffering servant.

Donne is not depicting the nativity as a charming, nostalgic scene. It is an unravelling of the very nature of God. It implies that, from the very inception of time, God has been and remains at the heart of all that is.

Then comes hurdle number one. "But O, for thee, for Him, hath the inn no room?" To put it bluntly, much of the world is uninterested in, or antagonistic to, the divine presence. The Christmas Gospel sums it up: "He came to his own home, and his own people received him not." This is a bleak, but sadly realistic picture.

We still fight wars, act inhumanely, disregard minorities, and lead lives that are ethically stunted or distorted. Godless regimes abound, and religion is confused with political idealism. It seems as if darkness has won the day.

Not so, Donne says. There are two glimmers of hope. The star that embodies the entire cosmic realm travels through the emptiness of space to rest over the stable, drawing the entire world with it. So do the Wise Men, who bring gifts and humility to the crib instead of rejection and destruction.

Just as the light is growing brighter, another malign event surges up. Herod is planning an appalling infanticide. At the last moment his murderous hand is forestalled, and the Bethlehem family is spared. The Magi complete their long journey, and the star arrives in the nick of time before the bloodshed starts: "Stars and wise men will travel to prevent The effect of Herod's jealous general doom."

THEN the poet urges us to contemplate in silent wonder the child in the manger, who represents both the God from the eternal realms of light, and the God centred in our world.

As if to underline the potency and sheer thrill of this message, Donne turns to irony. The nativity has a twist in the tale. God's pity is so profound that he chooses to up-end the equation and lie in a draughty stable, thereby bringing about a scenario in which we feel sorry for him rather than vice-versa.

So there is a reciprocity written into the Christmas event. Divine love shines out on humankind with a potential to kindle a flame of love in us. This flame, John Wesley states, can "burn with inextinguishable blaze, and trembling to its source return …". The God–humankind circle is complete.

The closing lines come as a vast reassurance. If we gear ourselves up to take a great leap of faith in the face of the world's secularity, if we are prepared to go on our knees, and kiss him, we can metaphorically travel with Joseph and Mary to the safety of Egypt.

There, with the Holy Family, we will be able to rest in the presence of the universal Christ, the Lord of glory, who shares our existential angst and co-suffers with the world.

> *Kiss Him, and with Him into Egypt go,*
> *With His kind mother, who partakes thy woe.*

Donne's message is universal, and beyond time. It rides high over the secular Christmas with its Santa, winking lights, canned music, and electronic tills. In all its poetic splendour, it proclaims that God is ever present — not only in the glory of heaven and the joyfulness of life, but in the sordid, hopeless caverns of human existence as well. And that is quite something to celebrate this Christmas.

(2014)

The long road of weariness

Malcolm Guite writes of his vision of Christ as a refugee child in poetry and prose

Refugee

We think of him as safe beneath the steeple,
Or cosy in a crib beside the font,
But he is with a million displaced people
On the long road of weariness and want.
For even as we sing our final carol
His family is up and on that road,
Fleeing the wrath of someone else's quarrel,
Glancing behind and shouldering their load.
Whilst Herod rages still from his dark tower
Christ clings to Mary, fingers tightly curled,
The lambs are slaughtered by the men of power,
And death squads spread their curse across the world.
But every Herod dies, and comes alone
To stand before the Lamb upon the throne.

THERE is always a danger of sentimentalising, and so trivialising, the nativity scene. Our houses are deluged in a cascade of cosy Christmas images, glittery frosted cards, and happy, holy families who seem to be remarkably comfortable in strangely clean stables, and we can lose track of the essential gospel truth: that the world into which God chose to be born for us was then, as now, fraught with danger and menace.

Indeed, we will not understand the light that shines at Christmas if we remove the dark backdrop. Richard Bauckham's poem "Song of the Shepherds" restores it for us in the line "The night was ominously black"; Christina Rossetti set the scene on Advent Sunday with "midnight, black as pitch". Herbert, even in the midst of his joyful "Glance", reminded us of "malicious and ill-meaning harm"; Donne's "Annunciation" spoke of "death's force"; Luci Shaw reminded us of "the felt rebuff … the lash … the sad heart of the human race". The feast of the Holy Innocents brings home with full force what might be called "the shadow side" of the Christian story.

217

THE story of Herod's jealous rage and the massacre of the innocents would be too appalling to bear were we not called upon to contemplate it almost every day in the news. What Herod did then is still being done around the world by tyrants who would sooner kill innocent people than lose their grip on power. Writing in 2015, we are still reeling from the appalling slaughter of children in Peshawar by the Pakistani Taliban, as well as the continued violence, much of it directed towards children, by Islamic State in Syria and Iraq.

This scarred and wounded world is the one into which Jesus was born, the world he came to save. Among those brought by his blood through the grave and gate of death to the bliss of heaven are those children of Bethlehem who died for his name without ever knowing him.

But he knows them, as he knows and loves every child in Syria, Iraq, and Pakistan, and he says of them, to every Herod, "as you did it to one of the least of these who are members of my family, you did it to me" (Matthew 25.40).

IN this sonnet, I have followed the narrative in Matthew 2.13-19, which goes out of its way to mention the death of Herod. The story of the flight into Egypt seems utterly contemporary. If we acknowledge the idea of *kenosis* — the self-emptying of God — then we must contemplate the experience of the Christ-child as being exactly the same as that of the disturbed and bewildered children we see being carried by their mothers in desperation out of war zones.

These children cannot possibly know the cause of the quarrel that has destroyed their homes; they could not name or articulate the label that has made them enemies of the state. Utterly innocent of the long, hideous adult agenda that has visited such devastation on them, they are "fleeing the wrath of someone else's quarrel".

Likewise, if we are to take seriously Christ's teaching at the end of Matthew, the same Gospel that gave us this appalling story — that he is really and substantially in the lives and bodies of those who are oppressed, and whatsoever is done to them is done to him — then we must become aware that the risen Christ is still a refugee.

But this is not to despair. It means that we can still meet him, and help him in his need. We cannot turn back through time to meet the Holy Family as they flee through the deserts of Egypt, but we can certainly meet them now. And there is one more thing that I tried to draw out in this sonnet. There is a judgement, there is finally an accountability, and, thank God, it is a judgement with mercy.

Perhaps the most profound and paradoxical image in the whole of Scripture is that of the Lamb upon the throne. We should never cease to be astonished by that verse; "for the Lamb at the centre of the throne will be their shepherd, and he will guide them to springs of the water of life, and God will wipe away every tear from their eyes" (Revelation 7.17).

The entire edifice of Scripture up to this point has been predicated on the difference between the shepherd and the sheep. "All we like sheep have gone astray" (Isaiah 53.6). God is figured in the Old and New Testament as the transcendent shepherd: in that sense, utterly different in kind from the sheep. But this verse of Revelation reveals one more meaning of Christmas, of incarnation.

We have a shepherd who knows what it is to be a lamb. He has himself been one of the vulnerable flock; he has been misled by false shepherds, and made victim of the wolf. And that is why he is able to wipe away the tears from our eyes, because he himself has wept them.

What might this mean for the Herods of this world? It certainly means that they will face judgement; they will meet their victims in Christ, and Christ in their victims, and know and have to acknowledge what they have done. In that final light, there will be no evasion, no spin, no propaganda, no polite euphemisms — only searing truth.

But right at the heart of the truth will be the Lamb, who died as much for the Herods as for their victims; and, even there, "the need and chance to salvage everything" (Seamus Heaney), the possibility in repentance, for the bloodthirsty themselves, to be "washed ... in the blood of the Lamb" (Revelation 7.14).

(2015)

The flight to Egypt: the Holy Family depicted as refugees in Edwin Long's Anno Domini *(1883)*

219

Music to take to heart

Handel's *Messiah* is a statement of faith, saying more about human responses to God than about Christ himself, says **Andrew Carwood**

IT is difficult to avoid a performance of George Frideric Handel's oratorio *Messiah* at Christmas. This masterpiece is such a part of the national heritage that having the festive season without at least the first part in your area is unusual.

Messiah deserves to be at the top of the charts. The music is of the highest quality, with a good mixture of style and pace, of ebullience and seriousness, and with a deft dramatic hand at work (Handel was first and foremost a composer of opera).

Oratorio and opera are two sides of a coin: opera is the secular side, and oratorio the sacred. In the Baroque period, they both had parts for soloists, and increasingly for instruments, and both were essentially dramatic, involving the retelling of a narrative. Unlike opera, oratorios could be performed even when the theatres were closed (during Holy Week, for example).

Composers and librettists took as their subjects the great characters of the Old Testament, or the lives of the saints. It is unusual, therefore, that *Messiah* is concerned with the promise of Christ's birth, the events of his life, and his glorification in heaven.

Musical settings of Christ's Passion had been heard regularly since the medieval period, but no oratorio, other than *Messiah*, deals with Christ's life, nor proclaims its subject matter so boldly. The man who chose this sequence of Bible passages, formed them into a coherent structure and presented it to Handel, was Charles Jennens.

JENNENS was an unusual man. Born in about 1700 into a wealthy Midlands family, he grew up to be a shy, cultivated, and sometimes irascible man, who became devoted to the arts. He also developed views that held him back from assuming a leading part in politics.

He was a non-juror (one who refused to support William of Orange and Mary's appearance after the Glorious Revolution of 1688) and he was anti-Settlement, preferring the Stuart claims to the throne to those of the Hanoverians. As a result, preferment was denied him, and he spent his time editing Shakespeare and supporting Handel.

George Frideric Handel (left) and Charles Jennens (right)

He was also worried by the rise of secularism, and the increasingly popular, anti-religious ideas of the Enlightenment, which sought to banish traditional Christian belief. He was most critical of the Deists, who believed (and still do) in the existence of God, but only as creator of the world, not as redeemer.

Jennens, secure in his traditional, Anglican, Bible-based beliefs, wanted to reassert God's relationship with us all; and that seems to be the main impetus behind his assembling various texts into a libretto that became *Messiah*. We know that it was Jennens himself who was the instigator of the project. He wrote on 10 July 1741:

> "Handel says he will do nothing next Winter, but I hope I shall persuade him to set another Scripture collection I have made for him … I hope he will lay out his whole Genius and Skill upon it, that the Composition may excell all his former Compositions, as the Subject excells every other Subject. The Subject is Messiah."

MESSIAH does not deal with narrative. There is no manger, no visit by the Wise Men, no miracles, and no mention of the Holy Spirit. It is rather a meditation on the events of Christ's life and how we react to them — and, quintessentially, it is about us, and our relationship with God.

After the instrumental overture (just like an opera), the first words that we hear are "Comfort ye, comfort ye". Jennens reminds us that we have the promise of being exalted, and of receiving comfort. But he then sends us off into the world of judgement in the recitative "Thus saith the Lord", the aria "But who may abide", and the chorus "And he shall purify".

The judgement that is to come is for us all, and none can escape it. So we are set up with the promise of comfort, and the threat of judgement. How are these two opposites resolved? The answer lies with the Virgin who "will conceive and bear a son", whose name is Emmanuel. We are already the centre of attention in this story. We are being comforted; we are being warned of the coming judgement; and we are being prepared for the arrival of "God with us".

Jennens uses only one narrative episode in *Messiah*: the scene from Luke's Gospel where the angels appear to the shepherds, tell of the birth of Jesus, and glorify God. Handel provides a little *scena*: a lilting, rural (or as rural as composers then could imagine) *Pifa* for the poor-but-happy shepherds, before the arrival of the angel.

By ignoring the actual birth, the Wise Men, *et al.,* Jennens has decided to highlight the moment when the good news is given to the ordinary people. It is the shepherds who are first told, not a political leader nor a military government. This Jesus is for us all, high and low, small and great.

IN the second part of *Messiah*, the focus moves to a meditation on the passion, a brief consideration of the resurrection, and then a final section on the spreading of the gospel, and how we react to it. Again, there is no narrative here: no crucifixion, no giving up of the ghost; rather there are various biblical verses that reflect on events with which Jennens assumes we are already familiar.

We are invited to gaze on an image of the Lamb of God in the first chorus, and after the poignant "He was despised", Handel provides us with a rollercoaster of emotion — from the angry, terse-sounding "Surely he hath borne our sins", to the uncomfortable "And with his stripes we are healed", before inviting us to one of the best musical parties in the business: "All we like sheep have gone astray".

In this F-major movement, voices swirl around in fast semiquavers, go off in the "wrong" direction, and love doing it — "We have turnèd every one to his own way". We lose ourselves in the euphoria of being sinful, and we love it — until a sudden crash into C minor at the words "And the Lord has laid on him the iniquity of us all". Christ is to suffer for our misdeeds.

Handel makes it even more real by using a "turba" chorus to follow. Turba choruses are the crowd reactions in the Passion narratives, which reach their zenith in Bach's *St John Passion*, where the crowd bays for the blood of Jesus. Handel sets Jennens's quotation from Psalm 22 with a sneering fugue: "He trusted in God that he would deliver him, let him deliver him if he delight in him".

The recitative that follows it is one of the most poignant ever written, reflecting on Christ's desolation and loneliness. We are not with him. We have abandoned him. We have been the turba, losing ourselves first in the enjoyment of sin, and then in the energy of a combative fugue which bristles with unbridled rage.

JENNENS lists only two short texts to deal with the resurrection, and one for the ascension. Handel underplays this still further by using a short recitative and a restrained aria, although he does produce one of his most memorable choruses ("Lift up your heads") for the ascension. The legendary "Hallelujah Chorus" — and let us clear up the fact that there is no evidence of George II's having ever being at a performance of *Messiah*, nor standing because he thought it was the end, thus prompting everyone else to their feet — does not follow the resurrection.

George Stevens, in his 1965 film *The Greatest Story Ever Told*, uses the Hallelujah Chorus as Easter morning breaks and the news of Christ's resurrection spreads. In *Messiah*, it appears at the end of Part II, and after Jennens has provided two other sections of texts: "The beginnings of gospel preaching" and "The world's rejection of the gospel".

It is after this final section, when we have witnessed the nations raging in a busy but ultimately futile aria, and when the Lord has "laughed them to scorn", that Jennens places his "Hallelujah Chorus". Handel is ending his Part II with the perfect closing item. Jennens, I suspect, is revelling in the triumph of faith over doubt and the routing of the Deists.

THE emphasis is back on us in Part III. It is about how we live our lives, and how we prepare for our death. "I know that my redeemer liveth" sings the soprano, in the same key as the first recitative and aria ("Comfort ye" and "Every valley") at the beginning of the piece.

"The trumpet shall sound and the dead shall be raised and we shall be changed" proclaims the bass in D major, with another backward glance to the recitative "Thus says the Lord", and the aria "But who may abide" — both in Part I, and both in D minor. Christ is the comfort promised, and the answer to how we face judgement.

The final chorus, "Worthy is the Lamb", where we worship the Lord in majesty, is proceeded by the exquisite aria "If God be for us, who can be against us". This is the sure, confident statement that we are saved, protected, and cared for.

Jennens, in his selection of texts for *Messiah*, assembles a powerful case for showing that we live in God, and he lives in us. In many ways, *Messiah* is more about us than it is about Christ. Handel amplifies Jennens's choice of Scripture, and, in *Messiah*, has created a piece of music that we can take to our hearts, and enjoy as our own statement of faith.

(2016)

Throwing out the bathwater
(but not the Baby)

Pamela Tudor-Craig investigates the disappearance of the
midwives from Christmas iconography

IN these days of alternative midwifery, some of the ancient lore of the "wise
women" who presided before the introduction, in the 18th century, of the
doctor and forceps into the delivery chamber, is being reassessed. The
patroness of the modem midwife should be Salome: not she who danced
before Herod, but the second of the two midwives whom Joseph sought out
while Mary was giving birth in the stable.

The Gospels have nothing to say of the midwives, though Mark 15.40
mentions a Salome alongside Mary Magdalene, and Mary the mother of
James the less and of Joses, among those who stood at the foot of the cross,
one of the group who had followed Christ and ministered to him in Galilee.
According to Mark 16.1, she was the third of the women who took sweet
spices to the tomb.

While acknowledging her Marcan appearance in this, the closest circle
of women around Christ at the end of his life, St Jerome was responsible for
quashing all possible association with the nativity. In his polemic *Against
Helvidius* of about AD 383, Jerome defended the doctrine of the Virgin's
perpetual virginity against what strike us as the understandable doubts of
poor Helvidius. In his tirade, Jerome declared: "No midwife assisted at his
birth; no women's officiousness intervened. With her own hands she wrapped
him in the swaddling clothes [Luke 2.7], herself both mother and midwife
… which … refutes the ravings of the apocryphal accounts, for Mary herself
wrapped him in the swaddling clothes …"

So the "ravings of the apocryphal accounts" were officially dismissed
from correct Christian reading. Despite the very ancient provenance of much
of it — in some cases only one or two generations later than the Gospels
themselves — the substantial, if fragmented, body of the New Testament
apocrypha is much neglected today. Nevertheless, its popularity throughout
the Middle Ages is witnessed by the strength of the visual tradition.

AMONG your Christmas cards this year there may be images of the nativity
where the foreground is occupied by two prominent ladies bathing the baby.
These are the midwives, named, according to the fairly late, perhaps eighth-
century, compilation of infancy narratives *The Gospel of Pseudo-Matthew*,
Zelomi and Salome.

They bathe the baby in countless representations of the nativity in the Eastern and Western traditions. After about 1430, they tend to become less common in the West, where the more vivid iconography of the Virgin kneeling before her new-born son deprives them of their moment. A predella panel by Gentile da Fabriano from his *Adoration of the Magi* altarpiece of 1423, now in the Uffizi, catches the transition: the midwives are tucked away just outside the stable, while Mary kneels before her baby in the foreground.

The primary account of the midwives is in the *Protevangelium of James*, an account of far-reaching influence, *pace* St Jerome. There survive more than 100 texts, some of the third century, and in languages as diverse as Syriac, Ethiopic, Georgian, Sahidic, Old Church Salonic, Armenian, and presumably Latin. It is generally accepted as originating in the second half of the second century, certainly before the references to it in Origen, and in Clement of Alexandria, who died in 215.

Here we read that Zelomi, the first midwife Joseph enlisted, witnessed the bright cloud over the cave, and uttered her own abbreviated Magnificat. She then met Salome and told her of the virgin birth, upon which the disbelieving Salome attempted a medical examination, and her hand was withered. Her repentance, "I have tempted the living God ...", was rewarded, and her hand restored. We sense the embarrassment of St Jerome. This incident is never depicted, to the best of my knowledge, in the visual arts;

Detail from The Adoration of the Magi *(1423) by Gentile da Fabriano, Uffizi Gallery, Florence, showing two midwives behind the Virgin*

but its vigorous survival is proved by its appearance in the Chester Cycle version of the mystery plays.

What is reiterated in the imagery is the bath scene. The puzzle is that it makes no appearance in the apocrypha. Even the great Emile Male, doyen of medieval iconography, could find no text for it, though he illustrated a very early rendering of the midwives bathing the Baby, occupying as much space as, and more prominence than, the recumbent Virgin behind them, on a sixth-century enamelled reliquary in the Vatican. Male was reduced to suggesting that the story could have been recounted in the cave of the nativity under the basilica at Bethlehem.

THE midwives did not go home on Boxing Day. In Gentile da Fabriano's painting of the adoration of the Magi, they cluster behind the Virgin at the entrance to the stable. In many renderings of the flight into Egypt, both (Antelami, over the inner door to the baptistry at Parma, c. 1180–1200) or one (Giotto, Arena Chapel at Padua) accompany the flight into Egypt. For this there is an apocryphal source, *The History of Joseph the Carpenter*, a probably Egyptian derivative of *Proto-James*. The narrative is given to Christ himself, who says of the flight into Egypt, "Salome was with us."

Here the plot thickens, for there was a lost *Gospel of the Egyptians*, which appears to have been of the early second century. Origen, though it did not please him, discussed it as an attempt, *antedating* St Luke, to write a Gospel, referring to Luke's opening lines. From the few quotations we have from it, in the works of Hippolytus and Clement of Alexandria, the *Gospel of the Egyptians* contained passages, probably substantial ones, of dialogue between Christ and Salome. They dealt with the issues of marriage and chastity, childbirth and death, appropriate for an interrogator who had been a midwife. According to Clement of Alexandria, when Salome asked Christ, "How long shall death prevail?" he replied, "As long as ye women bear children."

Hippolytus complained of the belief that "the soul is hard to find and hard to know. For it remains not in one fashion, nor also in one affection so that it could be called after one pattern or perceived in its nature. These manifold strange notions they find in the so-called Gospel of the Egyptians."

The loss of a Gospel whose message probably amalgamated early Christian and Egyptian thought about life and death, comments that we do not find "manifold strange" about the nature of the soul, and a dialogue purporting to be between Christ and the repentant midwife who would follow him to the end, is a loss indeed.

(2000)

Adventure falls on Christmas Knight

Nicholas Orme discusses Gawain's quest, and the medieval
Christmas scenes presented in *Sir Gawain and the Green Knight*

A KNIGHT in armour is riding alone through a forest in Cheshire in the late 1300s. It is Christmas Eve. He has been travelling across wild countryside for nearly two months, in distressing weather, and yearns for a refuge indoors — not for relief from his journey, but because this is a holy time, and he wishes to worship Christ on Christmas Day, as a good Christian should.

He prays as people did, repeating the *Pater noster* and *Ave Maria* in Latin, crossing himself three times and saying in English "Christ's cross speed me." No sooner has he done so than he sees through the trees a castle on a mound, glimmering in the winter sunshine. Around it is a park of great oaks fenced by palings: part of the landscaping that surrounded great medieval houses to set off the buildings and proclaim the status of the owners.

This scene comes from the poem now known as *Sir Gawain and the Green Knight*, written in Chaucer's day by an unknown author writing in the northwest of England. If the author lacks Chaucer's range, he rivals or exceeds him in other respects, writing in a rich alliterative verse that is both vivid in its descriptions and deep in the issues that it handles.

THE framework of the story is fantastic. A Green Knight — green in body as well as in clothing — comes to King Arthur's court on New Year's Day, and challenges anyone there to "a Christmas game". He will endure a blow from an axe, but he must give one in return. Gawain accepts the challenge, and cuts off the knight's head. The body then gets up, retrieves its head, and departs, warning Gawain to come for the reciprocal blow at the Green Chapel on the same day next year.

This is supernatural, as is Gawain's journey to find the chapel. He travels alone, which knights never did, and how he got his food is unexplained. But, within that framework, the story is highly realistic. The castle to which Gawain comes, and how it functions, reflect what might have been true of a wealthy and well-organised noble residence in Richard II's reign. The result is one of the best Christmas stories ever written — or, more accurately, the best midwinter stories, since it starts at one New Year and ends at another.

227

On reaching the castle, Gawain is immediately asked to stay and shown to a bedroom with a charcoal fire burning in a fireplace. A table and chair are set up, and food is brought, since he has arrived in the afternoon and dinner is over. A white cloth is spread, silver spoons are put out, and a lavish meal is served, consisting of fish — baked, stewed, and spiced. Fish, because this is the vigil of a major feast, as well as the last day of Advent, when the wealthy, at least, have followed a more austere diet.

His meal over, Gawain goes with his host to the castle chapel for first vespers of Christmas, as dusk falls in mid-afternoon — the time of the modern King's College carols. The service is preceded by "rich" bell-ringing — the ringing together of as many bells as there were — and the chapel closely resembles those that can still be seen at Haddon Hall, in Derbyshire, or at the Tudor/medieval house Cotehele, in Cornwall.

There is an antechapel with a screen through which the lord of the castle leads Gawain to a stall in the privileged chancel area. The lord's wife and her maidens watch from an upper window. It is a mark of Gawain's famously good manners that he sits "soberly" during the service, presumably not moving about, or talking.

THE author does not describe Christmas morning, which would have begun with more chapel attendance at matins and mass. Instead, he depicts the festal midday dinner in the castle hall. The chief people present are placed at a high table on a dais. The principal guest, an elderly lady (in fact, she is Morgan la Faye), has the seat of honour at the north end of the table. The lord of the castle sits on her left, facing the hall, with Gawain next to him, and then the lord's wife. Other guests are put at lower tables, according to their rank. Servants wait on them.

Hands are washed before meals, and grace is said. We are not told of the menu, but it would have consisted of two or three courses, each of numerous dishes of butchered meat, birds, or fish. In the later courses, tarts and custards would appear alongside the meat. Guests would taste several of the dishes, and there were interludes between the courses, partly for the convenience of the kitchen and partly to allow the guests to digest, and find room for more.

The interludes would be filled by entertainment from household members or visiting performers. Trumpets, drums, and pipes are mentioned, and there might have been jugglers, singers, dancers, or even short plays. After dinner, the guests dance or play active party games with blindfolds or forfeits, accompanied by laughter and high spirits. Eventually, they retire to a great chamber with a fireplace. There they sit, converse, and drink wine, and nibble fruit, nuts, and biscuits.

PRESENTS were not a feature of Christmas Day. They were given on New Year's Day, which was liturgically the "octave", or week after Christmas, and therefore an important feast in its own right, as well as the recognised start of the natural year (only the calendar year began on 25 March). Kings and lords gave presents such as pieces of silver to lesser folk, and received appropriate gifts in return. At Arthur's court prizes were given in games or guessing competitions.

Manners are formal, with an emphasis on good speaking. Gawain was renowned for his courtesy. When he first meets the lord's wife and her elderly companion, he bows to Morgan, embraces the wife, and asks, in the language of courtly love, if he may be their servant. Conversation is polite, careful, and full of compliments. Yet, as in the novels of Jane Austen, politeness is pregnant with meaning and issues. Gawain has not come to this castle by chance, or by choice.

The castle is indeed more perilous than the winter countryside from which it seemed to offer an escape. This becomes clear on the fourth day after Christmas, when most of the guests go home. The lord informs Gawain that the Green Chapel is close by. Gawain shall stay at the castle until New Year's Day, to recover his strength, while the lord spends his time hunting. At the end of each day, they will exchange their winnings, whatever these are.

NEXT morning, the lord leaves early for the hunt. Gawain remains in bed, and is horrified when the lady of the castle enters his bedroom — a breach of etiquette that means only one thing: seduction. He has to use all his diplomatic skills to avoid offending her and betraying his host. At length he escapes with a kiss, which he swaps with the lord for a pile of deer carcasses. The same happens next day, with two kisses for a wild boar.

On the last day, New Year's Eve, the lady slips under his guard. He is worried about his encounter with the Green Knight. She tempts him with the offer of a magic girdle that will make him invulnerable. When he has accepted it, she tells him that he must keep the gift secret from her husband, and kisses him three times. Later that day, he passes on the kisses, but not the girdle, and receives a dead fox. This determines what takes place next day at the Green Chapel — which I will not disclose, in case you have not read the poem.

Sir Gawain paints a brilliant picture of Christmas in a medieval castle. It is a time of hospitality; because in an age when travel is slow, guests must be asked to stay for several days. It is a time of devotion; each day begins in the chapel. The lord of the castle hears mass there at dawn before he goes hunting, and a second mass takes place at nine or ten for the late risers, such as Gawain.

There are recognised customs of merrymaking and behaviour, to which all must adapt themselves: what was known in later times as "Christmas rule". The festivity is the more enjoyable because it has followed four weeks of relative abstinence.

OUTSIDE, the poem's landscapes are sublime: now frosty and bracing, now desolate with fog and snow. "Near slain with the sleet, he slept in his irons More nights than enough in naked rocks, Where clattering from the crest the cold burn runs, Or hung high over his head in hard icicles." In four lines, the author evokes cold armour ("irons"), a waterfall cascading down a cliff, and the stillness and wonder of its icicles seen in the freezing air.

But the core of the poem is about identity. Gawain is asked more than once: "Who are you? Are you really Gawain?" He is aware of this question, and is anxious to be Gawain, and the right Gawain. He wishes to be loyal to his king, and polite to other people — especially ladies — and true to his host at the castle. He also aspires to be a good Christian: conscientious in his observances, and having faith that God will keep him safe.

But Gawain is not Galahad. The realism of the poem is also Christian, in showing that the perfection to which Gawain aspires must elude him. That is the fate of humanity. He makes mistakes like all of us, and pays for this in his final New Year encounter.

In the end, his efforts to do well, and God's protection, bring him through the worst dangers. The Green Knight praises him as "the most faultless fellow that ever went on foot". More wisely, Gawain comes out of the story aware of his own shortcomings, and ready to own up to them.

"A sad tale's best for winter," Shakespeare said; but Sir Gawain is not a sad tale. On the contrary, it is richly varied: now set indoors, now out of doors; now sinister, now humorous. At one point, it is full of sound and movement; at another, silence falls. The encounters that it describes are not just a string of events, but parts of an evolving plan whose meaning grows clear at the end.

There are many other great works of literature, but it is doubtful whether anything better has yet been written in English.

(2013)

The crib in the dark and the desert

Ben Quash escapes the traditional nativity narrative
through Berlioz's *L'enfance du Christ*

So he got up, took the child and his mother during the night and left for
Egypt, where he stayed until the death of Herod.

Matthew 2.14-15

"IT IS what you might call a Platform 9¾ picture." This was the observation
of one of the picture researchers working on a team I convene at King's
College, London, whose task is to identify images for inclusion in a planned
online visual commentary on Scripture.

Matching paintings from the world of art to particular biblical passages
has many challenges, but one of them is what to do with images that seem
to fall between those scenes that are explicitly described in Scripture. These
"in-between" images have often been the focus of rich and intense devotional
contemplation by Christians.

The image that elicited my picture researcher's Platform 9¾ comment
was comparable. It was a painting of *The Rest on the Flight into Egypt*. That
the Holy Family fled Herod's infanticide, and that they fled specifically to
Egypt, is recorded in the Gospels. No record exists in the scriptural canon,
however, of their having rested (though, presumably, they did), nor of what
that rest was like.

Nevertheless, the imagined scene had begun to become popular in
Western art by the 15th century, and remained so in the Romantic period.
It just escaped the strictures of the Council of Trent's clampdown on fanciful
and extra-canonical religious subject matter in favour of clearly decipherable
and instructive Bible-based art. Despite a little extrapolation, it was just
scriptural enough; so this halfway-house platform has remained open to
spiritual travellers.

INDEED, its survival has engendered more than an ongoing visual legacy.
One of the most touching musical compositions to associate itself with the
Christmas season is Hector Berlioz's *L'enfance du Christ*. It is a musical
triptych, which makes it comparable with many works of Christian visual
art. The analogy is helpful, for painted triptychs do not have a straightfor-
wardly linear structure, running from left to right. The centre of a triptych

231

makes sense of the outer panels; the outer panels amplify the meaning and relevance of the central scene.

At the centre of this work is a rendition of the Rest on the Flight into Egypt. It is the section of the piece that he wrote first. Despite Berlioz's acknowledged adult agnosticism, this central part is an expression of a lifelong and tender attachment to the Christianity that he encountered as a child.

Berlioz frames the narrator's description of the Holy Family at rest with the voices of singing shepherds on one side, and singing angels on the other. In other words, he creates in this part of his work what is, to all intents and purposes, a repristinated crib scene (there is even an ass). But he has set it up in the desert rather than in Bethlehem.

Thus, the atmosphere of Christmas is captured, but we come on it unexpectedly, and it gains a new freshness as a consequence. The meaning of Christmas is shown not to be bound by time, place, or even liturgical season: it travels, and can flower anywhere.

THIS is perhaps part of the power and the value of the Rest on the Flight into Egypt as a topic for artists, whatever their chosen medium. It stops Christmas from being a hermetically sealed moment, inoculated against contamination by the wider and darker biography of Jesus. In the Rest, Christmas pushes beyond its artificially imposed parameters, and displays important, challenging and contemporary connections with the things that come after the manger — while still identifiably "looking a lot like Christmas".

The glowing fireside of Rembrandt's painted version of the theme has the spellbinding quality of any crib scene, as Mary, Joseph, and Jesus share a moment of exquisite, reverential intimacy with their baby. But Rembrandt's great night landscape stretches in all directions, and its dark tones press threateningly on these tiny figures.

The expanse of darkness heightens our sense of their vulnerability: it suggests the murderousness from which they flee, and the alienation that they may face ahead. We are not allowed to forget (as stable scenes and nativity plays sometimes allow us to) that these are refugees — asylum seekers.

BERLIOZ achieves the same effect in his musical interpretation. As the familiar figures of the nativity reconvene around his desert tableau, there is one group notable by its absence. Here are animals, baby, parents, shepherds, angels — but no kings.

Subtly, he directs our attention to what is one of the greatest preoccupations of his work: the dangers of worldly power, and the devastating consequences of its corruption. How easily kings (like nativity playgoers) can

In-between images:
Rembrandt's Landscape with the Rest on the Flight into Egypt, *1647*

miss the political point of the incarnation. The only king we meet in *L'enfance du Christ* is Herod. He is the central focus of Part One (the "left-hand" panel of the triptych).

Berlioz's love of Shakespeare may well have had an influence on the *Hamlet*-like way in which a conversation between two guards on night duty is allowed to set the scene in this opening part. We learn of a corrupt state, and of the uneasy monarch within the palace walls. There is an overpowering sense that something is out of joint: a quality of nervous expectation asserts itself alongside the dreary plodding of the tired soldiers.

By contrast with Shakespeare's *Hamlet*, however, the "ghost" who appears in this city is no dead usurpee; he is an infant usurper — one who comes to enact the promise of Mary's Magnificat, which, through the narrator, Berlioz echoes in the piece's prologue: "The mighty trembled … the weak had hope". This child will put down rulers from their thrones not by force of arms, but by a new set of values: the shattering of pride, and the advance of the claims of love.

Herod is haunted by the visitations of this child, and teeters, as a consequence, on the brink of madness. We see him torn between radically different alternatives: an aching longing for the simplicity of the life of the woodland goatherd, and a fiercely possessive concern with his own "glory" (the rhyme in French poignantly juxtaposes "*gloire*" with "*croire*": selfish glory with the self-giving of faith). To believe, or not to believe? To cling to glory, or not to cling? Herod's decision for glory ensures that his destiny is, in his words, "to reign, yet not to live".

WHAT about the other panel in this triptych — the "right-hand" one? Like the bad and the good thief crucified on either side of Christ at Golgotha, Herod's character is contrasted in Berlioz's arrangement with that of an Ishmaelite householder, in whom compassion and the ethic of hospitality run strong. This Ishmaelite welcomes the migrants into his home.

All that Herod could not do and be, the householder does and is. He does not shut the door on the child whose parents plead entrance for him and for themselves; he is instantly wide open to them. This takes the very domestic form of simple charity: food, drink, music, and sleep. He does not have *gloire*, but he possesses the answer to Joseph's urgent plea for rest; a sort of urgent Agnus Dei ("*laissez-nous reposer!*"). He offers repose, and so Christ makes his home with him, with the implicit promise of an answering peace that passes all understanding.

IT is hard to deny the quality of devotional intensity that pervades this crystalline, jewel-like work. It gathers itself around a single, still point — the sleeping Christ-child, the very embodiment of peace. And yet it delineates the spiritual drama that shapes the whole human condition. Pride or humility? Violence or hospitality? The possession that destroys self, or the obedience that consecrates it?

Berlioz may have departed from the biblical story in inventing a Herod who seems never to have met the Magi, and an "infidel" household in Egypt to which no Scripture attests, but, in doing so, he does not seem to have acted merely in service of spicing up the entertainment value of his creation. Arguably, the ways in which he transgresses the letter of the inherited story actually make it more poignant and challenging in religious terms.

So thank goodness for Platform 9¾ images. St Francis may, as legend has it, have bequeathed to us the crib scene, but it so easily, in our culture, floats free of the larger story. Christmas's escape into the desert in the Rest on the Flight into Egypt makes us realise how seriously we still need to take it.

(2016)

A ridiculous day to choose for a stoning

Stephen Cottrell laments the untimely fate
of his first-century namesake

I HAVE an early childhood memory of being told that St Stephen was the first martyr of the Church, and then bursting into tears. This is one of those stories that gets retold, and probably embellished, at family gatherings, especially at Christmas. But I do remember it; for I was shocked to discover that I shared my name with the first person to be killed for being a Christian.

I do not quite know why I was so dismayed. I suppose it seemed unfair. Furthermore, of all the ridiculous days in the year to choose, his witness to Christ was celebrated on Boxing Day. How typical of the Church to dampen Christmas spirit so completely — what an intrusion! Why would the compilers of the church calendar choose this day to remember such a cruel and vicious death?

In T. S. Eliot's *Murder in the Cathedral*, Archbishop Thomas Becket, preaching in Canterbury Cathedral on Christmas morning, 1170, faces the same question. The Christmas Day mass, Becket reflects, is simultaneously a celebration of the birth of our Lord and a re-enactment of his death and passion. It is a strange paradox: "For who in the World will both mourn and rejoice at once and for the same reason?"

Yet this is the Christian mystery: at the same time as we rejoice in Christ's coming among us in human flesh, we also remember how this flesh was broken. We cannot celebrate the birth of Christ with integrity unless we also see where this birth leads: not just in Christ's own ministry — the manger at Bethlehem being the first step on the way that leads to the cross — but also in the lives of those who follow.

In Eliot's play, Becket sees this; the dark clouds of opposition are gathering. Terrible choices are to be made. In his sermon, Becket questions whether it is an accident that the day of the first martyr, Stephen, should follow hard on the day of Christ's birth. No, he concludes, for the death of Stephen echoes the same Christian paradox: "in a smaller figure, we both rejoice and mourn in the death of martyrs."

Here is the really hard part of Christmas: we are all called to martyrdom. To be a martyr means to be a witness. Mary submits to the will of God (Luke 1.38), and treasures in her heart all she experiences (Luke 2.19). The shepherds, who are the first to come to see Jesus, return "glorifying and

235

praising God for all they had heard and seen" (Luke 2.20). The Wise Men are overwhelmed with joy (Matthew 2.10).

SO it is with everyone who stops by this stable; it is a place of astonishing joy, but also a place where paths converge, and new journeys begin. No one wants to shed his or her blood for the sake of this Christ; but no one is exempt from the Christian vocation to become the place where God dwells.

We pause at the manger and see the story of God etched into a human life. Then, if we stay a little longer, if we are truly still and allow the mystery of God's presence among us to breathe its transforming grace into our own lives, we are invited to become the place where that story is told afresh. Like the Wise Men, we have the path of our life redirected — that is what being a witness means. Martyrdom is not first about shedding blood; it is about being faithful to truth.

We tell it as it is. We face the consequences. So this sort of Messiah — a God among us, born in this sort of manger, ambiguous and bright — leads to this sort of witness. We cannot be sentimental about this birth, and perhaps the real message of Christmas should be a health warning: don't linger for long in this stable if you want an easy life. But linger we must.

STEPHEN was ordained to wait at tables one day, but was preaching before the Sanhedrin and getting himself killed the next (so much for a New Testament pattern of ministry ...). This is where his witness leads. False charges are made against him, and, challenged by the council to account for himself, he makes the devastating and audacious Christian claim that God "does not dwell in houses made with human hands" (Acts 7.48).

Jesus is the place where we will now behold God. (Stephen has been to Bethlehem.) For this tenacious witness, he is dragged out of the city and stoned to death. Silent and serene before his accusers, he prays for them as he dies.

The Stoning of St Stephen, by or after Lorenzo Sabbatini (1530–76) (Wellcome Library, London)

Now all the connections are made. Stephen makes the prayer of Jesus his own: "Lord, do not hold this sin against them" (Acts 7.60). The forgiveness that Jesus extends to those who nailed him to the cross is now evident in the living and dying of those who follow him. A new pattern for humanity is established. The old madness of your eye for my eye, and your tooth for mine, is done away with. Stephen walks the same extra mile of love that we see in the passion of Christ.

"A martyrdom is always the design of God," says Becket; it is a demonstration of God's love for humanity, serving both as a warning and a means of leading us back to him. It can never be a human design, for the true martyr becomes the instrument of God, acting only through God's will and not their own – seeking not even the glory of being a martyr.

WHAT will we find at Bethlehem this year: how will our lives be redirected? More than anything else, what we need to find in the manger is Christ's uncompromising message of peace. We need to hear again the song of the angels that this peace can be known on earth. We need to direct our hearts and minds towards a peace that the world can never understand, because it is founded on the hospitality of a God who in Christ is drawing the whole creation into one.

This is a peace that reconfigures difference. Opposites are turned into complementary facets of a multifaceted and still-being-revealed truth. Diversity is cherished. God reaches out to Jew and Gentile alike. This is the truth we must witness to.

Maybe even the squabbles of the Anglican Communion can be redirected as a glorious and scrupulously honest attempt to live with disagreement, and to keep on walking and talking lest anyone be unnecessarily excluded. Is there another gospel our world needs to hear at the moment: that it is possible to live together with profoundly held disagreement?

Today, the word "martyr" too easily fills us with dread. It has become associated with those who might destroy us. Let it become again a word of hope, telling of those who will go on loving until the end, and whose faithfulness to the truth they find in Christ is boundless and full of joy.

Then there are all the other half-promises of peace that the world continues to peddle, symbolised most poignantly by the present-day walls around Bethlehem itself, and also by the billions our own country proposes to spend on more nuclear weapons. There is the new arms race that this stokes up, as others seek a place at the nuclear high table; the casual violence that is becoming a norm in the underbelly of so many industrialised cities, where astonishing wealth lives blithely side by side with appalling poverty; the mess that Iraq has become; the apathy that continues to betray the earth we inhabit, as we carry on plundering the sea, the land, and the very air we will soon no longer be able to breathe.

The God who comes to us in Christ, the one we find in the manger, breaks down these barriers of separation. "He is our peace," says the letter to the Ephesians. "He has broken down the dividing wall ... the hostility between us" (Ephesians 2.14).

CHRISTIAN peace is not just the silence after the guns have finished firing. Christian peace is true reconciliation, painfully embraced. Christ's peace means facing up to differences, confronting injustice, and repenting of those attitudes and actions that divide and devour the world. It means witnessing to what we see in Christ, the God who is with us.

When this does happen — in Stephen, in Thomas Becket, in the wonderful witness of so many Christian lives — Jesus is born again, the world is offered another way, and the invitation to be changed is offered afresh.

At the same time, however, there is also the dreadful possibility of martyrdom; for such a demonstration of tenacious loving will always strike fear in the hearts of those who have grown powerful by stirring up division. It is not the death of Stephen that is the first intimation of what following Christ may mean, but the terrible massacre of the innocents. What lengths some will travel to, to rid the world of love.

As Christians today, we are called to witness to peace in a time where fear and division seem to be winning the day. But they cannot prevail. Stephen sees the glory of God, and Jesus at God's right hand, as he offers his life in the service of God. This glory can sustain us, even when it is experienced in the midst of suffering.

So I did cry when I first learned about Stephen. But now St Stephen's Day is my favourite in the Christmas season — because it makes the connections. We mourn and we celebrate. The death of Christ and the death of his martyr, Stephen, is a sign of God's victory. Christ's birth and the awakening of vocation in the human heart is a sign of God's involvement with the world.

Yet I also like this day because it is usually a quiet day in the Church — a day when most people are still in bed, nursing hangovers or sleeping in. It is possible to come to the manger, to bend the knee, to get underneath the lintel of the door, to see how silently the gift is given, and then, away from all the hurried merriment of the day before, to receive it.

(2007)

It might soon be just two ...

Ian Tattum takes a look at the mixed fortunes of the turtle dove

THE Holy Spirit descended like a dove on Christ at his baptism, and it was a dove that brought to Noah the good news that the flood had receded. Members of the pigeon family have long been associated with hope and spiritual renewal in the Christian tradition.

But the same family of birds also gave us the dodo and the passenger pigeon, two familiar symbols of extinction. A startling statistic is that it took until 1850 for the global human population to catch up with the population of the passenger pigeon, and barely 60 more for the latter to be wiped out altogether.

The great Scottish-American conservationist John Muir left us a picture of the bird's abundance: "Of all God's feathered people ... no other bird seemed so wonderful ... I have seen the flocks streaming south in the autumn so large that they were flowing over from horizon to horizon in an almost continuous stream all day long."

Another of "God's feathered people", the turtle dove (*Streptopelia turtur*), the lover's gift on the second day of Christmas, has long been a poetic symbol of spring and love, as in the Song of Solomon:

The flowers appear on the earth;
The time of singing has come,
and the turtle dove
is heard in our land.

The turtle dove is so named because of its purring song, which people have long perceived as both mournful and consoling.

Now it, too, is in danger. About 250,000 visited Britain in the spring of 1966, but, today, barely 5000 make it to these shores each year, and the fall in numbers has sharpened in the past five years. It is a history that tells us something about our relationship with God's creation and the mysteries contained therein.

WHEN God answers Job from the whirlwind, he reminds him of the limits of human knowledge concerning creation and the lives of animals: "Do you know when the mountain goats give birth? Do you observe the calving of the deer?" (Job 39)

239

Job was expected to answer such a question with an emphatic "No." Those of us who live in the age of lushly filmed nature documentaries, in which drones and hidden cameras can probe such secrets, might be tempted to answer more positively. Such familiarity can, however, mislead us into thinking we know more than we do.

It is only with the recent advent of satellite transmitters that the exact migratory route of the turtle dove has been discovered. The birds that arrive in Britain in late April and early May have travelled three thousand miles from West Africa — Mali, Niger, and Senegal — across the Sahara Desert and the Atlas Mountains, before crossing the Mediterranean into Spain, and, finally, the English Channel.

The study of breeding behaviour has revealed one of the key factors in its decline. In the 1960s, each pair of birds was able to rear two or three broods a year. Now most pairs can barely manage one, and clutch sizes are falling, too. Although thousands of turtle doves are shot by hunters as they pass over the Continent, there is no doubt that this lack of chicks has a more significant impact on numbers. A fundamental reason for this, as is the case for most of the declining bird species, is that there is not enough food, or only the wrong kind of food.

It is easy to think that the animal behaviour we observe is in some way "natural" when it is inevitably affected by what humans do. It would be folly, for example, to conclude that chips are the traditional diet of gulls. When it comes to turtle doves, there is still uncertainty about exactly what they need to eat to flourish. Not long ago, an RSPB-led conservation project, based on the observation that the birds are known to glean the fields for grain, tried supplementing their diet by scattering supplies of what they believed were suitable seed. The project was not a success.

One conclusion is that the turtle doves only feast on grain because that is all that is left to them by modern farming practices. There is evidence that hard grain seriously damages the bird's throat, in contrast to the once-common agrarian flowers of the field, such as fumitory, clover, and vetches. This familiar bird, deeply embedded in our culture, has evidently still not revealed all its secrets.

GLIMMERS of hope can be found in rewilding, a process described by the author and conservationist Isabella Tree in her book *Wilding: The return of nature to a British farm* (Picador, 2018). The wilding project at Knepp, in Sussex, suggests that a more varied, untidy habitat can created a safe environment and bring back native plants which turtle doves need to prosper.

Ornithologists have also begun to ask whether too little attention has been paid to the turtle dove's African home, which is where, after all, it spends most of the year. There, it is a scrubland species, and has a varied diet including caterpillars.

The Book of Job assumes that wild creatures live outside human boundaries, eluding both our understanding and control. Wilding projects, and more modest, preferably untidy, attempts to give nature space, whether in churchyards or back gardens, are a means of restoration. We are, at last, learning that we need to allow the wilderness to return to allow "God's feathered people" to thrive.

Some Christians still think of the God-given relationship of humans with other sentient beings as one of utility, relying on a very narrow interpretation of the concept of dominion in Genesis 1.26; but the Hebrew Scriptures contain a great variety of alternatives, including the one in Job that the terrain and character of wild animals transcend human scope and are known fully only to God. Isaiah 40-41 reveals a creator who makes a path through the wilderness for the exiles to return, but fills the remainder with abundant non-human life.

When the English parson-naturalist John Ray pioneered the scientific study of birds in the 17th century, he saw his task as philosophical and theological. His project could be described as one of mapping the divine ecology, in which birds were observed and categorised, to discover where they fitted into God's scheme. To achieve his aim, he thought it necessary to put to one side the traditions, legends, and symbolic meanings that had come to be associated with birds, such as the belief that kingfishers could be used to predict the weather, and the wisdom contained in medieval bestiaries that pigeons represented the love of God and love of neighbour.

But symbolism has a way of reasserting itself in new ways. As the Victorians came to identify city-dwelling sparrows with the urban poor (who similarly scrambled for scraps in the streets), so the present-day plight of vulnerable birds mirrors humanity's present fragility.

In his book about Coleridge and the Wordsworths and their circle, *The Making of Poetry* (William Collins, 2019), Adam Nicolson suggests that Coleridge's sense of kinship with nature has come alive in the present time: "It was not a form of anthropomorphism — thinking that birds are like us — but the opposite, zoomorphism, that we are like the birds … The mariner shoots the albatross, and in doing so shoots himself."

The turtle dove has thus become more than a sign of spring and a token of romantic love, a symbol of loss and fragile hope. It has also magnified humanity's sense of connectedness to the whole natural world, which its actions threaten. The turtle dove is a reminder that, in this season, we celebrate God's outpouring of love for all of creation, in all its fragility.

(2019)

The blood of the martyrs

The calendar turns dark after Christmas.
John Pridmore reflects on the late-December feasts

St Thomas Becket

WE are watching the film version of T. S. Eliot's *Murder in the Cathedral*. It is 29 December 1170. A priest enters, then a second priest, then a third. Their speeches mark the sequence of the passing days, as do the banners they carry: St Stephen, first martyr (26 December); St John the Apostle (27 December); the day of the Holy Innocents (28 December).

The priests wonder what this fourth and nameless day can hold, a day so empty after days so highly charged. What can it offer, a day neither high nor holy, a day already fading?

Despite the gathering gloom, despite the sense of exhaustion and deflation after the celebrations of the past days, despite the bleakness of the season, one of the priests affirms his faith. "Even now, in sordid particulars, the eternal design may appear." At this point, four knights enter, the knights who later this same day will murder Archbishop Thomas Becket.

The medieval sources do not spare us "the sordid particulars" of Becket's death, from the first blow that sliced off the crown of his head to the final blow that scattered his brains and blood about the pavement. But the same principle — that the purpose of God is worked out in the appalling actualities of how things are — is shown by the testimony of all the saints, starting after Christmas with Stephen, John, and the Holy Innocents.

A 13th-century manuscript illumination, the earliest known depiction of Thomas Becket's assassination in Canterbury Cathedral

St Stephen

THERE is nothing new under the sun. The "sordid particulars" of the situation that led eventually to Stephen's stoning were threats of schism. In the church in Jerusalem, there were daily handouts to the destitute, particularly for the widows — always a desperately needy group in antiquity. A row was brewing in the church between "the Greeks" and "the Hebrews" about whether this relief programme was being administered fairly. Tensions between Brits and Poles, and disputes over entitlement to social services come to mind.

The apostles declined to be involved in the messy business of manning soup kitchens. They pleaded that they had sermons to prepare and prayers to say. So they appointed Stephen and six others to run the church's relief programme. But Stephen does not confine himself to the humble tasks of a "deacon", if that is what he was. He turns out to be something of a radical and a firebrand.

He is brought to trial before the Sanhedrin, accused of blasphemy. His speech in his own defence concludes with a searing attack on his accusers. By murdering Jesus they have proved themselves to be no better than their predecessors who persecuted the prophets. But what appears to have most outraged the hierarchy, and what sealed Stephen's fate, was that he dared to challenge the institution of the Temple itself (Acts 6, 7).

Stephen is the first martyr — or "witness". In the manner of his death, forgiving his enemies, he bears eloquent witness to his Lord, who did the same. But the story of Stephen shows, too, that from the start Christians have fallen out with one another. There was this spat over the daily handouts. But, reading between the lines, there were clearly more fundamental differences of opinion. There was disagreement over the importance of structures such as temples — over "houses made with hands". In a word, those first Christians disagreed about how far the way of Jesus needs special buildings with all the paraphernalia of "religion" — all the dressing up and ceremonial that goes on in them.

Persecution breaks out on Stephen's death, but — here's the significant point — we are told that this persecution does not touch the apostles (Acts 8.1). Why did they leave the apostles alone? The reason is that, so far from attacking the Temple, the apostles have been turning up there religiously — *religiously* — every day (Acts 2.46).

So then, as now, it seems, there were "the liberals" and "the traditionalists". The apostles erred on the side of caution, as some of their successors — wondering whether or not to come to Lambeth — do today. If contemporary Anglicanism faces schism, so, too, did the apostolic Church. Such are "the sordid particularities" of the body of Christ on earth. Thus it was in the beginning, is now, and — until the Lord comes again — ever shall be.

St John the Evangelist

JOHN escaped martyrdom. His last words, they say, were his last short sermon. "Little children, love one another. It is the Lord's command, and it is enough." John has his own term for the sphere of "the sordid particulars". It is that of "the flesh", the unlovely and variously hued substance, much pampered and indulged at Christmas, which the Word became in his incarnation (John 1.14).

We need to be specific. What precisely were "the sordid particulars" that Christ "assumed?" Whose flesh did he make his, in order that "the eternal design" might appear? To say that our Lord took his human nature from his blessed mother is at once most orthodox and most wonderful, but that statement does not exhaust the implications of John's audacious claim that the Word was made flesh.

Painting of Saint John the Evangelist in the Monastero del Sacro Speco, Subiaco, Italy

So whose flesh is his? We could start naming names, except that "were every one of them to be written, the world itself could not contain the books that would be written" (John 21.25). With whom would we start — suicide-bombers, homophobic bishops, and drug-dealers?

A salutary discipline would be to write down the names of those individuals who happen to get up our nose — and then to add by each name: "The Word became *his* flesh." "The Word became *her* flesh." Of course, not all sordid particulars are particularly sordid. We think of the "beloved disciple" who taught us these things, and of most readers of the *Church Times*.

Holy Innocents

STEPHEN is a deacon and a martyr. John is an apostle and an evangelist. We have some understanding of what these terms mean, but what, please, is a "holy innocent"? We have enveloped the infant victims of Herod in so much incense that we can no longer see them. Do we really suppose that the tiny tots skewered by Herod's soldiers were holier or more innocent, whatever those words mean, than the kids up the road who escaped the carnage?

Part of The
Massacre of the
Innocents
(c.1638)
by Peter Paul
Rubens,
Alte Pinakothek,
Munich

Here are the first children we meet in the story of Jesus, and already we sense the hesitancy and equivocation about the status of children that always seems to becloud Christian thinking about them and to bemire its ministry to them.

Hard heads soften. Even Augustine witters. These little ones, he says, are "buds, killed by the frost of persecution the moment they showed themselves".

One steadier voice speaks, that of Pope Leo the Great (400-461). "They were able to die for him whom they could not yet confess. Thus Christ, so that no period of his life should be without miracle, silently exercised the power of the Word before the use of speech ... He crowned infants with a new glory, and consecrated the first days of these little ones by his own beginnings, in order to teach us that no member of the human race is incapable of the divine mystery, since even this age was capable of the glory of martyrdom."

Not that there was anything particularly glorious in the "sordid particulars" of being butchered by one of those soldiers. But we take Pope Leo's point — and God help us if we do not. Whatever the calendar says, Bethlehem's slaughtered children are martyrs, a title and status that has nothing to do with their innocence or holiness. We used to say, before the law was belatedly changed, that those old enough to die for their country should be allowed the vote. By the same token, those old enough to die for Christ should be allowed the sacrament of his love for them.

So we return to St Thomas Becket. Beneath his vestments, we are told, he wore a hair shirt, swarming with vermin. Of your charity, pray for the one who today, hardly more comfortably, holds his high office.

(2007)

245

Remembered only for his cruelty

Jane Williams considers what is known about Herod the Great

HEROD does not get a very good press in the Christmas story. He is mentioned very briefly in Luke 1.5, just to fix a historical time. This confuses Luke's timeline horribly. Herod's reign lasted from about 40 BC to 4 BC, which is fine, except that the census that Luke mentions in chapter 2, carried out under Quirinius, the governor of Syria, happened in about AD 6 or 7.

Debate rages about whether Luke just got it wrong, or whether there can have been an earlier census, not mentioned in any other records, or whether Luke's sources were themselves confused. Since I can barely remember what I had for lunch yesterday, I incline to the view that Mary, in old age, got very tired of retelling the story of Jesus's birth, and simply could not remember all the external details. But we do not have to solve this puzzle here. Suffice it to say that Matthew agrees with Luke that Jesus's birth took place during the reign of Herod.

The New Testament mentions a number of different Herods, who should not be confused. The one most often cited is Herod the Tetrarch, or Herod Antipas, during whose time John the Baptist and Jesus began their public ministry, and who is also responsible for the imprisonment and beheading of John (Luke 3). It is also this Herod, Antipas, the son of Herod the Great, who plays a part in Jesus's crucifixion. Luke 23 tells us that Pilate sent Jesus to Herod, hoping to pass the buck.

IT is Herod the Great, however, who has such terrible associations with the Christmas story. Herod was a client-king of Rome, which meant he was given a free hand to rule, provided he paid a tax to Rome. He could — and did — raise far more than Rome required, and simply kept the surplus for himself.

Herod claimed to be Jewish, at least when he was among Jews. His people, the Idumaeans, had been forcibly converted about a century before, and practised circumcision and loyalty to the Law. Most Jewish people looked down on the Idumaeans as very much second-class. Herod had a life-long struggle with the aristocratic high-priestly family, who were, in effect, Jewish royalty. He was responsible for the execution and "accidental" death of more than one of them, including his brother-in-law, Aristobulus.

This young high priest made the mistake of being too popular; so Herod arranged for him to be drowned while swimming.

Although Herod got on better with the Pharisees, they never quite trusted him, and even his great building project, the Temple in Jerusalem, was viewed with mixed feelings, because of his association with it. He started to build it in about 20 BC, and it was not finished until well after his death; so it was complete for only a few years before it was destroyed by the Romans in AD 70.

Herod's family relationships were complex and bloody. He was married many times — probably ten — and had a great many children. His relatives were executed with remarkable regularity, including at least three of his own sons. It was said at the time: "It is better to be Herod's pig than to be Herod's son."

IT MIGHT not be immediately obvious from this description how he earned the epithet "Great". But Herod was an astute politician and an energetic ruler to those who did not annoy him or provoke him into insecurity. He owed his promotion to the rule of Judaea to his Roman patron, Mark Antony. Herod is briefly mentioned in *Antony and Cleopatra*.

Despite the fact that Cleopatra hated him, and manoeuvred to get rid of him and seize as much of his territory as possible, Herod managed to maintain his alliance with Antony. Cleopatra tried threats, and conspiracy with Herod's hated mother-in-law. When all else failed, she even tried to seduce him, but Herod survived. He calculated his moment to switch sides perfectly, submitting to Augustus when it became clear that Antony was going to be defeated, and so retained his title.

In the territory that Herod governed, he set up a number of projects that improved the quality of life for many of his subjects. In Jerusalem, as well as the Temple, he built an amphitheatre and a theatre. He was responsible for the construction of Caesarea, with its fine harbour, which brought prosperity to the region. He also built fortresses, such as Antonia in the Jerusalem region, and Machaerus and Masada. In the Gentile territories, he was just as generous in his provision of temples as he was in Jerusalem, and he was known to be a patron of Greek culture and philosophy.

IT IS paradoxical that he is chiefly remembered for an incident that is not witnessed to outside the New Testament, the "massacre of the innocents", as recorded in Matthew 2. But, although no other historians mention it, it is by no means implausible or out of character. There are records of his execution of a large group of wealthy and aristocratic Jews who had opposed him, and it is quite likely that the death of a few peasant children in an obscure village hardly seemed worth counting in the great lists of those who owed their deaths to Herod.

Matthew's picture of Herod as superstitious, vain, and insecure about his own power seems accurate. He liked the Essenes because one of their prophets had foretold that Herod would sit on the throne. He loved to be praised for his achievements, and he killed anyone who seemed a threat to his rule, including his own sons.

He was prone to extreme jealousy. He could not bear the thought that his second wife, Mariamne, might marry again if anything happened to him; so, on more than one occasion when he was going on a risky expedition, he arranged for Mariamne to be killed if he did not return. His suspicions about her faithfulness finally resulted in her death.

On his own deathbed, he could still not decide which of his remaining sons to trust with the succession, and changed his will backwards and forwards. It made no difference in the end, because Augustus refused to make any of his sons king in his place, but downgraded them and split the territory.

The final, macabre twist to Herod's story was a plan he concocted to ensure that someone would mourn his death. He gave orders that numbers of people should be killed when he died, so that the sound of tears would fill the city. Thankfully, once he was dead, no one felt compelled to carry out his brutal order. But there is something fitting about this bitter self-knowledge. Herod the King's raging had ensured that he died unmourned.

HEROD'S rule stands as the antithesis to Jesus's. Herod kills to maintain his power. Jesus dies to demonstrate his. Herod's whole life, even to his deathbed, is dominated by the insecurity that must be felt by any ruler whose supremacy has to be maintained by force. He could never be sure that anyone's love or admiration was genuine — so much so that he feared that no one would care when he died.

Jesus the King is born in a stable, to very ordinary parents. His only protection is their love. As he grows up, Jesus chooses friendship as his means of governance, entrusting the success or failure of his mission to a group of well-meaning but hardly bright or influential men and women. Not surprisingly, he is betrayed and killed. A triumph for the Herods of this world, surely?

But death cannot hold on to Jesus, because his way of living and reigning is God's way. Herod is always bound to fail in the end, because people cannot be enslaved for ever. They are created to be friends and co-heirs with Jesus the Son of God, not slaves of any other kind of king.

(2007)

Word from Wormingford

Ronald Blythe plans a quiet
St Odilo's Eve

NEW YEAR falls on a Saturday, but there will be no Saturnalia, unless those wet rompings in Trafalgar Square can be described thus. Nor on Sunday will there be an ancient liturgical expression of it, for such a service does not exist. But we will sing Timothy Dudley-Smith's fine "Lord, for the years your love has kept and guided" and Canon Ainger's "God is working his purpose out", and I will scrupulously avoid any mention of resolution in the sermon.

Poor saintly Dr Johnson, who cared for blind old Mrs Williams, and made a black servant his son and heir, lashed himself, figuratively speaking, every New Year's Day. He would get up early in the morning (he never did), he would work harder (how could he?), he would keep his eyes off actresses' shoulders (what a hope!), he would pray better (how could he?).

All these resolves he made on his wife's grave. What a mercy to know that on 2 January he was in the Cheshire Cheese as usual, terrifying his friends, then carrying oysters home for his cat. I chose Boswell's *Life of Johnson* for my book on Desert Island Discs, because of its endless sociability, its tries and failures where religion was concerned.

New Year's Day is the feast of St Odilo, the Cluniac abbot who created All Souls' Day on 2 November. New Year's Eve itself was all over the place until the 18th century, when it settled down as Watch Night. The followers of the Wesleys seem to have been the only part of the Church to have a New Year's Eve service.

No revels for me, no proper grasp of the calendar until February, but a sense of the strong

Engraving of St Odilo

jogging of Time, of the clanking date. No auld lang syne and a hangover —
not nowadays.

Primroses are in bloom by the wall, tiny flowers with the minimum of
stalk, nervous to stretch too far into winter. The hazels are pushing out a
lot of elementary catkins. The wind alternates between caresses and violence.
Henry the new Priest-in-Charge appears, the most welcome harbinger
imaginable of what is to come.

At the moment, his vicarage stares empty-mindedly across the valley.
Rooks whirr around the black wood behind it in a kind of "shall-we-or-
shall-we-refuse-to-build-here?" screaming mob of indecision. Black tomb-
chests glisten with grime in the churchyard opposite, where Georgian
farmers and millers make the most of their departure. They say that
medieval nuns used the nearby hall as a kind of holiday home, and I see
them lying in bed until five in the morning, cutting summer flowers and
eyeing shepherd boys.

Indoors, we eye the Christmas trash, the cards lolling against each other,
the red wrapping, the weary holly, not to mention the muddle in the fridge.
Dare we do a clear-up? Does God or custom allow it? Down the lane, in
the cold gardens, trees go on winking with electric blossoms. Not yet, not
yet. In any case, the Epiphany dawns. All the great religions are based on
enlightenment, and in spite of the darkness that they engender at times,
the world — humanity — would be spiritually and morally impenetrable
without them.

Such contrasting folk came to identify the Light that lighteth every
man, three kings you won't find in Scripture, King Gaspar, King Melchior,
and King Balthasar, with their serious birthday presents, and an old
couple checking each baby being carried by his mother up the Temple
steps: "Is it He — this one? Is it today that we will sing Nunc Dimittis?
How heavenly!"

(2004)

The circumcision of Christ

Jonathan Romain reveals a remarkable Jewish journey

JEWS have had a varying relationship with Jesus over the centuries. We met him first-hand in Galilee, and flocked to hear him preaching. In subsequent eras, the figure of him on a cross wielded by Crusaders and Cossacks became an image of oppression. In today's world of interfaith reconciliation, yet another picture is emerging.

I still remember the shock when I first walked into a church and saw the calendrical name for the next Sunday displayed on the notice board: "Feast of the Circumcision". A quick use of my fingers confirmed that if Jesus was born on 25 December, then he would be eight days old on 1 January — exactly the age at which all Jewish males are circumcised, in accordance with Genesis 17.12. It is a fact that is well known to some churchgoers, but will astonish others. Moreover, it prompts questions about Jewish practices and about Jesus.

It is puzzling that circumcision is not only the oldest of all Jewish traditions, dating right back to the first ritual command given to Abraham, but it is also the rite that is the most kept by all Jews to this day. Even those who never go to synagogue or who happily eat pork will still circumcise their sons.

IT is hard to pinpoint precisely why the tradition should have such a powerful effect on the Jewish psyche, and be the one that has such longevity, especially as it can seem so alien to those outside Judaism. Perhaps its power lies in the handing on of tradition — done physically — and is not just about the child, but is as much about the commitment of the parents, and their wish for their Jewish roots to carry on to the next generation, however well or badly they themselves have kept it.

Even if they are not especially observant, most Jewish parents have a sense of belonging and heritage that they value. It is about continuity, and ensuring that the baton is passed on and does not end with them. It also means that even if the child grows up to be not particularly religious, he will still have the mark of Jewish identity.

This is reinforced by the fact that the circumcision is usually done not in hospital, but in the home. It is also customary to invite family and friends to witness the event. Both of these would be inconceivable with any other medical operation. For the record, the person who does the circumcision — the *mohel* — is a highly trained and skilled individual, who becomes qualified only after a two-year induction period, and is very often a doctor. In fact, when the Queen had her sons circumcised, it was by a *mohel* rather than the court surgeon, as the former was considered to have much greater expertise.

But, while the medical aspects are carried out with every care —including sterilising the table on which the circumcision is performed — there is no doubting that the primary significance is to welcome the child into the community of faith.

In contrast to what happens in church, water is never used to greet the arrival of either boys or girls, as Jewish status is conferred automatically at the moment of birth by having a Jewish mother; so babies are "born Jewish". It is only when someone converts to Judaism that immersion occurs as a symbol of their entry into the faith.

THE contemporaries of Jesus, though, would have had no doubt about his status: born of a Jewish mother, and then, eight days later, circumcised in keeping with tradition. Moreover, a simple reading of the Gospels indicates that he was brought up in a Jewish environment.

Luke informs us that his parents took him to Jerusalem every year to celebrate the Passover; and it is clear that Jesus was educated in the Hebrew Bible, and was able to quote extensively from it. He was also familiar with the rituals of both the Temple and the synagogue. It is taken for granted that the Last Supper was a Passover meal, albeit one that became invested with new meaning.

Perhaps even more significantly, the vast majority of Jesus's teachings came from within Judaism, being based on either the Bible or contemporary rabbinic sayings, and are not in contradiction to Jewish tradition. The Sermon on the Mount, for instance, is a text that any rabbi, then or now, would have been proud to have constructed.

THIS recognition of the Jewishness of Jesus is doubly revolutionary. For many Christians, certainly in previous eras, and no doubt for some today, it would have been unthinkable that the founder of their faith could have been identified with a people who were reviled as stiff-necked and in league with the devil.

For Jews, too, until very recently, it was impossible to imagine that the person seen as responsible for centuries of persecution against them had come from a Jewish home. When a particularly forward-looking rabbi in the early-20th century suggested that Jews study the New Testament, he quickly withdrew the suggestion under an avalanche of criticism.

TODAY, however, most Jewish scholars accept that the great divide between Judaism and Christianity occurred not with Jesus, but with Paul. This was partly because of his introduction of Gnostic teachings, and partly because he was preaching to non-Jewish audiences who had little in common with the Jewish followers of Jesus. The latter saw him more as a super-prophet, such as Elijah, rather than as a deity, and did not regard their belief in him as incompatible with their Judaism.

The estrangement between the two faiths resulted in almost two millennia of Jesus's Jewish roots being hidden. They came back into view only in recent decades, thanks to the courage of those from both sides who were able to shrug off the toxic layers of myth and prejudice that had developed.

The rediscovery of "the Jewish Jesus" has great significance for both faiths. For Christians, it means that they can better understand the context of Jesus and appreciate the resonances of certain actions or phrases. The furore, for instance, over Jesus's healing someone on the sabbath was not a matter of his breaking the law against working on the sabbath. Instead, it was about Jesus's taking sides in a debate that was raging at that very time within Jewish thinking about how to redefine what was permitted and forbidden. It is clear that he was with those who declared that the saving of life took precedence over all other considerations — an opinion that eventually came to be the dominant one in Jewish law.

For Jews, the consequences of "the Jewish Jesus" are even more significant. It means that they need no longer shun the New Testament — to this day, most religious Jews never read it — but can benefit from a book that reflects a fascinating era in Jewish history, as well as enjoy the superb insights of the parables and other teachings.

The very notion, expressed above, that Jews can gain religiously from the Gospels will be seen by some of my co-religionists as outrageous, if not incomprehensible. Others will be delighted by the opportunity to "reclaim" Jesus, seeing him as a highly gifted Jewish preacher, shaped by both the prophetic writings of old and the rabbinic thinking of his time — a man who forged out of them a vibrant message that modern Jews might not endorse in every instance, but can still respect and admire.

(2010)

Countdown to Candlemas

Jeremy Fletcher explains the apparent confusion
in the Christmas and Epiphany seasons

"CHRISTMAS comes but once a year," sang Loudon Wainwright III, "and goes on for two months." Most people would disagree with him only by increasing the number of weeks. And it's not long after the first decorations have been spotted than the carol services seem to begin.

I confess to a sense of great relief at around 4 p.m. on Christmas Day, not only that the turkey appears not to have poisoned anyone, but that Christmas is over. No more herald angels have to be harked, and no more faithful must be told to come, at least until autumn next year.

The problem is that the liturgical celebration of the incarnation flies in the face of the popular one. Just as the holiday advertisements appear, the Church gives us the Sundays of Christmas. Then the schools go back, and we do gold, frankincense and myrrh. We're past the fourth round of the FA Cup before Christ is presented in the temple.

The liturgical Christmas may last six weeks, but they're not the six weeks everyone else does. Despite the popularity of the song, it's only the Church that makes anything of the 12 days. We start putting the partridge in the pear tree just as everyone else is shooing the lords a-leaping back to their stately homes.

IN an article on the calendar, the late Michael Vasey made the point that the Church's year is not a slave to the secular world, but a challenge to it. "Questions of calendar are integral to mission and identity," he said. The secular calendar has its principles and values, just as much as the Christian one.

The clash between the two can be a fruitful place of encounter, as long as the Church is not so blinkered in its own version of events that it cannot conceive that people might find reality in something else.

"Imagine", says the current Southwell Minster magazine, "what it would be like to sing your first carol in the darkness of Christmas Eve." But we have to acknowledge that to keep Christmas only after the 25th would be a bit like reading last week's *Radio Times*. The fruitful encounter can come when we do both: when we welcome those who need their carols early, and then offer them the riches of the great 40 days that follow.

The Presentation of Christ in the Temple *(c.1435), by Giovanni di Paolo*

This isn't made any easier by the way the Church's calendar messes up the chronology. In the coming weeks, Jesus is born, then he is taken to Egypt, then he's named, then we're back with the Magi in Bethlehem at Epiphany.

To those used to the natural progression of Palm Sunday, Holy Week and Easter, this is a pain. It's compounded in the Sundays of Epiphany, where Jesus is seen as an adult, before, on 2 February, we are jolted back to the presentation of the infant Christ in the temple.

There is no mistake here. It's just that the incarnation season, from Christmas to Candlemas, grew up in a different way from the resurrection season from Lent to Easter. It is less obviously linear, partly because the infancy narratives in Luke and Matthew contain different elements.

Here it is more important to explore the mystery of the Word made flesh than to re-enact the early life of Jesus. For example, what is revealed in the gifts of the Magi is connected to the ministry and passion of Jesus the adult. So the Epiphany has gathered other revelations to itself, notably God the Son, revealed in Jesus's baptism, and God's glory, revealed in the miracle at Cana.

COMMON *Worship* gives the Epiphany and its Sundays star treatment, so that the liturgical colour remains gold or white, and the revelation of Jesus as the Christ is explored in depth. As well as the revelations of the baptism and the miracle at Cana, Jesus is shown to be the Lamb of God who takes away sins, and the healer and teacher. All this sweeps us up to the light of the Gentiles and the glory of Israel at the presentation.

The incarnation is not restricted to a miraculous birth, and a secular world in its post-Christmas hangover needs to hear words of eternal life. It is possible to save some of the big guns for after the 25th. My former church always did Christingle in early January, and it is possible right up to the presentation, if you wish. An observance of the New Year could be tied in with the theme of revelation, with the gifts of Epiphany presented for the adventure of 2002.

Not only that, a church that might have been drawn too far into the materialistic whirlwind will need reminding, as on the First Sunday of Christmas, that the child in the manger escaped persecution by fleeing abroad. Christmas needs rescuing from unremitting jollity.

Of course, if you're really holy, you can go for the festivals as well: St Stephen, St John, the Holy Innocents, and the Circumcision of Jesus. One martyrdom, one massacre, one lifetime imprisonment, and one operation to make the eyes water. The Church knows how to have fun.

But one of my more profound moments was wrestling with the Holy Innocents as the readings for the First Sunday of Christmas. It seems to me that those who weep for their lost children need to know about the fragility of a baby born into danger. If the incarnation gives significance to all of life, if the child was born to raise the children of earth and give them second birth, then we can look horror in the face and say that there is hope.

THE Church proclaims the incarnate Christ, not the compliments of the season. The Church's year, as *Common Worship* has inherited it, gives us a glorious confusion: like Eric Morecambe's piano-playing, we have all the right notes, but not necessarily in the right order. No matter: we cannot leave Jesus in the manger; the child is born to die.

Naturally, we can make ourselves look foolish (and the argument that rages about the displacement of the Baptism of Christ every year when Epiphany is on a Sunday is a case in point). But a nod to the secular festival, as well as a courageous celebration of the life of Christ, just as people might really need it, can give us all the opportunity we need to make the 40 days to Candlemas a glorious song indeed.

(2001)

Does the date matter?

Robert Paterson asks why the Church transfers festivals

"WHATEVER happened to the Epiphany? I thought it was always on 6 January, but the notice sheet says it's 2 January this year. Please explain," writes one correspondent. It is all to do with the changing patterns of contemporary living, and with seeing the bigger picture of the cycles of the seasons.

In most parishes, it is the devoted few who take a keen interest in saints' days, let alone remember when most of them fall. Major festivals are generally better known: not many people will be unaware of Christmas, which, as we all know, is a festival celebrated between September and December by a commercialised riot.

Christmas Day, as a festival, was itself a late arrival on the scene, appearing between the fourth and sixth centuries. No one knows the exact date of Christ's birth, but the celebration was attached to the pagan Roman festival of the unconquered sun — or, we might say, "son".

The oldest and fundamental Christian festival is Easter — "Passover" in almost every other language — the celebration of the three great days of our redemption: the day of the cross, the day of the tomb, and the day of resurrection. Easter is a perfect example of the way Christians celebrate festivals. For the Church, a festival is not an anniversary, an annual reminder of something that happened in the past (a birth, a wedding, or a death, perhaps), but the taking of an event that has happened in the past, and bringing it into the present, so that it can be experienced today, and its effects may be felt.

So, when we use the world "Passover", we mean three things: the event of Israel's deliverance from slavery more than 3000 years ago, the three great days of our reconciliation 2000 years ago, and our celebration of Easter today, through which we find ourselves "dead to sin and alive to God, in union with Christ Jesus" (Romans 6.11). Sundays are weekly experiences of that death and resurrection at the heart of the faith.

THE revised Calendar recognises the importance of these experiences, and accommodates itself to the way we live today, with less time for churchgoing on weekdays. That is not necessarily a bad thing. If we respect Sunday as the resurrection day for rest and worship, it may be good that we spend more time in the week engaging with the world that God loves. Putting more into Sunday ought to equip us for our part in God's mission during the remaining six days of the week.

The first accommodation to the way we live today is that "red-letter days", such as the festivals of the Apostles, as well as other commemorations (such as those of the two Sts Augustine, or of John and Charles Wesley), can usually be moved at the minister's discretion to another weekday of the weeks in which they fall. This is common sense, particularly in multi-church parishes where midweek services are held on a fixed day every week.

The second accommodation is to acknowledge that the liturgical year moves through cycles. Advent begins the period characterised by God's coming to us; the theme develops in many ways, centred around the coming of the divine Word. From that first main cycle, we move into a period of preparation for Easter, the lengthening days in Lent.

BETWEEN these two cycles comes a single event that moves us on, the Presentation of Christ in the Temple (or Candlemas). At that event, we hear Simeon's words, which fulfil God's coming — "My eyes have seen the salvation you have prepared for all the world to see" — and look towards the future Passion — "Sorrow, like a sharp sword, will pierce your soul" (Luke 2.22-38). This is why the feast of the Presentation is so important, because it leads us from coming to redemption. This is why we encourage those churches that cannot get their congregations to turn out on weekdays to move it to the nearest Sunday.

The redemption cycle runs from the Presentation to Pentecost, the second ancient marker of the liturgical year, after which follows Trinity Sunday, and then an unthemed period "after Pentecost/Trinity".

At the other end of the year, the beginning of what many churches call the "Kingdom" season (four Sundays before Advent), comes the feast of All Saints', a joyful experience of belonging to "a chosen race, a royal priesthood, a holy nation, God's own people" (1 Peter 2.9) at the saddest time of the year. That, too, may be transferred to or shared with its nearest Sunday in order that as many as possible can enjoy the experience.

APART from Easter, Pentecost, and Sundays, the oldest Christian festival generally observed seems to have been the Epiphany, the revelation of Christ to Gentiles, and an important marker of God's mission. Unlike Christmas, this one has slipped out of many diaries; so the opportunity is given to move the celebration to a Sunday — but which one?

In four years out of seven, there are two Sundays in between Christmas Day and the Epiphany (the First and Second Sundays of Christmas). Since the Epiphany itself falls on a Sunday one year in seven, it means that the Epiphany cannot be held on the Second Sunday of Christmas twice in seven years; in those years, it should be celebrated everywhere on Friday or Saturday. As Anglicans are not quite as authoritarian as some, you might find that when 6 January is not a Friday, Saturday, or Sunday, your church has moved the celebration, and you might miss it.

For real liturgical geeks, there are rules about transferring festivals, but these are all made simple for the likes of me by the annual Lectionary booklet, produced by Church House Publishing.

But we shouldn't get too hung up on the date of the Epiphany — after all, the Bible doesn't give us a date; so it cannot be very important. Instead, we could discover again the stupendous glory of God's love in Christ, and let the Holy Spirit lead us to the Child who offers "boundless riches" to all the world (see Ephesians 3).

(2010)

The Star
by Kenneth Steven

The town was tight as a drum with strangers;
the nights sweaty with people and their flocks.
Then, that night, the star came;
bits of silver sprinkled over hills,
and everything else seemed suddenly dark.

I remember trying to sleep and cracklings of light
sparking the room, a strange and silent lightning.
I suppose in the end we forgot to remember —
the market was roaring, and there was another silver
to be made by the bucket-load. The star got lost
behind a host of other things.

But that one night I came home another way,
my head all smooth with wine.
A light in a stable; the gold of faces looking out at me
as in a painting. They had nothing;
I have houses, women, land —
yet for a second, one single moment,
I felt a different kind of emptiness,
was sure that they had more than I would ever know.

They're gone now. The town is just the same
and yet I feel their absence even yet —
a star is keeping me awake.

(2020)

Hemmed in with spears and crowds

The Adoration of the Kings by Pieter Bruegel is a painting for our times, says **John Drury**

T. S. ELIOT'S poem "The Journey of the Magi", written in the year in which he was received into the Church of England will be read in many churches over Christmas. It concludes with the narrating Magus's recording how, at the end of their journey, finding the young Christ put them so out of sorts with things at home that it was "like death, our death". The Magus muses that he would be "glad of another death".

The sombre poem has a visual counterpart in this very north-European painting by the pessimistic master, Pieter Bruegel the Elder. It had been in the National Gallery for seven years when Eliot wrote his poem; so perhaps it is a source, as well as a counterpart. Certainly the poem and the picture have a common temper.

With the momentous exception of the naked child set at the centre of it all, everyone is well wrapped up: soldiers and onlookers, jammed together at the back; Magi and mother and child on the hard ground at the front; burly old Joseph between the two groups.

Clothes are the painter's chance for colour. Bruegel has seized it with the predominant dull browns at the back, then the rich symphony of scarlet, lilac, pink, green and blue at the front. The two schemes are connected and modified by the pale buff of the black Magus's fine leather cloak.

It all leaves us with an ambivalent sense of glamour co-existing with drabness, even life with death, since the child seems to be drawing back into a shroud As in some of our Christmas hymns and carols, the celebration of the birth is shadowed by omens of the death.

These are present in St Matthew's story, the source of the picture. The massacre of the innocents, commemorated by the Church three days after Christmas, follows on the Magi's visit in St Matthew's Gospel. And the gift of myrrh, which is used for embalming the dead is ominous. Though last in the list of three in the Gospel, here it is the first to be offered. Its donor does so with a very long face, causing the child while smiling politely, to recoil and grasp his mother's hand.

For all that, there is much to enjoy. The gifts themselves are superbly desirable, above all the black Magus's incense, kept in the golden boat which holds a rare nautilus shell, surmounted by a little celestial globe (essential kit for a Magus star-watcher), with a tiny monkey emerging from its mouth.

The Adoration of the Kings,
by Pieter Bruegel the Elder,
in the National Gallery, London
(see www.nationalgallery.org.uk)

Detail: the gift of incense

And the people: each Magus represents one of the three continents. The scarlet Magus's thick moustaches, which fall from the corners of his mouth, denote the Asian. The pink Magus's hat, laid in homage on the ground with his sceptre, is European. The African stands magnificently on the right, gazing pensively out of the picture.

Then there are the people at the back, a gallery of the ugly and the ordinary in true Bruegel style. Above the Asian Magus, there is a kindly man with a crossbow, a happy man with a syphilitic face, and a cheery fatso. The man to the left of them, though, is sunk in melancholy. The soldier who stands guard over Mary gazes down at the myrrh.

Some very interesting interactions are going on on the right. A man who looks like a messenger is whispering urgently into Joseph's ear. It looks, from his face, like bad news: Herod's murderous intentions; scandal about the child's paternity? We cannot tell. But the man behind him in a white turban has an "Oh, my God" expression on his face — while his bespectacled neighbour gawps covetously at the expensive incense boat.

ALL human life and human nature is here: the good, the bad and the ugly, the base and the noble, the rich and the poor. For any baby to be born into such company is plenty of cause for anxiety, as well as celebration. Who knows what he will be caught up into? He is already hemmed in by people, as he was to be so often as a grown-up teacher and healer. The donkey in the shed its saddle ready on a beam, will take him away from it for a while, but not for long.

The only bit of sky to be seen is thick with jagged weapons. Of course, the Magi would need an armed escort, travelling with such treasure. But there could be more to it than that. The picture is dated 1564. Bruegel's Flanders had recently seen the departure of the Spanish army, which used it (and despoiled it) as a base for war against France. It was soon to suffer the terror of the Duke of Alva's persecution of Protestant heretics. This is a picture painted between outbreaks of violence — and so it is appropriate to us this Christmas.

(2002)

Three? Kings?
The uncertain story of the Magi

by **John Perumbalath**

THE story of the Magi has fired Christian imaginations since the earliest times. Their unexplained background provides abundant room to shape new narratives around the question of their identity.

Our primary source of the story, St Matthew's Gospel (2.1-12), does not even say how many of them were there. Matthew has given us only what is necessary to serve his theological purpose, leaving space for further questioning and inquiry.

Most Western traditions have assumed the Magi to have been three in number, but some oriental traditions consider them to be 12 or more. The background and names of the Magi have also varied throughout the world, especially in the East. An Armenian infancy gospel from the sixth century lists them as Melkon, King of Persia; Gaspar, King of India; and Baldassar, King of Arabia – closest to the Melchior, Caspar (or Gaspar) and Balthassar of the medieval Latin church.

The word *magi* is the plural of the Latin *magus*, borrowed from the Greek *magos*, which is used in the original text of the Gospel of Matthew. *Magos* itself might have derived from Old Persian *magâunô*, a priestly caste of Zoroastrianism. These priests studied the stars and gained a reputation for astrology. The word in its Greek form also came to be identified with royalty.

In the fifth century CE, the Byzantine emperor Zeno claimed to have discovered the remains of the Magi somewhere in Persia and brought them to Constantinople. The relics eventually reached the West during the Crusades, first traveling to Milan and then to Cologne in 1164. In the late 12th century, a shrine was built for them in Cologne, where they are known to pilgrims and tourists as the "Three Kings of Cologne".

The *Revelation of the Magi* — an apocryphal account preserved in an eight-century Syriac manuscript held in the Vatican Library, which purports to have been written by the Magi themselves — narrates the mystical origins of the Magi, their encounter with the luminous star, and their journey to Bethlehem. It has been claimed that the earliest versions of the text were written as early as the mid-second century.

In the *Revelation*, there are not just three Magi, nor are they Persian Zoroastrians, as other early traditions held. In Brent Landau's translation of the text, Magi are defined as those who "pray in silence". They were a group of monk-like mystics from a far-off mythical land called "Shir", possibly China, and numbered as few as 12 and as many as several score.

They were descendants of Seth, the third son of Adam, and the guardians of an age-old prophecy that a unique, bright star would some day appear "heralding the birth of God in human form". The Magi who visited Jesus returned home and preached the Christian faith to their brethren, ultimately being baptised by the apostle Thomas.

A later tradition was recorded by the Venerable Bede, the Anglo-Saxon historian and theologian of the eighth century, that the three Magi signified the three parts of the known world — Africa, Asia, and Europe — and that they might be linked with the sons of Noah, who fathered the three races of Earth (Genesis 10).

EARLY Church fathers interpreted the story in the light of the Old Testament. Justin Martyr considered the Magi to be the fulfilment of Old Testament prophecy regarding the coming of the Messiah. Some popular interpretations, reflected in art, linked the Magi with the three youngsters in the furnace (Daniel 3).

Origen suggested that the Magi discovered the prophecy of Balaam about a star coming out of Jacob (Numbers 24.17). Many found echoes of Psalm 72 in the story of the gift-bringing wise men: "May all kings fall down before him, may all nations serve him." Seen in this light, the Magi perform a unique role as witnesses to the true faith, and as a sign that the salvation that Jesus brings is universal.

Magi also figured in the discussions about the Trinity in the Early Church. Some Church fathers considered them as the first witnesses to the Trinity — or thought that the Magi themselves came to represent the Trinity.

All the evidence we have suggests that the Early Church attached great theological significance to the story of Jesus's first visitors. In art, this story appeared earlier and more frequently than any other part of Jesus's infancy narratives.

The practice of celebrating the Magi's arrival as the Feast of Epiphany on 6 January, 12 days after Jesus's birth, was established by the fourth century. In this feast, the Church celebrates Christ's manifestation to the world.

This Child, who until now was known only to his immediate surroundings and people, is now being worshipped and recognised by some wise men from foreign lands. The world outside Judaism is brought into the story to emphasise that Jesus is not a Jewish Messiah, as many would have expected, but is the Lord of the whole world, receiving homage from non-

The Three Magi (1618), by Peter Paul Rubens

These three studies were painted by Rubens for his close friend
Balthasar Moretus, head of the largest press in Europe at the time.
Balthasar and his two brothers, Gaspar and Melchior, were named after
the Magi, in the hope, according to their father, that they would "seek
to do honour and glory to Him after the example of the Three Kings".

Jewish visitors. The story of the Magi is actually the Christmas story for the gentile world.

WHAT, then, does the story of the Magi say about God, the people of God, and those outside the household of the Christian faith?

The story of the Magi reveals God's universal intentions, and that God has several and varied ways of dealing with humanity. God's message to the wise men initially came to them as a star. It seems an unusual form of revelation. This is not the way God spoke to his people either in the Old or New Testament.

But assuming that these wise men had a keen interest in astronomy, as traditionally assumed, then God was speaking to them in a language that they would understand. Contrary to the understanding of the people of God at that time, Hebrew was not the only language that God used.

The story warns us that we cannot place restrictions on God's chosen channels of communication. The God of the Magi does not sanction any monopoly of spiritual experience, nor insist on stereotypical expressions of human response.

The story also reminds us that we can lose sight of God even when he is so close to us. Jesus was born among the Jews. By the time the visit of the wise men took place, the holy family must have made friends with the people of the locality. Matthew 2.11 does not mention a babe lying in a manger but implies a child living with his parents in a house.

Matthew is undeniably implying the failure of the people of God. They knew God would send a Messiah for whom they were long waiting. They had Scripture in their community to reaffirm God's promises. Now the Messiah is growing up right in their midst, but no Jewish wise man is shown paying homage to him.

The wise men among the people of God — the chief priests and the teachers of Scripture — advised Herod without any hesitation about the place where the Messiah was to be born. They studied Scripture and found the vital information about the Messiah. Yet none of them seems to have any interest in paying homage to him.

Busy advising Herod, they exhibit a false confidence in existing systems. They fail to see God at work outside those systems which they defend and venerate. The Jewish leaders were expecting something spectacular and appealing — a noble and royal birth, at least — and would no doubt have responded well to that.

The Magi, on the other hand, with no Scripture or tradition to guide them to the Messiah, are open to whatever God is doing in the world. Astronomy was considered a field of science, a valid form of enquiry in antiquity. These wise men were ready to go wherever their study and inquiry led them. They undertake a long journey, to a place unknown to them at the beginning of the journey, only to find themselves paying homage to a child in a cultural and religious context totally unfamiliar to them.

God does not disappoint those who search diligently, and honours the hunger for learning wherever that happens.

The Magi's journey appears to have been one of persistence and perseverance. They were probably unclear about what they were heading for. They had a sign but lost it on the way, judging by their enquiries of Herod. They were misled by the circumstances. At that point, it was possibly a path of uncertainty and darkness.

But they did not give up. They did not abandon their journey, even though they made mistakes, ending up in the wrong place. Their persistence took them to witness a special manifestation of God.

Matthew's narrative invites the readers to consider the contrasting responses to this divine revelation. King Herod is seen as visibly disturbed, anxious and angry. The religious scholars of the nation are indifferent and bound by tradition. But the Magi are joyful and willing to pay homage.

For Matthew, this symbolised rejection of Jesus by his own people. In a theological system that consigned outsiders to eternal condemnation, Matthew sets his theological agenda — showing how God's manifestation in Jesus breaks down the dividing walls between races and cultures.

(2021)

Star of wonder and of science

Andrew Davison balances the astronomical explanations
for the Star with its cosmic significance.

ASTRONOMERS — among them two luminaries of early modern astronomy, Tycho Brahe (1546–1601) and Johannes Kepler (1571–1630) — have had the Star of Bethlehem in their sights for some time. Indeed, even to translate St Matthew's account, you need to decide whether there's a hint of stargazing vocabulary in his Gospel. The Authorised Version ("We have seen his star *in the east,* and are come to worship him") suggests not. In contrast, the NRSV gives us "We observed his star *at its rising,*" which is favoured today.

To the modern eye, there are two distinctive aspects of Matthew's account. On the one hand, the sky *announces*, informing the Magi of the birth of the King of the Jews. That is all they need to direct them to Jerusalem. Once there, Micah's prophecy would suffice to send them on to Bethlehem.

At this point, however, the star plays its second part, as *pathfinder*: "There, ahead of them, went the star that they had seen at its rising, until it stopped over the place where the child was." Astronomically plausible contenders for what Matthew might be describing are varied, but they tend to fit better with the first aspect than the second.

SOME discussions — though not all — mention a meteor, but generally only to dismiss it. Meteors fall too often to be remarkable, and last only seconds. A comet is another possibility, popular with artists. Giotto's depiction, among his frescoes for the Arena Chapel, in Padua, is particularly notable. Painted just into the 14th century, the inspiration is Halley's Comet, which had appeared in October 1301. It is moving to see this artist, who was so instrumental in bringing the observation of nature and a new naturalism into Western art, recalling that event in paint.

A comet, however, is a poor contender for the story. The appearance of a comet — something new, and out of kilter within the otherwise ordered systems of the heavens — was associated with disaster.

A further possibility is the brief appearance of a "new" (previously invisible) star: a nova, or supernova. The former are more common, flaring up during the life-course of some two-star systems. Supernovae are far rarer, but entirely more spectacular. They are the final stage in certain sorts of star death, and convert mass into energy so rapidly that a single star, at its passing, can momentarily outshine a galaxy of maybe 400 billion stars. Records from China suggest a nova in 5 BC, but of a relatively modest kind. (That, we should note, is in the right time-frame: the birth of Christ is probably best dated to about 7–2 BC.)

Within the Epiphany story, a nova-burst in the sky might fit the bill, lasting for a while before fading. As with a comet, however, this unexpected event would likely not be seen as propitious. Better to turn to our final, and favoured, contender for catching the ancient imagination (whether of Magi, or of Gospel-writer): a planetary conjunction.

Thanks to light pollution, few of us are in touch with the changing sky. If we were, we could distinguish two sorts of motion. The backdrop is composed of stars, which seem to pan across the sky over the course of an evening, as the earth rotates. (There are also some gentle changes over the cycle of a year.) Across that background move the planets — the word derives from the Greek for "wanderer". Their remarkably complicated courses are set by the interrelation of their orbits with ours.

Kepler was a lucky man: he was alive during a rare supernova, in 1604. The year before, however, he witnessed the conjunction of Jupiter and Saturn in the night sky (the Christmas night sky, no less), and that sent him to his calculations. He was able to determine that something similar had happened in 7 BC, and with spectacular effect, since those planets then drew near three times in rapid succession.

Another candidate for the wondrous sight, the following year, would have been the clustering of three planets: Jupiter, Saturn, and Mars. Both of these events happened in the constellation of Pisces (said to be associated, for reasons I cannot fathom, with Judaea and the Jews). If we want to tie Matthew's story to an astronomical event, something like this seems to be the best candidate.

Planetary conjunctions — or novae, for that matter — perform what I called the star's first task: tipping off the Magi that something was afoot. That would suffice to get them to Jerusalem, where Micah would point them to Bethlehem. What it might mean, however, for the star to perform the second task — to "go ahead of them", or to "stop over the place where the child was" — is far less clear. On the planetary hypothesis, the best fit may be the pause of a planet, as it changes direction in the sky.

THIS is probably as far as we can go, and it may already be too far. The temptation to ask scientific questions of an ancient claim about the night sky is strong and obvious, but, in doing so, we risk anachronism. Neither Matthew nor his contemporaries thought in terms such as supernovae. Their purpose was theological.

On that front, at least two principal themes emerge. First, we see both that there was a message for those who would hear it, and that those who did included Gentile magicians from the ends of the earth. Matthew's Gospel, which is considered the most "Jewish", here seems to take up themes from Isaiah (for instance), with its interweaving of the particular and the universal; and the idea of one nation — even of one representative figure — as the hope for the whole world. In our days of happily constructive interfaith relations, we might think of the Magi as the patron saints of dialogue and recognition across traditions.

The second theme is creation responding to the incarnation of the Son of God as the pivotal event in earth's history. Even if a nova is not the best candidate for the Star, there is an informative link to be made with the medieval Christmas carol whose refrain is "*Nova! Nova!*" A new thing has happened — radically, world-changingly new — and creation, even the unchanging heavens, is caught up in its own act of homage.

The development of astronomy since the time of Copernicus, Kepler, and Galileo is indisputable and magnificent; but, if we approach the story too much in astronomical terms, we may diminish elements that Matthew, his first readers, and subsequent generations thought important. In particular, modern astronomy offers a story that unfolds, relentlessly, over billions of years.

Planetary conjunctions, we now know, are baked into the celestial mechanics of our solar system. That might suffice to tip off observant watchers (the first theological angle), but it offers little of creation's responding to God's new gift (the second). If heavenly messages are all we look for in the story, the facts familiar to modern astronomy might still fit the bill. If, however, we want something more dynamic, with creation making its response to God's work, we will be left wanting, and the astronomical explanation may simply look like a divine stage effect.

A parallel approach to the darkened sky on Good Friday is even more crushing, reducing it to the somewhat brief and partial lunar eclipse (there can be no solar eclipse near the Passover) on Friday 3 April AD 33. Better than that to have the sun occluded in horror for three whole hours, even if only in the story. Better to have creation recoil in horror at the crucifixion of God incarnate — even if only as literature — than to have celestial stage machinery grinding its billion-year course.

So, too, perhaps, with the Star of Bethlehem, although the choice is less stark. A planetary conjunction has poetry, but I would only reluctantly give up on a tale of the sky's bursting into amazed and grateful light, as Christ grows within his mother's womb. We may do better with the story as story than with the story as science.

(2019)

A story by **Evelyn Underhill**

KING Melchior walked the hanging gardens that terraced his palace walls. He was very lonely, old, and tired. Desire still lived in him, though its inheritor despair had long been born. He looked out upon the empty desert in which his city was set, and wished for death, for there alone he hoped to find reality. He was King of the Spirit of Man.

He walked the terrace with a certain air of impatience: for midnight was past, and he awaited the rising of the new star which, as he remembered with sardonic pleasure, had upset the calculations of the court astrologer. It shone with a peculiar splendour, and Melchior, who embellished a taste for science with some of the sentiments of an aesthete, felt himself drawn towards it with a rapidly increasing affection.

Its light fell upon a patch of sand, very far away; and it seemed to the king that this spot then became a focus of infinite peace and satisfaction. He had suspected of late that the walls of his comfortable city were barriers, which kept him from this radiant emptiness; where, as he was sure, old age and loneliness would no longer bear the disheartening significance that they had at home, and the profitless wisdom which had made his court a celebrated centre of learning would at least meet the Reality which it sought.

Because he could not bear the long and solitary watch, and the dark, unfriendly sky, he left his terraced garden, and went through sleeping streets to the temple that was in the heart of the town. There an ever-living lamp burned before an empty shrine; for the king had set up many gods only to dethrone them, and the flame and the temple waited a Divine Guest. The place was very dreary, and the dusty symbols which his priests had erected were singularly meaningless. It increased his latent longing for great and empty spaces: for the desert, that was less desolate than this admirably appointed sanctuary, and for that object of a limitless adoration which his lonely kingdom could not provide.

He took a censer and lit the coals within it by the flame of the ever-living lamp. The perfume and smoke ascended, wrapped him round, shut him from the world; so that he forgot his kingship and the careful dignities of his little court, and became filled with the ardours of some unknown, incredible quest.

He left the temple, and saw the star that he longed for. It had risen over the desert whilst he lingered by the empty shrine. It called to him insistently; and a voice within answered the call. It drew him to a little postern in the walls of his city; and so he left his sleeping kingdom, abruptly almost, and without deliberate intention, and descended by steep paths to the wilderness.

As he walked he swung the heavy censer, in long and rhythmic beats. The burning perfume filled the air with strange and elusive desires, dim suggestions of ineffable peace. The hot coals cast a light on his path, slowly, for he was very old, and had lost the habit of solitary pilgrimage.

THE star stood in mid-heaven. Melchior could no longer see the patch of sand that it lit; but its pale and steady fire drew him, as a lamp set in a window draws the lover across the dark and menacing desert towards some adorable and irresistible event. Because his face was set towards it, and all practical things were left behind, some of the ardours of the lover awoke in him — joy, desire, and unrest. He had forgotten his kingless city on the hill, and the strange folly of this undertaking. He looked with infinite satisfaction on the silent wastes before him, glad to know himself alone.

It was therefore with considerable annoyance that he presently perceived a patch of darkness, which crawled over the face of the desert as clouds crawl over the sky. His solitude was over. There were other wayfarers abroad, fellow-travellers, for the dark patch followed the star; and soon from another quarter came another moving shadow that would join it, and within it the moving lights of many lanterns and the glitter of polished arms. The wilderness, which he had loved for its desolation, teemed with life.

King Melchior drew near to the first company, and saw in its midst a great prince surrounded by his escort; tall and dark, the lord of mighty empires. He recognised his neighbour, Balthasar, the King of the Will of Man.

When they were come near enough to hear each other's voice, Balthasar cried, "My cousin, what do you seek?"

Melchior answered, "I seek an escape from life, for it is illusion and weariness. What do you seek, cousin?"

271

Balthasar replied, "I seek this star, for I am assured that it offers an escape from death, which threatens to destroy me, and with me all my power and joy."

Melchior said, "You believe that you will die? I congratulate you on your good fortune."

Then he turned, and saw that the third wayfarer had joined them: a pretty youth in fair clothing, who came surrounded by his camels, hounds and horses, his dancing girls and boys. He had great wealth, but little dominion, for he was Caspar, the King of Man's Body, and Caesar's feudatory. Melchior said to him with great courtesy, "And what, cousin, do you seek?"

Caspar replied, "Life brings pain, and death takes joy away. I seek in this star the satisfaction of perfect love eternally renewed."

Then, because their road was the same, though the end of their adventure clearly different, they went on together, and so continued many days; a strange trio, set on a threefold quest. Melchior, the king of one lonely stronghold; Balthasar, who ruled great countries; Caspar, the royal slave. All were stricken with a vague and fevered craving, a dim knowledge of something that they must seek.

AND after a long while the star led them to the confines of the desert, and they saw a great road which ran away to the horizon, with cornfields and thick woods on either hand. Far off, the black shafts of many mines and factories, the smoke and gloom of human habitations, lay dark in the curve of a hollow valley, and above them very great and awful hills. With the coming of the dawn the star had faded from the sky. There was nothing to guide them in this world.

The King of the Will looked up at the veiled summits of the mountains. "There", he said, "is the ending of our pilgrimage; for those hidden peaks must dominate the world. There I shall pay my tribute, and be at peace."

So they went all day upon the road that led to the hills: past the pleasant woods, and past the fields of hay and green corn. The crested grasses waved in the breeze, offering a scented resting-place. Small enticing paths wandered away to the shaded and flowery forest. Caspar looked at them with regret. The mountains were austere and terrible; as the day fell, they took on a peculiar majesty. He feared them; but Balthasar marched with eagerness and determination, as if to the conquest of a desirable kingdom.

Melchior went alone, swinging the smoking censer which gave to his journey the air of some secret and mystical rite. The Kings of the Will and the Body smiled at his curious fervour. They perceived him to be an eccentric and possibly senile person, who would have fared ill without their protection on the road.

But when night was come, and they were at the foot of the hills, Balthasar saw with disappointment that the star had turned aside. It shone over the smoky town in the curve of the valley, and was reflected in a thousand twinkling lights. Caspar said, "It is well! Warmth, joy, and the fulfilment of desire are in the lowlands. There I shall break my jars of myrrh and precious ointment, for the honouring of perfect beauty and the adornment of undying love."

So they followed the star; and it brought them, whilst the night was still dark, to the city, where furnace fires blazed, and hammers rang incessantly upon anvils, and a pall of smoke shut out the sky.

The aspect of the place was not encouraging. But they went on, for though its precincts were unlit, the

burning coals in Melchior's censer cast a light on the muddy pathway; and presently they were caught in a network of mean streets and dingy tenements, ill-suited to the tastes of royal travellers.

Caspar and Balthasar turned this way and that, to find some decent road by which their camels and men-at-arms could pass. Thus, becoming entangled in the narrow courts and alleys, they soon lost one another; and when dawn came, each, looking for his companions, found himself alone amongst an inquisitive and ill-mannered population, which gave more ridicule than reverence to this pilgrimage of strange kings who had come down many worlds and countless centuries on a vague and unpractical quest.

NOW, about mid-day the King of the Spirit, having wandered for many hours through the dreary by-ways of a prosperous manufacturing town, came out with a great sense of thankfulness on to the waste ground on the far side of the city.

There he found by the roadside the King of the Will, who sat alone under the shadow of a great block of dwelling which was the last outpost of the poorer quarters. There were draggled women and screaming children all about him. He seemed very tired; his torn robes were soiled by the refuse of the streets.

273

He looked at King Melchior, and perceiving that he no longer carried his censer said, "What has happened to you, my cousin, and why did you forsake the quest? I have looked for you all day."

Melchior answered, "I followed the star."

Balthasar said, "That cannot be, for I went with it all night in solitude; and it brought me very early in the morning to the greatest king in all the world, even he who rules over this town."

Melchior replied, "Yet all night I saw it go before me, shining very faintly through the smoke; and it brought me at last to the Ineffable Mystery, which is without doubt the true end of this quest. For after many weary hours, it stayed before a house in a wide street, where there was great business of buying and selling, and a concourse of people going to and fro with much jostling and noise.

"I knocked, and a man came to the door and took me in; and I saw a table set out with white and shining Bread, and a Cup that was filled with wine like fire. And many poor folk stood round the table, that they might be nourished; and the man of the house gave freely to all. And each, as he ate that Bread and drank of the Cup, left all his pain and unrest, which are but illusion, and opened his eyes on reality and peace.

"Then I knew that my quest was accomplished, and I knelt, and adored, and received; and so I stayed till the fire in my censer was spent. And after that I came out of the house, the star moved from the door and went before me; and it brought me to this place, whence no doubt I shall return to my kingdom in due time."

Balthasar laughed, and said, "You were deceived, cousin. I too followed the star, and some of my men rode with me. It brought us by sorry places, and past the tavern that you speak of; a foul place it seemed.

"The man that dwells there came out, and bade us enter. He is a charitable fellow, who nourishes poor travellers with broken victuals. He would have given us a meal of his rye-bread and sour wine; but my men mocked at such entertainment, for we had better things in our saddle-bags.

"So I rode on, and the star went before me, and when day broke it brought me to an open place in the midst of the city.

"There I saw a strange sight indeed, and glorious; even a King, who ruled from a Tree. He was poor and mean of aspect, without royal robes or any sign of sovereignty. His limbs were cruelly maimed. Yet he was set high above the earth, that all might do him homage, and none disputed his dignity. When I came near, I saw that he was dead; but none the less he continued his reign.

"Then I said, 'This is the King of kings whom I seek, for his rule has triumphed over the grave.' And I left my tribute of gold at the foot of the Tree. And when I had so done, the star went on, and brought me out of the town."

WHILST they spoke together, they saw with great surprise the King of the Body, who came out of the many-storied tenement near which they sat. He was alone and empty-handed. He wept as he walked. The King of the Will said to him with great kindness, "Alas! my poor cousin, you had better have followed the star: for now I perceive that you have lost all and found nought."

Caspar replied, "Not so. The star has been with me, even to this moment; and it has shown me perfect beauty and eternal love, which is the most piteous sight in all the world."

Balthasar said, "What! Beauty in this foul dwelling?"

Caspar replied, "By many busy streets and by a poor house of refreshment, where the host offered me coarse food, and by the market-place, where a felon hung stark upon the gallows. And my pages and dancing girls were weary and frightened, and lagged behind, so that at last I lost them all in the tangle of the streets, and found myself alone. And a little after dawn, when the star was very faint and hard to see, it brought me to the door of this tenement.

"I went in, and climbed many stairs. I heard a sound of bitter weeping, that grew louder as I climbed; till I came at last to a little attic, and there I saw a marvellous Child, which lay dead on its mother's knee. She wept, and

her tears fell down on its white body like diamonds upon snow.

"I said to her, 'Who is this child, and why is he so beautiful? For he is formed like a king's son.' She answered, 'He is the fruit of perfect love. With pain he was born, and with pain he was taken away.' Then I knew I had found that which I sought, the beauty which is eternally renewed: and I broke my jar of myrrh and anointed that perfect little body for its burial, weeping because I had seen the fulfilment of desire, which is the child of love and

275

pain. And when I had so done, the star moved from that place and brought me here."

King Melchior smiled, and said, "You have behaved with much condescension. As for me, I dislike the children of the poor. They disturb my meditations."

Balthasar retorted, "Yet you found the food of poverty strangely sweet."

Melchior answered, "At least I did not mistake a felon for my king, nor a pauper woman's grief for perfect love." Thus they sat and disputed, and cloaked their very natural anxiety with recriminations; for their servants were lost, and their beasts, and all provisions for the homeward journey, and they found themselves reduced to the condition of any poor pilgrims on the road.

Each believed in his heart that he had achieved the quest, and was eager to return to his kingdom; but without guidance of the star they could not find the way. Each was very sorry for his companions, knowing that they had mistaken the sign and been duped by vulgar deceits.

BUT the star did not move. It stood with singular obstinacy above the thatch of a miserable outhouse that was by the wayside, and shone with ever-increasing splendour on the briars and brambles which grew over its door. And whilst they waited, very hungry and disconsolate, a messenger came and stood before them, and said, "Will you not come in?"

They said, "Where would you take us?"

He answered "To that which you seek." Each replied quickly, "But I have found!"

The messenger said, "No! for that which you found was Three, but the consummation of the quest is One."

Then the three kings were full of distress, saying, "Alas! it is too late, for we came on this adventure bearing rich gifts to him whom we sought but now all that we have is spent, and we are empty-handed as the poor. It is not fitting that we should come in."

The messenger answered, "What gifts did you bring?"

Melchior said, "I bore incense to the God."

The messenger replied "Its perfume is yet about His feet."

Balthasar said, "I brought tribute to the King."

The messenger replied, "At daybreak it was laid before His throne."

Caspar said, "I brought myrrh to the Man."

The messenger replied, "Even now it was poured out upon His limbs."

And he went before them to the little outhouse on which the star still cast its light. And they were greatly displeased at it, for they were heartily tired of the sight of squalid dwellings, and this was a shelter ill-suited indeed to mighty kings.

Nevertheless for very weariness they followed him: and seeing it now to be all grown about with fragrant roses, that shone like living flames by the light of the star, each said in his heart, "Without doubt this is an hallucination produced by excessive fatigue; for we are yet upon the edge of the city, and this place is but an outhouse where drovers coming to market herd their beasts."

The King of the Spirit was forced to stoop low that he might pass under its lintel; so low, that the briars which grew across it did not touch him at all, only a rose brushed his forehead very softly as he passed. The King of the Will and the King of the Body came after; but because Balthasar stood very tall and stooped not, he was compelled to remove his crown before he could go in, and the briar that hung below the lintel checked Caspar's hasty entrance, and tore his brow.

But when they were come in, they forgot straightway all their weariness and the miseries and illusions of the way; being seized by the passions of adoration and service and love.

For the beams of the star lit the place with a light that was exceeding sweet and glorious.

And there they found Mary, and Joseph, and the Babe.

This short story was first published by G. J. Palmer & Sons (proprietors of the Church Times*) in their magazine* The Treasury, *January 1907, and was reprinted in the 2020* Church Times Christmas *issue. The illustrations were early work by Francis E. Hiley (1878–1927).*

Looking backwards for Christmas

The end is where we start from, says **James Alison**

WHO appears in our midst during midnight mass? I suppose most of us, nudged along by the ceremony of the placing of the babe in the manger, assume that it is the infant Christ. But the one who is present in our midst at midnight mass, as at every eucharist, is the crucified and risen Lord. We are, in fact, as at every holy communion, celebrating Easter.

I don't say this to be iconoclastic: there is clearly nothing wrong with celebrating the birth of our Lord also. I want to meditate on the curious piece of shorthand in which we often engage when we celebrate the birth of our Lord — as if Easter were yet some way off.

We are less likely to appropriate Christmas into our own tame scheme of things, and more likely to find ourselves approaching it with the reverence that will allow it to become something capable of shaking and shaping our lives, if we dwell not on the order of logic ("Jesus was clearly born before he died, so we must celebrate the one first and then the other later"), but on the order of discovery ("it was because of the death and resurrection of Jesus that it became possible and necessary to tell the story of his life, including the story of his birth").

To put it crudely: if Jesus hadn't died, been raised from the dead, and appeared to the disciples, there would have been no interest at all in his birth. With most of us, who live and die unheralded and unsung, there will be very little interest in the place or time of our birth. It is only if we "become something" — a great artist or politician — that someone will research our birth, write a biography, and put up a plaque somewhere.

These will not reflect what was known about us at the time of our birth, but will tell the story as of one heading towards becoming a great prime minister, a renowned artist, or the inventor of the galvanised sprocket. The end of the story will determine both whether the story is told at all, and in what light it will be told.

We would have avoided much scandal at the "demythologising" of the infancy narratives a few years back if we had remembered what we should always have known: that the infancy narratives in Luke and Matthew are the reading back, by authors close to the apostolic circle, of elements designed to enrich their hearers' understanding of Jesus's death and resurrection, and what it was that these achieved.

BUT the infancy narratives are more than mere literary devices. They are the recognition that we cannot adequately begin to indicate what Jesus's death and resurrection achieved unless we see that, largely unknown to and certainly misunderstood by those who knew Jesus in his life, there was a dynamic project at work, which became apparent only after the end of his life.

Jesus, by dying and being raised from the dead, showed that, for God, there is no such thing as death. We do not need to live in the shadow of death.

Jesus did not just happen, as an adult, to cotton on to something interesting. All along, there had been a purpose to his being alive — a purpose not comprehended at the time, and comprehended only gradually afterwards.

That purpose turned out to be the rescuing of our capacity to be the fulfilment of God's creation, a capacity that was so snarled up in us that we did not even know what being created was about.

In telling us the infancy stories, the apostolic group are saying something about what they have understood as the whole purpose of the life, death and resurrection of Jesus. The desire that was behind it all could be told only by telling the story. After the event, their very capacity to imagine what had been expected was altered, and an open future taught them to re-imagine the past.

But that they did so re-imagine it was not simply an act of piety, let alone a pious fraud. If the apostolic circle had merely borne witness to Jesus's death and resurrection, it might have been understood as an account of a divine thunderbolt, or rescue from a ghastly trap. That would have meant imagining the rescuer relating to creation in a certain way: as one not liking it, not being patient with it, not being delicate with it, but rushing in to sort it out. That would have been the story not of God but of a god.

Instead, the apostolic witnesses appreciated a vital aspect of Easter. Although it is the story of a violent murder, it cannot be told except as the fulfilment of something very gentle, delicate, and quite immense. It was a plan made by someone who likes humans as they are, and wants to involve them — cowards, murderers, liars, addicts of death and security — in becoming something greater than they can imagine.

This delicacy could be shown only in a working-out of the history of Israel, and not in a sudden suspension or cancellation of that history — just as the history of Israel was not a suspension or cancellation of the history of sacrifice and idolatry that it learned to overcome.

THIS is the importance of Matthew's genealogy, and of Luke's portrayal of a small group of off-centre Jews who can pass, without rupture, into the time of the Messiah.

It is a hugely delicate project, worked out over a vast expanse of time, and suggesting, not the power of one who puts things right, but the greater power of one who loves us into being and for whom time is not a concern.

When, at the Christmas eucharist, we hear the words: "The people who walked in darkness have seen a great light," we would do well not to think it refers to people in the past, and that we are the ones who have seen the light.

Rather, as we are taught by the crucified and risen Lord to understand our own complicity in darkness, and as so we continue with our own gradual, ambivalent steps into living in the light, we are taught by the Christmas eucharist to look back at the project of love that comes into being; to consider the painful birth, in our midst, of a truth (and that means a capacity to learn to tell the truth) which is not ours, and which we would not be, of ourselves, inclined to recognise.

We can come to revere the unexpected and improbable nature of the project, which we scarcely comprehend now. We can rejoice in the gift we are being given, a gift unrelated to our worthiness or our belonging.

It is a gift whose first sign is the vulnerability of God, in an offstage corner of the world, of which — but for the life which it turned into, and for the lives it turned around — we would never have heard.

Then perhaps, duly Easterfied, we can kneel at the manger.

(2001)

Author details and index

Numbers in square brackets refer to pages where the author's work appears.

James Alison is a Roman Catholic priest and theologian. [278–80]

Dennis Bailey is an Anglican priest. [14–17]

Margaret Barker is a Methodist preacher and biblical scholar. [59–63]

John Barton is a priest, Emeritus Oriel and Laing Professor of the Interpretation of Holy Scripture in the University of Oxford, and a Senior Research Fellow of Campion Hall. [93–6]

Sister Wendy Beckett (1930–2018) was a religious sister, art historian and TV presenter. [181–2]

David Kirk Beedon is a prison chaplain and formerly a parish priest. [18–20]

Ronald Blythe is an English writer, essayist and editor, whose weekly column *Word from Wormingford* appeared in *Church Times* between 1992 and 2016. [10–11, 166–7, 200–2, 249–50]

David Bryant is a retired priest living in Yorkshire. [214–16]

Kate Bruce is an RAF chaplain, who used to teach preaching at Cranmer Hall, Durham. [154–7]

Andrew Carwood is the Director of Music at St Paul's Cathedral. [220–3]

Richard Coles is Priest-in-Charge of St Mary the Virgin, Finedon, in Peterborough diocese. [146–9]

Stephen Cottrell is the Archbishop of York. [235–8]

Andrew Davison is Starbridge Senior Lecturer in Theology and Natural Sciences at Cambridge University. [79–83, 106–8, 267–9]

Malcolm Doney is a writer, broadcaster, and Anglican priest. [150–3]

Susan Dowell is a journalist and author. [142–5]

John Drury was Dean of Christ Church, Oxford, from 1991 to 2003, and has been Chaplain of All Souls College, Oxford, since 2003. [260–2]

Gillian R. Evans is Emeritus Professor of Medieval Theology and Intellectual History at the University of Cambridge. [97–101]

Jeremy Fletcher is Vicar of Hampstead Parish Church. [254–6]

Catherine Fox is the author of *The Lindchester Chronicles*. [40–3]

Rod Garner is a retired priest and honorary fellow of Liverpool Hope University. [109–10]

Robin Gill is a priest and theologian, and is Emeritus Professor of Applied Theology at the University of Kent. [192–4]

Paula Gooder is Chancellor of St Paul's Cathedral. [1–3, 21–4, 44–7]

Elizabeth Goudge (1900–84) was a British author of novels, short stories and children's books. [25–33]

Malcolm Guite is a priest, poet, and Honorary Fellow of Girton College, Cambridge. [39, 88, 217–19]

Cally Hammond is Dean of Gonville and Caius College, Cambridge. [134–41]

Helen-Ann Hartley is the Bishop of Ripon. [34–9]

Hugh Hillyard-Parker is Series Editor of Church House Publishing's *Reflections for Daily Prayer* and a lay clerk in Edinburgh.

John Inge is the Bishop of Worcester. [119–22]

Simon Jenkins is an author and a newspaper columnist and editor. [189–91]

James Jones was Bishop of Liverpool from 1998 to 2013. [56–8]

Nick Jowett is a retired priest in the Diocese of Sheffield. [64–6]

David Keys is the archaeology correspondent of *The Independent*. [183–5]

Adrian Leak is an Anglican priest and freelance writer. [168–71]

Sara Maitland is a novelist and short-story writer. [123–5]

David Martin (1929–2019) was a priest and professor who wrote extensively about the sociology of religion. [102–5]

Mark Oakley is Dean of St John's College, Cambridge. [111–14]

Nicholas Orme is Emeritus Professor of History at Exeter University. [227–30]

Pádraig Ó Tuama is a poet, theologian and conflict mediator. [180]

Robert Paterson is the former Bishop of Sodor and Man (2008–16). [257–9]

Neil Patterson is Rector of Ariconium, Herefordshire, and Director of Vocations and Ordinands (Hereford). [195–7]

George Pattison is Professor of Divinity at the University of Glasgow. [12–13]

John Perumbalath is the Bishop of Bradwell. [263–6]

John Pridmore was the Vicar of Hackney until his retirement and previously lectured at Ridley Hall, Cambridge. [126–30, 242–5]

Ben Quash is Professor of Christianity and the Arts at King's College, London. [231–4]

Hugh Rayment-Pickard is Chief Strategy Officer and co-Founder of IntoUniversity. [115–18]

Jonathan Romain is a rabbi, writer and broadcaster, and director of Maidenhead Synagogue. [251–3]

John Saxbee was Bishop of Lincoln from 2002 to 2011 and is now Assistant Bishop in the Diocese of St David's. [89–92]

David Scott is an Anglican priest, poet, playwright and spiritual writer. [203–6]

Kenneth Steven is a poet, novelist and children's author, with numerous book-length collections of poetry. [20, 47, 259]

Kenneth Stevenson (1949–2011) was Bishop of Portsmouth from 1995 to 2009. [8–9]

Ian Tattum is Vicar of St Barnabas's, Southfields, Priest-in-Charge of St John the Divine, Earlsfield, and Area Dean of Wandsworth. [198–9, 239–41]

Barbara Brown Taylor is an American Episcopal priest, professor, author and theologian. [48–53]

Angela Tilby is a Canon Emeritus of Christ Church Cathedral, Oxford, and Canon of Honour at Portsmouth Cathedral. [67–70]

Howard Tomlinson is a writer and historian, and was formerly Headmaster of Hereford Cathedral School. [163–5]

Pamela Tudor-Craig (1928–2017) was an eminent British medieval art historian. [207–13, 224–6]

Evelyn Underhill (1875–1941) was an Anglo-Catholic writer known especially for her works on spiritual practice and Christian mysticism. [270–7]

Paul Vallely is Visiting Professor in Public Ethics and Media at the University of Chester and Senior Honorary Fellow at the Global Development Institute at the University of Manchester. [161–2]

Robin Ward is Principal of St Stephen's House, Oxford. [71–4]

William Whyte is an Anglican priest and Professor of Social and Architectural History at the University of Oxford. [172–6, 186–8]

David Wilkinson is Principal of St John's College and Professor of Theology and Religion at Durham University. [84–8]

Jane Williams is the McDonald Professor in Christian Theology at St Mellitus College. [4–5, 6–7, 75–8, 131–3, 177–80, 246–7]

Lucy Winkett is Rector of St James's, Piccadilly. [158–60]

Tom Wright was Bishop of Durham from 2003 to 2010 and is now senior research fellow at Wycliffe Hall, Oxford. [54–5]